D1486803

WITHDRAWN

Offender Restitution in Theory and Action

Offender Restitution in Theory and Action

Edited by

Burt Galaway
University of Minnesota

Joe Hudson
Minnesota Department of
Corrections

Lexington Books
D.C. Heath and Company
Lexington, Massachusetts
Toronto

Library of Congress Cataloging in Publication Data

National Symposium on Restitution, 2d, St. Paul, Minn., 1977.
Offender restitution in theory and action.

Bibliography: p. 203
1. Reparation—United States—Congresses. I. Galaway, Burt. II. Hudson, Joe. III. Title.
HV8688.N37 1977   364.6'8   78-54700
ISBN 0-669-02328-0

Published simultaneously in Canada

Printed in the United States of America

International Standard Book Number: 0-669-02328-0

Library of Congress Catalog Card Number: 78-54700

Contents

Acknowledgments

We are very grateful to the many people whose work has contributed to the success of the Second National Symposium on Restitution and to this volume. Authors of these papers have provided a very stimulating and exciting set of ideas regarding restitution programming. Special appreciation goes to Marlene Beckman of the Law Enforcement Assistance Administration whose suggestions and support were essential to the project, to Keith Brownell, St. Louis County (Minnesota) Attorney, and to C. David Hollister, Acting Dean, University of Minnesota, School of Social Development, for their active encouragement and permission for their respective organizations to cosponsor the symposium. And, most importantly, appreciation is extended to the persons who spent many hours to insure that the project ran smoothly, including Paul Gustad of the St. Louis County Attorney's Office, Peggy Hendrickson from the School of Social Development, office staff of the School of Social Development, and editorial staff from Lexington Books.

This project was supported by Grant #77-ED-9-021, awarded by the Law Enforcement Assistance Administration, United States Department of Justice. Points of view or opinions stated in this publication are those of the authors and do not necessarily represent the official position of the United States Department of Justice.

1

Introduction
Joe Hudson and
Burt Galaway

The papers included in this volume were first presented at the Second National Symposium on Restitution held in St. Paul, Minnesota, on November 14 and 15, 1977. The purpose of the symposium was to provide a forum to assist in the thoughtful and orderly development of restitution programming in the criminal justice system. An earlier symposium on restitution held in 1975[1] focused on issues associated with implementing restitution, and since that time, interest in the idea of offender restitution to crime victims has continued to grow with a wide variety of formal program efforts implemented at different points in the justice system. As the use of restitution increases, a variety of issues have arisen about the relationship of restitution programming to the multiple purposes of the justice system, the role of restitution within the emerging field of victimology and victim service programs, and the place of restitution within behavioral change theories. In addition, criminal justice practitioners are interested in available research about the use of restitution as well as in information about the experience of pilot programming efforts. It was to address these major concerns that the Second National Symposium on Restitution was planned and it is to these areas the invited papers were directed.

The Concept of Restitution

Attempts at defining restitution frequently result in confusion. Much of this confusion seems to occur around the relationship of restitution to programs in which offenders are required to engage in some form of community service or, alternatively, differentiating between restitution and victim compensation schemes. For the purpose of the symposium, restitution was defined as a sanction imposed by an official of the criminal justice system requiring the offender to make a payment of money or service to either the direct or substitute crime victim. This definition is broad enough to include restitution programs involving community services as well as financial restitution.[2] A clear distinction, however, is made between restitution and victim compensation. Restitution is an offender-oriented sanction involving offender payments to the crime victim or some substitute victim. The restitution process is typically monitored and supervised by an official of the justice system. Victim compensation, on the other hand, is more directly victim oriented, involving a state agency using tax monies to make a payment to the victim so as to cover losses resulting

1

from the victimization. Although practically all victim compensation schemes are limited to losses resulting from injuries due to violent crime, restitution is most commonly used for crimes against property. The focus of this volume is clearly on restitution, not victim compensation.

Recent Developments in Restitution

Within the past few years, many legistlative, policy, and program developments have occurred around the use of restitution as a criminal justice sanction. A brief discussion of these major developments as well as an identification of some of the problematic features associated with the rapidly expanding interest in restitution programming should provide a useful context for the papers to follow.

Legislation

A wide variety of legislation that explicitly refers to restitution has been introduced in several states during the past few years. This legislation supplements older legislation incorporated in statutes in most states and generally falls into three major categories: restitution as a component of the routine sentencing of adults; restitution as a specific condition of the disposition of juveniles; and restitution as a purpose or objective to be achieved through special correctional programs.

Legislative references to restitution as a sanctioning consideration to be used in the routine sentencing of adults are generally of two types, seeing restitution as a part of the general sentencing power of the courts, or as a mandatory sentence for specific types of crime. As part of the general sentencing power of the courts, restitution is incorporated in statutes that emphasize the use of this sanction as a condition of probation, suspended sentence, or parole. In such contexts, restitution is often pointed to as a factor to be considered in mitigating the sentence. For example, the Colorado Crime Victims Restitution Bill,[3] passed unanimously by both houses of the Colorado General Assembly and signed into law by the governor in May 1976, explicitly aims at encouraging the establishment of restitution programs for sentenced offenders, parolees, or offenders incarcerated in local correctional and detention facilities. This statute expresses the clear legislative intent that restitution be used wherever feasible to restore losses to the crime victim as well as to aid in the rehabilitation of the offender.

Statutory references to restitution as a mandatory sentence can also be found in recent legislation. For example, 1974 Iowa legislation requires that restitution be a disposition condition of either a deferred sentence or probation.[4] A restitution plan is stipulated and must be presented to the court for approval, including both the amount of restitution to be made and the schedule of payments. In addition, this legislation requires that restitution be made as a supplement to the probation or deferred sentence disposition, not as an alternative for offenders who would otherwise have been incarcerated.[5]

A second major category of restitution legislation involves the use of the sanction as a condition in the disposition provided to juvenile offenders. Although only a few of the state juvenile codes make explicit reference to restitution, almost every state has a statute providing for juveniles to be placed on probation "under such conditions as the court sees fit to impose," or some similar language. An examination of case law in these states would undoubtedly reveal that restitution is commonly ordered as a probation condition, especially for offenses against property. Supporting evidence of this is available from the recently completed survey of American juvenile courts by the Oregon Institute of Policy Analysis which found that 86 percent of a random sample of American juvenile courts commonly used restitution.[6] This apparent widespread use of restitution in the juvenile courts may at least partially explain the infrequent references to restitution for juveniles in more recently introduced legislation. The discretion exercised by the juvenile court is much broader than in the adult courts and therefore specific statutory language about restitution may not be seen as necessary.

A third category of legislation identifies restitution as a purpose or objective to be accomplished by special programs. Both victim compensation and corrections programs are identified in such legislation. Victim compensation statutes most commonly provide for state subrogation rights in victim tort claims on any restitution or civil damages recovered by the victim from the offender. A somewhat different type of statutory reference to restitution provides for the payment of restitution to a state compensation fund out of monies earned by offenders while under corrections supervision. For example, Assembly Bill 1983 introduced in the 1977 California legislature[7] and House Bill 79 introduced in the 1977 session of the Mississippi legislature[8] tie together restitution and compensation. The California legislation would create a Release and Restitution Board within the Department of Corrections and provide for the release of offenders on parole to the custody of the board if an agreement were negotiated with the victim to repay damages or to make payments into the compensation fund. The Mississippi legislation would establish a state compensation fund and authorize the commissioner of corrections to deposit 10 percent of the wages received by offenders participating in the work release program into this fund. In short, both these pieces of legislation directly involve restitution payments from offenders to the state compensation fund. From the perspective of the history of reparations, what this amounts to is that the circle has been closed: it has gone from offender or kin group responsibility for making restitution, to state administered forms of compensation, to offender restitution to state compensation programs.

Restitution has also been incorporated in legislation dealing with corrections programs. Statutes of this type make restitution either a major focus of correctional activities or a deliberate purpose or objective to be accomplished by such programs. This type of legislation appears to be increasingly common as evidenced by bills recently introduced in California,[9] Colorado,[10] Mississippi,[11] Nebraska,[12] Tennessee,[13] and Washington.[14] Legislative Bill 221 introduced in the 1977 session of the Nebraska legislature, for example, provides that adults and juveniles convicted of property crimes be eligible for restitution employment furloughs. Each county board in the state would be responsible for hiring a furlough administrator to implement this legislation. Eligible offenders would then meet with their crime victims and establish furlough contracts with provisions that the offender agree to repay the victim for losses. While on furlough, offenders would work with the earnings going to the county furlough administrator who would distribute money due to the victim with the remainder going to the offender. The recently passed Restitution Centers Act in Tennessee[15] authorizes the commissioner of corrections to establish residential restitution centers to facilitate felony property offenders' reimbursing their crime victims for the value of the property stolen or damaged. The centers may be established within or outside prison settings, but only property offenders who have committed a felony in which the actual sentence is no more than five years would be eligible to participate in the program. All money earned by offenders while in the centers is to be turned over to an account administered by the state for payment to crime victims.

Policy and Standards

In addition to legislative enactments, the use of restitution has received support from several national policy and standard-setting bodies. For example, the 1973 National Advisory Commission on Criminal Justice Standards and Goals identified restitution as one of the factors warranting withholding a sentence of incarceration for nondangerous offenders and recommended that fines not be imposed when they might interfere with the offender's ability to make restitution.[16] The second revision of the Model Sentencing Act by the Council of Judges of the National Council of Crime and Delinquency explicitly recognizes restitution as a sanction to be used alone or in conjunction with other sanctions.[17] Restitution is also recognized in standards established by the American Bar Association[18] and the American Law Institute[19] and recommended as an alternative to prison by the 1972 Annual Chief Justice Earl Warren Conference on Advocacy in the United States.[20] In Canada, the Law Reform Commission has issued several recent reports advocating the use of restitution and negotiated settlements as methods for diverting offenders from the criminal justice system.[21]

Programming Developments

Formal restitution programs have recently been implemented at various points in the adult and juvenile justice systems. The prototype for many of these programs was probably the Minnesota Restitution Center.[22] This program was established in 1972 by the Minnesota Department of Corrections as a community-based, residential program for adult, male property offenders diverted from the state prison after four months of incarceration. Prior to arriving at the center, offenders were involved in face-to-face negotiations with their victims concerning the amount of damages done as well as the form and schedule of payments to be made following release to the center. Based to some considerable extent on the Minnesota program were the four restitution shelters established by the state of Georgia in 1974.[23] These shelters receive probationers directly from the courts as well as parolees from state prisons. While in the program, residents are required to live in the shelter, work in the community, and make the required restitution. Research information on both these programs is contained in the article in this volume by Joe Hudson and Steven Chesney.

A recent survey completed by the Minnesota Department of Corrections identified forty formal restitution programs currently operating in this country.[24] For the most part, these programs are explicitly identified as restitution programs, rather than general corrections programs using restitution as some type of incidental sanction. These restitution programs are largely nonresidential and involve adult, property offenders. The relatively few residential projects generally serve adult offenders who have penetrated the justice system to at least the level of incarceration and in such cases, restitution is used as a condition of parole or work release. Most commonly, the surveyed restitution programs are administered by state corrections agencies. A major characteristic of these operational restitution programs is the use of restitution as a supplementary sanction to other penalties. In short, restitution is commonly added as a probation or parole condition and, as a consequence, results in the use of conventional probation or parole supervision along with the requirements of restitution.

The Law Enforcement Assistance Administration (LEAA) has provided the major impetus for the use of restitution within the criminal justice system and discretionary grants have been provided for the establishment of restitution programs in California, Maine, Georgia, Oregon, Massachusetts, Colorado, and Connecticut. These programs operate at different points in the criminal justice system and involve different target populations.

The California project is administered by the California Department of Corrections and involves adult male and female parole violators ordered returned to prison. In such cases, the restitution program is instituted as a special parole condition as an alternative to prison return. The Colorado Crime Victims Restitution Program is much broader in scope. One of its components involves offenders sentenced to the state prison on the basis of property crimes. Victims and offenders are to be jointly involved in the development of a formal restitution agreement with the offender held responsible for making restitution from prison earnings as well as from monies earned while in the community on parole status. A second program component focuses on felony offenders convicted of property crimes and placed on probation. Eligible offenders are to be involved in the development of a service restitution plan to be included as part of the presentence report presented to the sentencing judge and incorporated in the probation order.

The Connecticut Restitution Program is administered by the State Judicial Department. At the request of the trial judge, a restitution plan is developed and, upon acceptance by the judge, incorporated as a condition of probation or deferred sentence. The Georgia Sole Sanction Restitution Program includes both pre- and postplea program components. In the preplea program component, negotiations around restitution and the development of a formal restitution plan are used as a part of the plea bargaining process. A restitution plan acceptable to both the offender and the prosecuting attorney is recommended to the court and, if accepted, the plan becomes a special condition of the probation order. The postplea program component involves similar procedures with the exception that the offender has been convicted prior to the development of a restitution plan. A restitution plan is developed and incorporated in the presentence investigation report and presented to the court as a factor to be considered in the disposition. Similar procedures have been implemented in the Maine Restitution Project with a restitution plan developed and included as part of the presentence report and incorporated in the eventual probation disposition.

A different type of restitution scheme has been implemented in the Massachusetts Parole Board Victim Restitution Program. Restitution is part of an institutional, work release program being operated out of three county correctional facilities and one state correctional institution. Eligible offenders are given an opportunity to develop a restitution plan as a condition of the Mutual Agreement Programming Model with the offender released to work release status and expected to make restitution from earnings. The seventh program funded by the Law Enforcement Assistance Administration is located in the Multnomah County (Oregon) Office of the District Attorney and involves screening cases for eligibility after the preliminary hearing or arraignment with restitution requested as a condition of the probation disposition.

Overview of the Volume

The papers in this volume are organized around common themes. The first set of papers examines the role of restitution in relation to commonly perceived purposes of the justice system. The two papers in Part II consider restitution from somewhat different psychological perspectives and the papers in Part III relate restitution to the field of victimology. Research on restitution is reviewed in Part IV followed by a description of service restitution programs in Part V and of financial restitution programs in Part VI. The paper in Part VII presents a summary and suggests future directions for restitution programs.

Restitution and Criminal Justice Purposes

General agreement does not seem to exist about the primary purpose to be achieved within the criminal justice system. Instead, different system actors emphasize the different, and frequently conflicting, orientations of punishment, deterrence, and rehabilitation. A similar situation exists with regard to the use of restitution. Different writers have emphasized both punitive and rehabilitative uses for the practice and undoubtedly different restitution programs emphasize different purposes. A crucially important issue, then, is how compatible use of restitution is with the different purposes of the criminal justice system and the extent to which different types of program applications are most useful in achieving these purposes.

The papers by Paul Keve, Patrick McAnany, and Charles Tittle address questions about the relevance and use of restitution to the system purposes of deterrence, rehabilitation, and punishment. In addition, these papers discuss the relationship of restitution to other sanctions that might be used by the justice system so as to enhance the respective rehabilitative, deterrent, or retributive purposes.

Psychological Perspectives

Equity theory formulations have been extensively discussed in the social psychological literature and supported by the body of evidence that has been generated primarily from laboratory experiments. Although such an approach may be useful for the development of a theoretical foundation for the practice of offender restitution, this possibility has not been directly addressed by restitution programs. What is the relevance, if any, of equity theory formulations for the operational use of restitution? What program implications can be generated from such theoretical formulations and how can the use of restitution be structured so as to more effectively generate and test theoretical propositions? Elaine Hatfield and Mary Utne address these types of questions; they identify central concepts of equitable and inequitable relationships relative to the concept of harm-doing and discuss some of the specific psychological consequences seen by equity theorists as following from the notion of harm-doing and the restoration of equity. In particular, Hatfield and Utne identify the relevance of restitution as a method for reducing the psychological effects resulting from inequitable relationships.

The paper by O. H. Mower addresses the general question of using restitution as a method for effecting interpersonal change. Among the specific issues discussed are the extent to which restitution can be incorporated in alternative methods for bringing about change in behavior as well as the relevance of restitution to self-help behavioral change strategies.

Restitution and Crime Victims

Pilot victim-service programs have been established in many parts of the country, some operating within established components of the criminal justice system and others located in organizations external to this system. In addition, scholars and practitioners have been forging out the discipline of victimology as involving a sustained focus on the crime victim. Given these developments, several questions arise: What is the relationship between victim services and the use of a restitution sanction? Does restitution provide a vehicle for increased victim input into the criminal justice decision-making process? What impact does the extensive use of restitution have upon established practitioner roles in the justice system? These questions take on added importance for planners and administrators who require information about possible links between restitution programming, newly developed victim service programs, and the developing conceptual framework within the field of victimology.

The two papers by Emilio Viano and William McDonald address questions about the relationship of restitution to the emerging field of victimology and victim service programs and the role of the crime victim in settling criminal disputes through arbitration, mediation, and at the point of sentencing. Viano provides an overview to the field of victimology and suggests that restitution has the potential for more fully integrating the victim into the operation of the criminal justice system. McDonald's paper addresses the place of the crime victim in the settlement of criminal disputes. McDonald considers the issues of victim involvement within arbitration and mediation processes, and the structuring of direct victim and offender contacts in sentencing and dispute settlement procedures, as well as within formal criminal justice dispositional processes.

Restitution Programming and Research

Like many fast-changing fields of practice, restitution programs appear to be operated in relative isolation from each other with the potential danger that newly funded and implemented programs continuously reinvent program applications of the concept and engage in repeatedly resolving significant issues. In many cases, program models exist and significant issues have been identified and at least partially resolved in various jurisdictions around the country. Consequently, a major objective of the symposium was to provide descriptive analyses of selected restitution programs utilizing both financial and community services. Three programs using community service restitution and three involving financial restitution are included here. The programs are implemented at a variety of points within the criminal justice system and are both residential and nonresidential. The papers by Robert Keldgord, Anthony Macri, and Dennis Challeen and James Heinlen describe community service restitution schemes as presently being operated in Pima County (Tucson), Dade County (Miami), and Winona County (Minnesota). Primarily financial restitution programs are described in papers by Camden Raue, Mike Patterson, and Ted Nelson. Each of these program descriptions deals with the initiation and development of the program, the manner in which the concept of restitution is operationalized, the population served, the extent and form of victim involvement, and major problems.

Research regarding restitution needs to be undertaken and findings disseminated to program planners and administrators. Marguerite Warren describes the evaluation research currently underway on the seven LEAA-funded adult restitution projects. She describes the types of information that will be available from this research effort as well as some of the difficulties encountered in conducting the evaluation. Although research in the field has not been extensive, a few studies have been completed within the past few years. Many of these have not been released in published form and there has been little effort made to integrate systematically what is currently available about the use of restitution. Consequently, a priority need for the symposium was to review systematically research on restitution that has been completed, identify substantive knowledge gaps and deficiencies, and suggest additional research needs. The papers by John Gandy, and Joe Hudson and Steven Chesney summarize and analyze research concerning the use of restitution. Gandy deals specifically with research conducted on attitudes as held by criminal justice officials and citizens toward the phenomenon of restitution while Hudson and Chesney supplement Gandy's paper by reviewing the major pieces of descriptive and evaluative research that have been completed. A description of the methodology used in these studies is presented along with a summary of the major findings and an assessment of the deficiencies associated with each work.

The final paper by Alan Harland summarizes material presented at the symposium and suggest some future directions for restitution programming efforts. It is hoped that this volume will contribute toward the more rational and systematic use of restitution as a sanction for crime.

Notes

1. For proceedings of the First Symposium on Restitution, see Joe Hudson and Burt Galaway, *Restitution in Criminal Justice,* Lexington, Massachusetts, D.C. Heath, 1977.

2. For further discussion of this definition of restitution, see Burt Galaway, "Toward the Rational Development of Restitution," in Joe Hudson and Burt Galaway, *Restitution in Criminal Justice,* pp. 80-81.

3. House Bill 1237, 50th General Assembly, Second Regular Session, state of Colorado.

4. Senate File 26, 65th General Assembly (1973), state of Iowa.

5. For a discussion of this legislation, see Bernard J. Vogelgesang, "The Iowa Restitution in Probation Experiment," in Joe Hudson, *Restitution in Criminal Justice,* St. Paul, Minnesota Department of Corrections, 1976 pp. 134-145.

6. Peter R. Schneider et al., *Restitution Requirements For Juvenile Offenders: A Survey of the Practices in American Juvenile Courts,* Institute of Policy Analysis, Eugene, Oregon, 1977.

7. Assembly Bill 1983, state of California, 1977.

8. House Bill 79, state of Mississippi, 1977.

9. Assembly Bill 1206, Senate Bill 725, state of California, 1977.

10. Assembly Bill 1237, state of Colorado, 1976.

11. House Bill 18, House Bill 436, state of Mississippi, 1977.

12. Legislative Bill 221, state of Nebraska, 1976.

13. "The Restitution Centers Act," state of Tennessee, 1976.

14. Senate Bill 2664, state of Washington, 1977.

15. "The Restitution Centers Act," state of Tennessee, 1976.

16. United States National Advisory Commission on Criminal Justice Standards and Goals, *Corrections,* Washington, D.C., U.S. Government Printing Office, 1973, p. 150.

17. National Council on Crime and Delinquency, Council of Judges, "Model Sentencing Act, Second Edition," *Crime and Delinquency,* 18, October, 1972, pp. 356-359.

18. American Bar Association, *Standards Relating to Sentencing Alternatives and Procedures,* New York, Office of Criminal Justice Project, Institute of Judicial Administration, 1968, 2.7(c)(III); American Bar Association, *Standards Relating to Probation,* 1970, 3.2(c)(VIII).

19. American Law Institute, "Article on Suspended Sentences, Probation and Parole," *Model Penal Code,* 1962, 301.1(2)(h).

20. Annual Chief Justice Earl Warren Conference on Advocacy in the United States, *A Program for Prison Reform,* Cambridge, Massachusetts, Roscoe Pound-American Trial Lawyers Foundation, 1972, p. 11.

21. Law Reform Commission of Canada, *Working Paper No. 3: The Principles of Sentencing and Dispositions,* Ottawa, Information Canada, 1974, pp. 7-10; Law Reform Commission of Canada, *Working Papers 5 and 6: Restitution and Compensation; Fines,* Ottawa, Information Canada, 1974, pp. 5-15.

22. Joe Hudson and Burt Galaway, "Undoing the Wrong," *Social Work,* 19, May, 1974, pp. 313-318; Robert M. Mowatt, "The Minnesota Restitution Center: Paying Off the Ripped Off," in *Resitution in Criminal Justice,* Joe Hudson, editor, St. Paul, Minnesota Department of Corrections, 1976, pp. 190-215.

23. Bill Read, "The Georgia Restitution Program," in *Restitution in Criminal Justice,* Joe Hudson, editor, pp. 216-227.

24. Minnesota Department of Corrections, "Known Restitution Programs in the United States," St. Paul, 1977.

Part I: Restitution and Alternative Purposes of the Justice System

2

Restitution as Idea and Practice: The Retributive Process
Patrick D. McAnany

Introduction

Restitution as practice and as theory has ridden on the coattails of a larger phenomenon in criminal justice: the reinvention of the victim. Prior to a decade ago in this country, restitution was not an uncommon occurrence as a condition of probation. But one would look in vain for articles about this practice. Even sizable books, such as Sol Rubin's *The Law of Criminal Correction,* devoted only a few sentences or paragraphs to the practice and offered no conceptual basis at all.[1] But beginning about 1970, the victim's absence from the system of justice began to be noted.[2] It is this growing phenomenon of victimology to which restitution has become attached and in light of which it seems worthwhile to examine its retributive prospect.

Not unlike restitution, the practice and theory of retribution has undergone a *volte face* of late. In 1967, when a colleague and I undertook a survey of penal philosophies being practiced, we searched almost in vain to discover a practicing retributivist, at least in the United States.[3] Later, when we edited a book of readings on the subject, the chapter devoted to retribution had only a single American, Professor Jerome Hall.[4] Although the practice of sentencing in the United States had never totally eschewed the notion of retribution, very few scholars were then willing to undertake its exposition, much less its defense.[5] Particularly averse to the notion were those in the professional corrections community.[6] Then, quite suddenly, or so it seemed, otherwise reputable professional persons began to convert to a retributive explanation of criminal sentencing, as we shall see below.

Although the practice and even the theory of restitution seems simple and acceptable, the same cannot be said for retribution. Retribution is not simply vengeance, though this is a popular, and even sensible, explanation. No less an authority than the Supreme Court has thought the concept might well be exhausted with this description.[7] In fact, retribution is a moral concept grounded in the notion of desert and requital. In some sense, it is pedestrian common sense. In another sense, it is high metaphysical intuition.

The question I wish to raise is whether restitution as a practice can be reconciled with a theory of retributive punishment for the very obvious reason that the practice tends to be formulated in terms of rehabilitation of the offender, rather than in terms of justice for the victim. But even if we could reconcile

15

these ideas with practice, one must wonder whether the victim has any role in a system that is public in mode and punitive in thrust.

Sentencing and Persons: An Historical Analysis

Victims and the Public Management of Crime

The disappearance of victims from the criminal justice process begins with the decline of feudalism.[8] Somewhere in the fifteenth century, the gradual evolution from a system of private dispute settlement to a system of public crime was completed in England. The former system involved a victim or his family seeking redress through the courts. The form of redress could be either compensation in satisfaction for the harm inflicted by the accused; or in punishment inflicted by private parties, but under legal authorization, on the offender; or both.[9] But the moving party was the injured private person or family.

The gradual transition from a private dispute settlement mechanism to a public criminal one appears to be tied to several social-institutional factors. The first is the emergence of a separate branch of law that we have come to call the law of torts or personal injuries.[10] Prior to the fourteenth century, the law of crime and of tort were inextricably mixed. Only gradually were the courts able to develop principles that distinguished between intentional harms and negligent ones, and even after hundreds of years, courts have not drawn a definitive line separating the two.[11] The victim's right of recourse was lost with the emerging field of tort.

Another contributing factor was the preemption of the criminal process by the Crown. At issue in the sixteenth century was injury to the "King's Peace" rather than the injury to the victim.[12] It is not certain that the emergence of a central authority and the resulting social cohesion was the sole cause of the transformed view of who the victim really was. Some suggest that the displacement of the victim by the state as the litigant in interest was no more than a move by the Crown to enrich itself through the cooptation of all fees derived from the criminal process.[13]

The displacement of the victim from the criminal courts except as complainant and witness could also be seen as a consequence of the breakup of the communal society of feudalism and its replacement by the modern commercial state.[14] In such an analysis the economic interests of the state displace the economic interests of individuals. A later development of this same theme would be that victims of all the harsh consequences of social organization are treated alike in a welfare formula that repays in the dole what had been denied to people in the major social institutions. Thus the victims of crime, if they have paid a price by being victimized by other victims of society, will be subsumed into a general victim class by social welfare.

In more contemporary settings, the victim has tended to be excluded for reasons of system that may have escaped attention at the time. Under the dispensation of the rehabilitative school of thought, the victim was often viewed as the very embodiment of revenge, rehabilitation's antithesis. By excluding the victim and his desire for revenge, the system promoted healing and return to social integration by the offender. Further, behaviorism often dictated that offenders had no responsibility in committing the crime, and thus victims were unfortunate captives of circumstances beyond their, or their aggressor's, control. If anyone owed them something, it was the society that had allowed the criminal events to occur.

If one approached the problem of crime from a utilitarian perspective, the victim also counted for little. The foucs was not on past acts and their consequence, but on future crimes which the judicious use of punishment was intended to deter. Although the burden of punishment might be increased by adding restitution, the principle of economy in penalties and the judges' wide scope of discretion for choosing among sentences, left small room for restitution as necessary punishment.

Finally, a sense of justice displaced victims from courts. Offenders were regarded as themselves victims whose plight often made their victims' plight pale by comparison. Because many offenders were the poorest of the poor, and because the criminal justice system tended to concentrate, for whatever reason, on them, many critics found cause to favor the offender over society with its legitimate claims, and especially over his victims. It seemed wrong to take away from the poor to give to the not-so-poor.

This historical sketch suggests some reasons for the displacement of the victim from the system and for his prolonged exclusion. In the late 1970s, however, the victim has regained a certain prominence in the criminal justice process. Many programs were created to give some recognition to the fact that he is more than a key vitness; among them are the restitution programs discussed here.[15] Historically, it is too soon to define precisely the reasons for this phenomenon, or to predict how long it will last or how far it will go. (But indicative of the earnestness with which the law now pursues the interests of the victim is a recent amendment to the Juvenile Court Act of Illinois that makes it mandatory that the identity of the juvenile adjudicated a delinquent be made known to the victim despite the confidentiality of juvenile records.)[16] One reason frequently given is that the victim has gained because the defendant had gained during the fifties and sixties from the Supreme Court's due process revolution. Simple justice seemed to demand that we give some rights to the victim when we had given (apparently) so many to defendants.

American Sentencing and the Debate on Goals

American criminal law in its institutional form has not dwelled on goals. In fact, even under the leadership of their most eminent scholarly group, the

American Law Institute, professionals in law have eschewed the question of what goals they were pursuing, as evidenced by the statement in the Institute's Model Penal Code on the purposes of the reformed criminal law.[17] This section of the code was cast in the broadest and vaguest of language, inclusive rather than precise, and without any hierarchy of goal choices. The explanation of the wishy-washy approach was that it appealed to pragmatic considerations; the drafters wished to elicit the endorsement of both sides of the then establishment, the deterrists and the rehabilitationists.

When decisions on goals were forced by decisions on how to handle offenders, the Model Penal Code chose a general framework of deterrence with an aspiration to rehabilitation. How much the punitive/preventive philosophy prevailed was pointed out in the sharp critique made by Sol Rubin, counsel for the National Council on Crime and Delinquency (NCCD), the guardian of the rehabilitationist philosophy of criminal law and sentencing.[18] The language of the code did not rule out a retributive interpretation entirely, as Professor Henry M. Hart, in his benign interpretation, tends to show.[19] But it was fundamentally deterrence that prevailed. This was 1962.

At about the same time, the NCCD put out its Model Sentencing Act which enlarged upon the basic indeterminate sentencing structure reflected in the Model Penal Code. It did so by creating a category of sentences for dangerous offenders under which they could be incarcerated for up to five times the average sentence length for a felony.[20] While offering a safety valve so that the courts could protect society against the truly dangerous, they took from them the power to sentence many felons to prison at all, or placed a limit of five years on prison terms in most cases. Thus, the Model Sentencing Act expressed the basic philosophy of rehabilitation, with a caveat clause for the protection of society. This combination of rehabilitation and social defense or restraint directly rejected retribution under its sentencing provisions.

The debate until the late sixties was thus joined between a preventive/punitive approach and a restraint one, with both groups willing to place the largest rhetorical emphasis on rehabilitation.

This general support for rehabilitation as the primary goal of sentencing prevailed without challenge into the seventies. There were, however, several important dissents registered during the waning years of the sixties. Professor Herbert Packer saw in the behaviorist wing of rehabilitation a development which, given a fast-growing technology, might threaten to break down the protective barrier built by the criminal law between the individual defendant and the state.[21] That barrier was reflected in the basic structure of criminal responsibility. The behaviorists were convinced that choice and blame, summarized in the word *guilty*, were either anachronistic or out of place.[22] If there was any need to determine the role the defendant's choice played in committing the crime, it could be reserved for sentencing and be established by psychological evidence for purposes of protecting society against dangerous persons. Packer felt that missing from this approach were the protections of a philosophy that said that the state could encroach only on individuals who were guilty because they chose to commit an offense. Without this safeguard, individuals were subject to being used by the state for the socially beneficial purpose of crime prevention. Put another way, Packer was willing to adopt a retributive approach insofar as it said flatly that punishment was justified only against the guilty. But he added that retribution was only a limiting principle of distribution of punishments whose primary aim was the prevention of crime. This, I suggest, is one of the early recognitions of the values that retribution may offer to a criminal law system in a democratic society.

The first blood drawn in the seventies on the sentencing goals dispute was the work of the American Friends Service Committee. Its report delineated a criminal justice system that was discretionary, and unjust along lines of class and race.[23] The problem was not the familiar one that the correctional systems lacked the resources for rehabilitation. Rather it was that the system served as a means of control over classes of persons, minorities, who were considered a threat to society. The solution offered by the Friends was the elimination of all discretion from sentencing and corrections. Flat-time was the type of preferred sentence: a judge would, guided by carefully drawn norms, sentence all like-situated offenders to like sentences, based on the seriousness of the offense and not upon the character of the offender.

Although the Friends acknowledged that this looked like a thoroughgoing retributive system, they suggested that it might be as well a system in which the vengeance of society is channeled into limited punishment, a type of deterrence.[24] Further, they had raised in a direct fashion the issue of social justice which had lurked in the background of earlier rehabilitationist reforms.

By 1973 there begins a full-scale attack on the sentencing structure and the correctional system that is its progeny. Though many of such authors do not express themselves in terms of goal choices, such as deterrence, retribution, and the like, they all add to the movement away from the choices made earlier in the century. For instance, James Q. Wilson offers a return to the old verities of punishment when he scathingly attacks the social welfare aspects of penal reforms during the decade from 1965 to 1975.[25] On examination, however, Wilson turns out to be a social defense programmer rather than a retributivist.[26] Further, Judge Frankel makes short work of the sentencing structure: it is beyond the law because totally at the discretion of individual judges.[27] While he suggests several basic reforms for sentencing, he does not offer a single-purpose system. Dean Norval Morris, in examining the prison of the future, rejects the parole release decision as unavoidably unfair and unjust.[28] He deals directly with goals and suggests that we pursue both deterrence and rehabilitation within a framework of retribution. He would accomplish this by making the outside limit of sentences reflective of the seriousness of the offense. Finally, David Fogel makes the attack on the rehabilitation stronghold of corrections forthrightly in his book *We are the Living Proof,* in which he proposes a "Justice Model" for corrections instead of a rehabilitation one.[29] Yet the book and the subsequent legislation drawn from it lacks precise goals. Although rehabilitation is rejected as a goal of sentencing and corrections, punishment is never defined as either retribution, deterrence, or social defense, though all of these are discussed.[30] In general, however, one could call Fogel, as well as most of the others, practicing retributivists in that they opt for equality of treatment for all offenders.

The most recent chapter to this saga of retribution came from the Committee on Incarceration in its report, *Doing Justice,* authored by Andrew Von Hirsch.[31] This group confessed, in an introduction to the report, that they had, as it were, backed into the position of advocating retribution as the primary goal of criminal law and sentencing. They did so by eliminating all the other goals. Rehabilitation is rejected both because it has not worked and because it creates threats to individual freedom. Further, restraint is rejected because it is based on a type of prediction about human behavior that may be inaccurate and false. Finally, deterrence, while not rejected outright, is given a secondary role since there is almost no proof that punishment works as a preventive device. Positively, the committee suggests that retribution is a basic goal of sentencing because people feel obligated to punish the guilty based on desert.

Retribution as a Value System

Some Types of Retributive Thought

This paper has suggested that over a period of fifteen years professional persons, both lawyers and nonlawyers, have moved toward an acceptance of retribution not only as *a* justification of criminal sentencing and correction, but as *the* justification. At this point it will be helpful to examine the meaning of that concept for some contemporary writers.

Retribution in popular usage is most often equated with revenge.[32] It expresses the hostility victims feel at being victimized and is intended to satisfy that feeling.[33] In terms of system, punishment of offenders is taken over by the state to prevent the behavior that one might expect from an outraged person— taking two eyes for one, and the like. The common sense on which such an explanation is based has also been described in psychoanalytic terms by several authors.[34] The Supreme Court in its recent death penalty decisions has drawn heavily upon this idea of punishment as revenge.[35]

At another level, retribution as revenge comes to take on the meaning of deterrence, or at least prevention. By satisfying an instinctual blood-lust among victims and victim constituencies, the system deters people from taking the law into their own hands.[36] At an even higher level, the satisfaction derived from seeing the offender suffer his just deserts has the valuable consequence of creating and reinforcing social conformity.[37] Revenge is the glue that holds the social fabric together.

In each of the above descriptions is apparent a certain element of consequential value, that is, the idea that we punish because we derive from doing so certain social values. This is to be strongly contrasted with the view of retributive thinkers who insist that punishment can be justified only by past acts of the offender, not future results of the punishment. But this particular divergence illustrates the elusive nature of the distinction among the various schools of thought about punishment. There is no easy way to draw lines across a reality as dense and primal as the need to punish, as many modern authors have suggested.[38] Their conclusion, an eminently sensible one, is that every system will tend to collect all justifications within it. But the caution is that we should try to be as precise as possible about how and where these justifications are invoked.

Expressive retribution would describe a system in which the basic justification for punishing lies in its denunciatory value, since it expresses our rejection of the wrong done by the offender whom we punish.[39] It is true that mere denunciation might suffice without adding to it the sentence in which pain is inflicted on the offender. In such a system, judges would be called upon to pronounce judgment against the offender and the offense after a determination of guilt, but would not necessarily be called upon to levy other punishment if such denunciation were sufficient. The problem with this truncated system is that few persons would consider denunciation sufficient. Insofar as the punishment consisted in measures added to condemnation, it, too, would be justified as a symbolic expression of rejection of the wrong by the community.

Formal retribution would describe a system in which the only justification needed for punishment would be that the law was broken.[40] No questions would be allowed as to the justness of moral rightness of the law itself. This description of retributive theory reduces the issues to formal consequence of law breaking.

The Kantian argument can be portrayed as one of unjust enrichment.[41] Thus, we might describe *equalizing retribution* as that in which the punishment tends to return the offender to a position before the law (social contract) equal to others who have obeyed the law. Through crime, offenders place themselves above others who have obeyed the law, as well as above their victims from whom they have taken certain goods. Not only is it right and fair that offenders be made to disgorge the profits of the crime to the victims, in whatever form, but it is also fitting that offenders be made to pay a price for the undeserved privilege of committing an act against the code. By suffering punishment, they are returned to a place of equality with others.

Desert retribution reflects a theory of punishment that justifies infliction of pain on offenders as their just deserts.[42] Because offenders have chosen to offend by wrongdoing, they deserve blame from society. They deserve to be punished. The measure of desert rests on both the seriousness of the harm done and the degree to which the offender was engaged in an act of choice. This triple element of blame, harm, and choice, must be reflected in a range of penalties for different levels of gravity. For the most part, the range is predetermined by legislative choices arranging crimes into levels of seriousness.

Requital retribution is a theory of punishment in which the basic justice to be accomplished is replacement of the morally wrongful act by a morally rightful act.[43] Just as it is right to reward the morally good act of persons with a return of moral good, so it is right to return the morally evil act through punishment. In the punitive process morality is required or upheld by the symbolic repudiation of evil. At bottom the punishment is something that we owe to the offender. He need not accept the requital as a moral order value, but he may, and it is this opportunity for moral reform that grounds retribution.

Common Value Characteristics of Retributive Theories in a Sentencing System

The above exercise indicates that retributive theory represents far from a monochromatic response. Yet among all these theories of retributive justice, certain common themes emerge, and can be related to the sentencing structure in which they are reflected.

Justice. Virtually all the above schools of retributive thought are based on an acknowledged justice relationship between the offender and the victim and/or socity. Unlike the deterrist or rehabilitationist, the retributivist is concerned that a just order be restored, rather than that future crimes be prevented or that offenders be changed. This characteristic makes retributive sentencing structure much clearer in relating the punishment to the offense. It also underscores the role of the courts as institutions of dispute settlement, rather than as media of treatment or social control. One of the sobriquets chosen by one author for a new approach to sentencing is the "Justice Model." Here justice is opposed to discretionary decision-making based on a medical model of clinical diagnosis.[44]

Morality. In addition to showing a justice orientation, the retributive sentencing models tend to underscore the moral justification of punishing criminals. While aware that contemporary society emphasizes plurality of moral codes and privacy of conscience, the retributivists insist that criminal law reflects a moral consensus on the basis of which it is morally right to punish wrongdoers. This is contrasted with a utilitarian approach, or positivism, where moral values are subsumed into an ethics of beneficial social results or made irrelevant in a jurisprudence of the legitimacy of power.[45] The retributivists insist that punishment needs moral justification because it raises truly moral questions. Granted that the morality involved is of public order, the retributivist will still claim that this makes it no less—indeed, more—a morality commanding assent of conscience. From the unexpected source of radical social critics has emerged a broadly accepted understanding that the legitimacy of our legal system depends heavily on a common morality.[46]

Equality. One of the most serious problems addressed by penal reformers is the absence of equality of treatment among offenders. The "disparity" problem draws the retributivists very much into the center of things. Their principle of "treating like cases alike" reflects the justice nature of the issue and tends to be expressed in the further principle of proportionality—relating the punishment to the seriousness of the crime. This equality suggests, indeed probably implies, a mandatory quality to the sentences set out by law. Although there is room for mercy in such a system, this is not to be mistaken for mere leniency. The result would ideally be a uniform system of sentences in which all offenders would be treated alike insofar as their crimes were alike.[47]

Responsibility. At the center of any desert-type argument lies a theory of personal choice and responsibility. If an offender could and did choose to commit the crime, then he deserves to be blamed and suffer the consequences. This contrasts sharply with scientific determinism, at least as expressed early in the development of the social sciences relating to crime and punishment.[48] Several thinkers who otherwise sympathized with the goals of a preventive approach to crime came to see the harm in discounting human choice.[49] If a person is considered incapable of responsible action, then some other person or institution will act for him. The opportunities for oppressive manipulation are obvious.

Backward looking. A retributive approach to sentencing is concerned with what an offender *has done*, not what he *might do*. This backward-looking quality is characteristic of trial proceedings. The trier of fact is asked to determine whether the defendant committed a certain act under certain circumstances. Punishment in retributive terms is related to that act, not to some act that the offender might commit. Other systems—indeed, all other justifications—have an element of prediction buried in them. The sanguine assertions about predictive powers in rehabilitation, restraint, and deterrence systems have withered under scrutiny and left us with the notion that we know little about how persons will act tomorrow, though this has not discouraged us—nor should it—from trying.[50] Much of the power of retributive advocacy lies in its simplicity of approach and the unyielding resistance to the technologies of control that many contemporary Americans find threatening to constitutional freedom.[51]

Act based. This final quality of retribution indicates that punishment does not depend on who the offender is, but on what he did. Making the punishment fit the crime means that attention of the sentencer is directed to the crime and its circumstances, rather than to the social history of the offender. In one sense, this may seem to undermine the social justice arguments advanced in favor of minorities where a deprived background might be grounds for relief from harsh sentences. On the other hand, the argument has been tellingly made that in actor-based systems in which character and personal qualities are weighed in assessing dangerousness, the very same considerations lead to longer sentences.[52] There seem to be more limits placed on selection of sentences based on act than on the uncertain assessment of character by judges and others.[53]

Restitution in a Retributive Structure of Sentencing

The Level of Compatibility

Looking at a retributive-based sentencing system and the virtues it endorses, my general intuition is that restitution as a practice would fit in quite well. In fact, the fit is so nearly exact that the reinvention of the victim in criminal justice and the return of retribution as the primary explanation of why we punish appear to be manifestations of the same social movement.

For instance, restitution clearly is based on a justice relationship between victim and offender. To restore the basic order that existed prior to the criminal act, restitution must be made that places the victim back in the same position as before, through either return of the object taken, its replacement, or analogous replacement by damages. The retributive system reflects this same primary concern for justice, as opposed to treatment of the offender.

Further, the emphasis on the moral rightness or wrongness of the criminal act, the blame element in criminal law and sentencing, is carried over in restitution practice. The actual goal of most programs appears to be the offender's recognition that what he did was wrong because it injured someone.[54] This centrality of responsibility acceptance in restitution is intended to reinforce the message of the law that the accused is proven guilty of wrongdoing and stands condemned by the community for his freely made choice.[55]

Like the retributive system above described, restitution is grounded on a backward-looking, act-based approach to responsibility. Just as the criminal trial focuses on the historical actions of the defendant and assesses punishment on the basis of the seriousness of the act as proven, so the restitutionary process asks questions of an historical order and bases payments on a scale of magnitude related to the act. This contrasts sharply with the perspective of rehabilitation-ists or social defense thinkers who measure treatment by the present condition of the defendant, and shape outcome on predictive measures of future be-havior.[56] Even with deterrence, the past is important only insofar as it allows one to predict an individual recurrence of the crime or the measure that will maximize disutility for others inclined to it.

Finally, the equality among offenders that retribution underscores as essential to a system of justice is clearly present in restitution. The measure of restitution is the measure of harm, as perfect a proportionality as can be achieved within the human range. Like offenders are treated exactly alike because they are measured by the amount of harm they have done to their victims. Although there may not be a perfect symmetry among offenses—for it is difficult to compare the harms of rape and robbery—there is an attempt in the objective order of money damages to assess these harms in a mode that makes them somehow comparable.

One would, after this brief excursus, be led to believe that the two move-ments of retribution and restitution are really a single development. I have no doubt that this is true to a degree yet unrecognized by many authors on both subjects. Yet, there are conceptual problems that make the two systems appear incompatible or at least uncomfortable together. Further, there are problems of practice.

Conceptual and Practical Problems

Conceptually, restitution is the return of the *victim* to a preevent status through return of the object taken or through damage. Punishment, on the other hand, is the payment to the *state* of something over and above the goods taken or the harm inflicted. It is added to the simple justice between the parties whereby the rights of the victim are restored. Wrongdoing always deserves a special objectifi-cation that goes beyond the return of things due to others. It simply would not be punishment to make the criminal disgorge his illegal gains or even to pay for the harm of his crime. We sense the two things to be related but different.

Would it be possible to bring them together by adopting a concept of punitive damages for crimes? In such a system, victims would be awarded com-pensatory damages based on their out-of-pocket expenses, as well as on pain and suffering. But a set of damages would be explicitly added on to the award as punishment of the offender. Some tort suits rely on punitive damages in this manner to emphasize the gross injustice of the actor's behavior.[57] In a sense, such a system would comprehend both elements of justice, distributive and retributive. Yet it neglects a facet of punishment that is essential to criminal justice—the societal. One of the problems with the private dispute settlement common to England before the fourteenth century was the interpersonal focus of the process. The criminal was regarded as the debtor of the victim in the larger sense we have given to a system of punitive damages, but this does not include the full sense of being also the debtor of the community.[58] Although the victim has suffered the wrong in a physical sense, it is the common code that the criminal has violated. Society as victim has suffered a loss of consortium, a breach of the common bond among its citizens. Repayment of the victim, even punitive amounts, misses this point.

Also overlooked in such a system is the nature of the repayment that punishment implies. In a way, money payment in place of other types of punishment mars the relationship between wrongdoing and justice. While one must pay one's debts to others, as we have settled for a common denominator of money damages, it is another thing to pay one's debts to society. This injury will not translate as easily into money damages, however carefully worked out. Quite apart from the practical problems of trying to equalize damages across a range of economically differentiated offenders,[59] there is the issue of the purchase of justice. Restoration of the moral order is not a commercial transaction. The use of money as symbol of the moral order seems strained at best, except perhaps in totally commercial crimes. The violation of the ordering among citizens is restored by symbolizing the harm that the wrongdoer caused, not in the very terms of the crime committed, but in a way that requites the disorder of the immoral action.

Restitution differs considerably, insofar as the repayment of the victim tends to exhaust the debt owed. Even where restitution exceeds just the return of the thing to the victim, still we have left it at that.[60] But with punishment, we have insisted on the restoration of the moral order, at least symobolically, by the offender suffering his just deserts. Whether or not he returns to the moral order through a change of heart and rejection of his wrongdoing, the opportunity is there and is owed to him.[61]

Conceptually, then, restitution and retribution do not fit together as nicely as we have supposed. But further, there are some practical problems that make their compatibility subject to doubt.

The economic inequality among offenders makes restitution in practice difficult to administer evenhandedly. Even with the use of symbolic restitution through work programs, there are obstacles to achieving equality. Victims are not always ready to participate. Crimes differ so drastically that for some restitution is not ordinarily used at all. And even where restitution is mandatory, judges are given no guides for administration. A major catastrophe for a restitutionary system would be if the rich were allowed to pay and go, and the poor were made to stay. Such a result would directly contradict what many of the major retributive thinkers are trying to achieve in sentencing—equality of treatment for like offenses.

Another threat inherent in promoting restitution in a retributive framework would be the displacement of punishment by the repayment of individuals.

The sentencing process could begin to take on the aspect of a collection agency and lose its ability to convey a moral message. On the other hand, when both restitution and retribution were practiced together, there would be an element of double jeopardy or revenge unmistakeably present. The fine balance between extracting the pound of flesh and doing justice is not easily struck.

The problem of morality of the law arises in the restitutionary situation in which the victim is a large corporation and the offender is a marginal individual in an economically disbalanced society.[62] It may be justice in a certain sense to insist that the offender pay the victim for his theft. Yet the social injustice that preceded the crime may eviscerate the moral message. This problem of social justice appears also in a retributive system and tends to make the moral assertions of those insisting on justice somewhat hollow.[63] When restitution orders repayment across highly differentiated economic levels, this same effect would take place. In those instances it would appear valuable to remit restitutionary payment or direct it toward the more socially needy. Yet by doing so one may forfeit equality of treatment among offenders.

The goals of the two systems might also clash in their differing emphases upon victims and offenders. While restitution as a theory clearly has the victim in mind, its primary interest has remained the offender.[64] Many programs seem to select offenders for restitution on the basis of merit and need, rather than selecting victims for either reason. Restitution is looked upon as a valuable program for offenders and where it is not, offenders are not placed in the program. But this surely has turned the justice model upside down in retributive terms.

Conclusion

We raised the question at the beginning of this paper whether restitution could fit within the retributive framework of sentencing. Although I assert that it can, there are elements of both conception and practice that militate against any easy fit between the two notions. It is too early yet really to say that either retribution or restitution will long remain a central focus of the courts. Retribution is a dangerous idea whose value to the system can quickly turn into threat. No more immoral pronouncement can be made than in the name of justice, as we all know. The problem of how retribution can be properly applied in sentencing remains to be fully worked out. The whole issue of assessment of personal responsibility has yet to be addressed.[65]

As to restitution, the idea is old and solidly grounded in probation practices. Yet the notion that restitution should bring victims into the criminal process as participants on a regular basis is too new to be fully appreciated. We all await the outcome of various experiments being undertaken in this country to test the impact that victims have on the process.[66] Like retribution, restitution as a practice has its own limitations which, if exceeded, turn a method for fuller justice into one full of injustice.

Notes

1. Sol Rubin, *The Law of Criminal Correction* (St. Paul, Minn.: West Publishing, 1963). In his second edition (1973), Rubin has devoted substantially more pages of the topic. See pp. 231-232; 295-297.

2. Stephen Schaffer, *Compensation and Restitution to Crime Victims* (Monclair, N.J.: Patterson, Smith, 2d ed., 1970).

3. Rudolph Gerber and Patrick D. McAnany, "Punishment: Current Survey of Philosophy and Law," *St. Louis University Law Journal* 11 (1967): pp. 491-535.

4. Rudolph Gerber and Patrick D. McAnany (eds.), *Contemporary Punishment: Views, Explanations, and Justifications* (Notre Dame, Ind.: University of Notre Dame Press, 1972) excerpting Hall's *General Principles of Criminal Law* (Indianapolis: Bobbs-Merrill, 2d ed., 1960).

5. See, for instance, the then rare foray into a retributive explanation of criminal law, Henry M. Hart, "The Aims of the Criminal Law," *Law and Contemporary Problems* 23 (1958): pp. 401-441.

6. See, for instance, the statement on purposes of the criminal law in the otherwise balanced account by Henry Weihofen on "Punishment and Treatment," as chapter 18 in Rubin (1963), supra n. 1.

7. Andrew Von Hirsch, *Doing Justice* (New York: Hill and Wang, 1976).

8. Several basic references for this analysis are: O.W. Holmes, *The Common Law* (Boston: Little, Brown, ed., Mark DeWolfe Howe, 1963); Theodore Plucknett, *A Concise History of the Common Law* (London: Butterworth, 5th ed., 1956); Egon Bittner and Anthony Platt, "The Meaning of Punishment," *Issues in Criminology* 2 (1966): pp. 79-99.

9. Plucknett, pp. 463-475.

10. Plucknett, pp. 455-462.

11. Plucknett, pp. 463-470.

12. Bittner and Platt, supra n. 8, at p. 87.

13. Plucknett, pp. 421-423.

14. Mark Kennedy, "Beyond Incrimination," *The Catalyst* 5 (1970): pp. 1-37.

15. For an analysis of contemporary restitution programs, see, e.g., Anne Newton, "Alternatives to Imprisonment," *Crime and Delinquency Literature* 8 (1976): pp. 368-390; Joe Hudson, Burt Galaway, and Steve Chesney, "When Criminals Repay Their Victims: A Survey of Restitution Programs," *Judicature* 60 (1977): pp. 312-321; Gallaway, "The Use of Restitution," *Crime and Delinquency* 23 (1977): pp. 56-67; Allen M. Linden, "Restitution, Compensation

for Victims of Crime and Canadian Criminal Law," *Canadian Journal of Corrections* 19 (1977): pp. 3-49.

16. *Ill. Rev. Stat.,* Ch. 37, Secs. 702-10.1

17. American Law Institute, *Model Penal Code* (Philadelphia, Penna.: American Law Institute, P.O.D. 1962), Secs. 1.02. For further analysis of this section, see Gerber and McAnany, supra n. 4 at pp. 532-533.

18. Sol Rubin, "Sentencing and Correctional Treatment Under the Law Institute's Model Penal Code," *American Bar Association Journal* 46 (1960): 994 et seq.

19. Henry M. Hart, Jr., supra n. 5.

20. National Council on Crime and Delinquency, Council of Judges, *Model Sentencing Act* (New York: NCCD, 1963) Sec. 5.

21. Herbert Packer, *The Limits of the Criminal Sanction* (Stanford, Calif.: Stanford University Press, 1968).

22. See, e.g., Gregory Zilboorg, *The Psychology of the Criminal Act and Punishment* (New York: Harcourt, Brace, 1954), and Lady Barbara Wooton, *Crime and the Criminal Law* (London: Stevens, 1963).

23. American Friends Service Committee, *The Struggle for Justice* (New York: Hill and Wang, 1971).

24. O.W. Holmes, supra n. 8 at pp. 35-36.

25. James Q. Wilson, *Thinking about Crime* (New York: Basic Books, 1975).

26. Wilson invokes a return to punishment, but his notions of the values that imprisonment holds are in the main incapacitating rather than punitive. Ibid.

27. Marvin Frankel, *Criminal Sentences: Law Without Order* (New York: Hill and Wang, 1973).

28. Norval Morris, *The Future of Imprisonment* (Chicago: University of Chicago Press, 1974).

29. David Fogel, *We Are the Living Proof* (Cincinnati, Ohio: Anderson, 1975).

30. McAnany, Merritt, and Tromanhauser, "Illinois Reconsiders 'Flat-Time': An Analysis of the Impact of the Justice Model," *Chicago-Kent Law Review* 52 (1976): pp. 621-662.

31. Supra n. 7.

32. This same restricted notion of retribution is extended into the recent Supreme Court decisions on capital punishment: *Gregg* v. *Georgia, Profitt* v. *Florida,* and *Jurek* v. *Texas,* 428 U.S. 153; 242; and 262 (1976). For an analysis of this retributive basis of capital punishment, see Patrick D. McAnany, "Death as Just Punishment: Retribution, Capital Punishment, and the Supreme Court," *St. Louis University Law Journal* (forthcoming).

33. Homes, supra n. 24.

34. Alexander and Staub, *The Criminal, The Judge, and The Public* (New

York: Macmillan, Zilboorg trans., 1931); Karl Menninger, *The Crime of Punishment* (New York: Viking, 1968).

35. Supra n. 32.

36. Ted Honderich, *Punishment* (Middlesex: Pelican Books, 1971).

37. Jackson Toby, "Is Punishment Necessary?" *Journal of Criminal Law, Criminology and Police Science* 55 (1964): pp. 332-337.

38. Several of these authors favoring a "pluralistic," approach to purposes of punishment are collected in chapter 6 of Gerber and McAnany, *Contemporary Punishment,* supra n. 4.

39. Joel Feinberg, "The Expressive Function of Punishment," *The Monist* 49 (1965): pp. 397-423. These ideas are elaborated in his later book, *Doing and Deserving* (Princeton, N.J.: Princeton University Press, 1970).

40. J.D. Mabbott, "Punishment," *Mind* 48 (1939): pp. 152-167.

41. J.G. Murphy, "Kant's Theory of Criminal Punishment," in L. Beck (ed.), *Proceedings of the Third International Kant Congress* (Dordrecht: D. Reidel, 1971), pp. 434-441.

42. John Kleinig, *Punishment and Desert* (The Hague: Martinus Nijhoff, (1973); Andrew Von Hirsch, *Doing Justice,* supra n. 7.

43. Joel Kidder, "Requital and Criminal Justice," *International Philosophical* Quarterly 15 (1975): pp. 255-278.

44. Fogel, supra n. 29.

45. Lon Fuller, "Positivism and Fidelity to Law—A Reply to Professor Hart," *Harvard Law Review* 71 (1958): 630 et seq.

46. See, e.g., Richard Quinney, *Critique of Legal Order* (Boston: Little, Brown, 1973).

47. The Twentieth Century Fund Task Force on Criminal Sentencing, *Fair and Certain Punishment* (New York: McGraw-Hill, 1976).

48. Francis Allen, *The Borderland of Criminal Justice* (Chicago: University of Chicago Press, 1964).

49. H.L.A. Hart, *Punishment and Responsibility* (London: Oxford University Press, 1968); Herbert Packer, supra n. 19.

50. Norval Morris, supra n. 28.

51. See McAnany, review of Nicholas N. Kittrie, *The Right to be Different: Deviance and Enforced Therapy* (1971), *Journal of Criminal Law, Criminology and Police Science* 63 (1972): pp. 557-560.

52. American Friends Service Committee, supra n. 23. Ernest Van den Haag, *Punishing Criminals* (New York: Basic Books, 1975), argues that the poor are not treated any differently than others, or if they are, it is because they are more prone to crime.

53. Frankel, supra n. 27.

54. The way this is expressed may be broader than mere acknowledgment of responsibility for wrongdoing, but this appears to be a central notion among program personnel. See Hudson, Galaway, and Chesney, supra n. 15 in which

they report that ten of nineteen programs surveyed acknowledged rehabilitation of defendants as a major goal of restitution. Also, see Linden, supra n. 15, for similar affirmative evidence about Canadian programs.

55. Henry M. Hart, supra n. 5 at pp. 404-406.

56. L. Radzinowicz, *Ideology and Crime* (New York: Columbia University Press, 1966), pp. 29-59.

57. See, e.g., Morris, "Punitive Damages in Tort Cases," *Harvard Law Review* 44 (1931): 1173 et seq.

58. Plucknett, supra n. 8.

59. In a cognate area of criminal justice, the Supreme Court ruled against courts confining certain individuals who could not pay fines, as a violation of equal protection under the Fourteenth Amendment. *Williams* v. *Illinois,* 399, U.S. 235 (1970).

60. In discussion of 100 percent restitution in several programs, Hudson, Galaway, and Chesney suggest that this is a figure that does not included a punitive element. Hudson, Galaway, and Chesney, supra n. 15.

61. Kidder, supra n. 43.

62. Hudson, Galaway, and Chesney, supra n. 15.

63. Von Hirsch, supra n. 7.

64. In a survey of nineteen programs, ten responded that rehabilitation of the offender was the major purpose, whereas only four indicated that victim compensation was a major goal. Hudson, Galaway, and Chesney, supra n. 15.

65. Most retributive proposals suggest that seriousness of the offense is the norm, without going on to explain that seriousness will include the mental state of the offender at the time of the crime. A recent article has developed this understated theme in retributive sentencing with suggestions as to how courts can assess moral responsibility. See Gardner, "Renaissance of Retribution—An Examination of *Doing Justice*," 1976, *Wisconsin Law Review,* p. 781.

66. Several interesting evaluations are being undertaken in the Chicago area. One is an attempt to assess the impact of making the victim a participant in the plea bargaining process. This study is under the auspices of the Center for Studies in Criminal Justice at the University of Chicago Law School (contact Mr. Wayne Kerstetter). The other is a description of various victim advocacy programs funded in the metropolitan area by the Illinois Law Enforcement Commission. The report, *Fourth Power in the Balance,* is issued by the Chicago Law Enforcement Study Group (1977).

3

Restitution and Deterrence: An Evaluation of Compatibility
Charles R. Tittle

This essay assesses the potential impact upon criminal deterrence of various schemes that would require offenders to provide restitution for harm caused by their criminal acts. Almost everybody agrees that a major objective of any system of criminal justice is to secure general conformity by deterrence of illegal conduct. But scholars do not agree about the meaning of deterrence.[1] Some theorists think that deterrence includes any curtailment of illegal behavior accomplished by sanctions or sanction threats, no matter what the mediating process by which prevention is brought about. Others use a narrow definition that restricts deterrence to those situations in which illegal conduct is inhibited by fear of punishment.

For example, by reinforcing the moral status of laws, sanction threats may cause some people to conform. A significant proportion of citizens may believe that particular acts are morally wrong precisely because the law imposes a penalty for violation,[2] and this belief may in turn influence them to comply. Those with a narrower view of deterrence would claim that it is not involved in such a case since these conforming individuals are obeying the law not specifically because of perceived fear of the consequences of disobedience. Theorists who favor a restricted definition prefer to think of compliance produced by sanctions or sanction threats through mechanisms other than perceived fear as "preventive effects." But since the definitions seem arbitrary, and the relevant empirical data rarely permit such distinctions, I shall consider the potential effects of restitutive schemes using conceptualizations of deterrence.

Deterrence Through Fear

Meaning

The idea of deterrence through fear is simple enough—that people will refrain from illegal acts if they perceive that they will be caught and punished. The underlying rationale is that humans are motivated to maximize their advantages and minimize their disadvantages, and that they will make rational choices in the pursuit of those goals. The law provides a penalty for violation that is designed to outweigh the rewards of illegal behavior. Achievement of general conformity through deterrence by fear, then, requires that the potential penalties be greater than the rewards of illegal behavior and that they be implemented

33

frequently enough that the possibility of sanction becomes credible to all people in the social unit.

Assumptions

Although the deterrence doctrine is ostensibly straightforward and plausible, its actual validity is far from established,[3] and it is much more complex than appears at first. Most of the assumptions on which the doctrine is based are questionable. First, people are not always rational: they often make choices that are disadvantageous in the long run in the pursuit of proximate goals. Second, much human behavior stems from immediate response to social influences or internal stimuli and is closer to reflex action than it is to contemplative decision making. Third, perceptions of possible penalties are often incorrect and may bear little relationship to actual probabilities of suffering punishment. Fourth, people differ greatly in their assessment both of cost and of reward associated with particular behaviors in specific situations, so that it is almost impossible to devise a system of sanctions that will apply to all persons in a political unit or to all situations in which illegal behavior might occur.

Fifth, imposition of penalties may actually generate deviant responses that are stronger than those that were to be deterred initially, or the conditions of punishment may in fact neutralize sanction fears.[4] For example, punishment (or even processing) of offenders can in some cases stigmatize the individual and create secondary deviance. Widespread imposition of penalties may intensify deviant actions by causing those with deviant inclinations to organize to promote their activities and to protect themselves. And imprisonment may expose one to a subculture that undermines the threat of sanctions. Finally, implementation of a system of sanctions with high enough probability to produce credible sanction threats for all, or even most, citizens is almost unthinkable, especially in a democratic society.

For these and other reasons sanction threats can never be more than partially successful in insuring conformity. And without more extensive and careful research than has been done so far, we cannot say even approximately how successful fear-inducing efforts are or under what conditions their success is maximized. Therefore, assessing the potential impact on deterrence of modifications in the legal system may be futile simply because we don't yet know how much effect sanctions have or by what mechanisms apparent effects occur. Sanctions may, in fact, be largely irrelevant to the degree of conformity. Or, if they do have significant consequences, it may be because frequent offenders are incapacitated while incarcerated rather than because people fear sanctions.[5] If this is true (and remember that we don't know whether it is or not),[6] then substituting restitution for imprisonment would be disastrous.

This does not mean, however, that it is useless to contemplate the possible effect or legal change on the deterrent goals of a criminal justice system. We can speculate about the implications of certain legal modifications in light of what we think to be true about the realities of sanctioning. And we can consider whether the general objectives of the criminal justice system that are presumably achieved by sanction threats could logically be accomplished without deterrence. If nothing else, such an analysis will alert us to the weaknesses of the deterrent system, and it may convince us that any reasonable change might be worth a try.

Restitutive Plans

There are many ways that a restitutive scheme could be formulated, and the particular method used will determine the extent to which the principles of deterrence can be maintained. Some plans may call for restoration in addition to ordinary penalties and some may envision compensation in lieu of incarceration. In addition some restitutive systems may allow compensation either from an offender's own resources or through some form of regulated labor,[7] while others might permit restoration only through regulated labor. Moreover, some plans might call for full restitution of all damages and perhaps even of state costs of investigation, trial, and administration, while others would require only partial compensation to the victim which could be accomplished by regulated labor while incarcerated. And, of course, there are many types representing combinations of these different elements. Seven various types will be examined here.

Punishment and Restitution

In simplest general restorative scheme, compensatory requirements would be added to ordinarily imposed sentences. Three variations of this general approach are of interest. In one plan (A) those convicted would be required to compensate for costs of the crime from their own resources or by regulated labor until the full obligation was met. For example, an individual convicted of burglary of a home where he took items worth one thousand dollars would be tried and if convicted sentenced just as he would have been if there were no restitutive requirements—perhaps to two years in prison. But in addition he would be obligated to compensate the homeowner (or the state, which had already repaid the victim) by paying one thousand dollars of his own money or by working in prison-based industries or for private business under contract while serving his usual sentence in prison or on probation. And if the mandated compensation exceeded that which could be earned during the period of the sentence, he would be required to continue regulated labor until all reparations were complete.

A second variation (B) of this basic approach would prohibit offenders from meeting restorative mandates with their own resources. Rather, in the interest of fairness, it would require that all offenders provide compensation through regulated labor. Thus, each person convicted of assault would be sentenced as usual—some to prison and some to probation—and each would be required to make restitution by regulated work in amounts appropriate to the damage done.

A third punishment/restitution combination (C) would demand only partial compensation for the victim—that which could be generated during the term of the sentence. For example, a person convicted of rape might be sentenced to fifteen years in prison and assessed a compensatory obligation for psychological damage to the victim equivalent to that which could be earned in regulated work while imprisoned or on parole. Here the length of the sentence and the period of time that the restitutive requirement was operative would correspond.

Effects of Plan A. The first of these alternatives would probably have several consequences relevant to deterrence. Because it demands punishment as well as compensation to the victim, the net effect would probably be interpreted as an *increase in the magnitude of penalties.* An offender would suffer ordinary deprivation of liberty, and in addition he would be assessed something akin to a fine. Moreover, since most convicted offenders are not people of means, reparation of damage might well necessitate regulation labor for years after the actual sentence expired, particularly if compensation included state costs of processing as well as victim harm. Therefore most offenders would no doubt experience restricted freedom for much longer periods of time than they would under the existing system.

But at the same time, this restitutive scheme would probably lead to *reduced rates of conviction,* at least for more serious offenses. This would come about in two ways. First, since compensation would have to be linked to an identifiable injury, conviction would have to correspond to the specific crime that presumably produced that injury (unless enormous legal fictions could be tolerated). This would make plea bargaining, the chief means by which conviction is now achieved,[8] extremely difficult, or at the very least change its character.

All bargaining would have to be based on possible reduction of sentence. Prosecutors could perhaps negotiate on the promise that they would recomment lower sentences to the judge, a recommendation that would have some force.[9] Or perhaps negotiations concerning sentence length could be in direct consultation with judges. But it is unlikely that bargaining on that basis could be as successful as negotiation is now. For one thing, where damage was great, judges would no doubt be reluctant to reduce a sentence very much because control over restitutive efforts would be maximized while the offender was in custody. And offenders, knowing that they would face heavy compensatory obligations if convicted, would probably be less willing to concede their guilt without a trial. Prosecutors, in turn, would be unlikely to try the case before a jury unless it was especially strong—stronger than it would have had to be for a guilty plea under current plea bargaining procedures.[10] Consequently many of the cases that are now resolved through guilty pleas would be dismissed under a restitutive system.

Moreover, if past experience with extremely long or mandatory sentences is a reliable guide, juries would be reluctant to convict in serious cases, even when they were brought to trail, just as jurors presently are reluctant to convict in capital and life sentence cases.[11] Thus the probability of sanction for serious offenses would almost certainly deteriorate under the restitutive plan being considered.

Further, a system that allows those who can afford compensation to escape with less obligation than those who cannot afford it is likely to generate some feelings of injustice by citizens in general and by the less well off offenders in particular. Although the present criminal justice system is itself viewed by many as unjust because it allows great inequities in the probability of conviction and in the kind and length of sentences imposed, a justice system in which differences could be measured directly and visibly in monetary terms would command even less respect.

Finally, this type of restitutive plan would surely induce strong incentives for further crime among many convicted offenders. Imagine a man convicted of assault who knows that after serving two years in prison, he must continue to forfeit a large proportion of his earnings for years to compensate a victim for injuries suffered. Would not such a person be inclined to obtain large sums of money quickly by illegal means, even if reparations had to be proven to have come from legitimate sources?

Plan A would, then, probably have four consequences relevant to deterrence: it would increase the severity of punishment, lower the probability of sanction, magnify belief that the criminal law is unjust, and provide stronger incentives for further illegal behavior among those convicted. In principle, increasing the severity of sanctions ought to improve deterrence, and decreasing the certainty of conviction ought to erode it. Therefore, applying one brand of theoretical argument, the overall effect ought to be negligible. Certainty and severity of punishment are said by some to be additive,[12] standing in a reciprocal relationship so that they compensate for each other. If severity is high, certainty can be low and if certainty is high, severity can be low. However, evidence suggests that these two sanction characteristics are not independent and additive but rather that certainty of sanction is independent and conditional for the operation of severity.[13] This means that in the absence of a reasonable degree of certainty, severity is irrelevant as a deterrent and where certainty is high, severity can be relatively low and still induce conformity. Thus although plan A would affect one sanction characteristic positively and another one negatively, it would appear to have its adverse effect upon the more important of the two.

Moreover, the potential impact of reducing sanction probabilities is heightened by the presumed magnification of general feelings of injustice that would probably follow implementation of plan A. Most legal theorists maintain that the vast majority of people comply with the law voluntarily, particularly if they perceive the law to be fair, legitimate, or beneficial and where they perceive its implementation to be just. And most deterrence theorists argue that sanction fear is most relevant where volunatry compliance is minimal.[14] That is, if people are motivated to conform out of moral commitment, recognition of mutual benefit, or general perception of the justice of the laws, sanction threats are irrelevant because individuals do not contemplate deviance and therefore do not take into account the potential risk. If this reasoning is sound, it would follow that plan A would intensify people's tendency to fashion their behavior in accordance with sanction risks at the same time that it weakened the major deterrent feature of sanction threats—the certainty of imposition.

Furthermore, it has long been a basic tenet of deterrence thought that the success of sanction threats in curtailing deviance depends heavily upon the strength of motivation to engage in deviance. The forefathers of deterrence thinking recognized that the utility of behavior (its value to the potential actor) determined the nature of sanctions needed for deterrence.[15] Even now, theorists almost all concede that the stronger the motivation to do something, the greater the probability and magnitude of penalty needed to deter it, and under ordinary circumstances the less likely it is to be deterred.[16] Hence if plan A would enhance incentives for illegal behavior among a significant proportion of the population, it would lessen the deterrent success of the law, even if sanctions remained as they are now.

It would appear, therefore, that implementation of restitutive plan A would substantially reduce the deterrence of illegal conduct. It would erode the probability of sanctions while simultaneously inducing larger numbers of people to organize their behavior in light of sanction possibility. And in addition it would cause criminal behavior to acquire even greater utility for a significant proportion of the population, thereby weakening the ability of the law to deter violation, particularly with deterioration of the certainty factor. Although it would, in most cases increase the magnitude of penalties, there is good reason to believe that in the context of reduced certainty of punishment severity would be of little consequence.

It should be noted, however, that the accuracy of these projections depends upon several unknowns. First, the analysis assumes that individual perceptions of certainty of sanction bear a reasonable correspondence to the actual certainty of punishment. At this point we do not know whether this is true. We do know that many people far overestimate and that some underestimate the probability of their being caught and punished. But we do not know how changes in the actual certainties of punishment would be related to perceptions. It is at least conceivable that most might be unaffected by actual reductions in conviction rates.

Second, the validity of the projection assumes that the probability of conviction is an important factor in producing deterrent fear within a population. But actually, some evidence suggests that conviction probability adds scarcely anything in deterrent power to that achieved by arrest probability.[17] And, there is little in the restitutive plan that should have any bearing on arrest probability (except perhaps declines in police morale because of the drop in conviction rate). Moreover, the probability of conviction for any given criminal act is already so low that it is hard to believe that even drastic reductions would make much difference for the general population.[18] Some evidence suggests that arrest certainty itself, at least in some types of places, has no deterrent effect until it reaches a particular threshold level—a level that is already far above the conviction rate for most crimes in most places.[19]

Thus the argument that the net effect of plan A would be to reduce deterrence is perhaps shaky. However, these qualifications assume that the general population is usually deterred, even though most theorists argue that sanction fear is not really relevant to most people since the majority conforms for other reasons. Rather, it is said that only those who are unconventional—who have criminal inclinations ("marginal groups")—are affected by sanction threats.[20] To the extent that this is true the qualifying assumptions mentioned above are less important. It is precisely marginal individuals—those who frequently come in contact with criminal justice agencies—who are probably most likely to alter their perceptions of sanction characteristics in the light of changes in conviction rates, to consider conviction possibility as a relevant threat, and to feel that a restitutive plan is unjust. In addition, it is they who have the greatest probability of being sanctioned and feeling magnified incentives for further illegal conduct. If only the "criminal element" is potentially deterred, then plan A would probably have even greater impact upon deterrence because its consequences would be most applicable to precisely that category of citizens.

Effects of Plan B. Plan B differs from plan A in one essential respect. It allows convicted offenders to meet restorative requirements in only one way—through some form of regulated labor. Three of the probable consequences of plan B would be similar to those of plan A. As with plan A, the magnitude of penalties would be increased. Indeed, since all convicted offenders would be required to compensate through regulated work, the length of obligation would be extended for even larger numbers of people. The probability of conviction would also decline, probably more than in plan A, because the prospect of extended work commitments, even among the wealthy, would no doubt discourage more of the accused from pleading guilty. And, just as with plan A, those individuals without personal means to maintain their lifestyle while fulfilling compensatory requirements would feel greater need for further illegal behavior. However, there is no reason to think that those people of means who were required to make restitution through labor would develop such incentives. Thus the two plans would have essentially the same effect on criminal incentives.

But the two approaches would differ in their effects on concepts of justice. Since according to plan B, all would be somewhat equal in the manner by which restitution could be made, initial differences in wealth could not give unfair advantage to some. Therefore plan B should produce some increase in belief in the justice of law, which would translate into greater amounts of voluntary compliance and less awareness of sanction characteristics. Although this is likely, it is worth noting that a completely equal system of regulated labor would be impossible or impractical. For example, if a physician and a gas station attendant were both obligated to pay ten thousand dollars in reparations after release from prison, theoretically both could be required to labor at jobs such as highway maintenance. But as a practical matter, they would probably be required to perform tasks appropriate to their skills. The physician might work in a public hospital while the laborer worked on a highway maintenance crew, both forfeiting a portion of their pay. These differential conditions of work would in themselves probably be considered unfair by some. But the fact that the physician would discharge his obligations rather quickly while the laborer would be deprived for much longer would no doubt be perceived as wrong by many people.

Plan B, like plan A, would lead to increased penalties, decreased conviction rates, and enhanced incentives for illegal behavior. But unlike plan A, it should make sanction characteristics less relevant for most people. The overall impact on deterrence ought, then, to be a little less than for plan A. Although conviction rates should be even lower under scheme B than under A, and criminal incentives should be increased about the same amount, enlarged belief in justice should override some of the negating influences. And as with plan A, the fact of even larger penalties should be of little consequence in view of decreased conviction rates. Therefore, the net effect of plan B would in all likelihood be some reduction in deterrence, but not as much as for plan A.

Effects of Plan C. Plan C would differ from the other two alternatives in several ways. It would require only partial compensation by the offender, and it would link the amount of restitution to the length of the sentence. In principle this would seem to have few pejorative consequences for the deterrent purpose. There is no reason to imagine that it would generally imply greater severity of sanctions. Theoretically, the same sentencing policy now in effect would continue. The only thing that would change would be the activities programmed for offenders while they were serving sentences. But once the sentence was served, the compensatory obligation would also cease. Hence reparation would not be considered as additional to standard penalties, but would become part and parcel of the sanction.

Although the same sentencing policies practiced now would presumably continue, it is a good bet that after a while sentence length would come to bear a linear relationship to the amount of harm perpetrated on a victim. If the damage were serious, a judge would more than likely impose a longer sentence so that a greater portion of the damage could be restored by the offender's labor. But if the actual harm were slight, the sentence would probably be shorter since the only rationale for it would be the traditional one, and in the context of restitutive thinking those justifications would probably lose force. The overall effect on average sentence length would therefore be negligible.

Second, there is nothing about plan C that would be likely to affect conviction rates negatively. In fact, there is some reason to believe that it might increase conviction rates a little. Since restorative requirements would not be directly linked to the criminal act, plea bargaining could proceed as it does now. Of course, knowledge that the judge is likely to impose a sentence as nearly commensurate with the harm done to a victim as possible, regardless to the actual charge, might undermine some of the bargaining appeal of reduced charges. But statutory limitations on possible sentences would still make lesser charges attractive. Moreover, when cases did go to trial juries would probably be more willing to convict. They would know that conviction would not mandate endless obligations even where costly damage was done, and at the same time they would know that conviction would provide some relief for a victim (or the state if it had already compensated a victim) as well as some punishment for an offender.

Third, nothing about this approach would seem to affect ideas of justice in a negative way. Whatever variables now influence conviction and sentencing would presumably continue to operate. And if the system is now considered unfair it would continue to be so. But to the extent that sentences came to reflect more about the amount of harm done than about the characteristics of the offender, the system might come to be perceived as more just. Hence if plan C had any effect on justice perceptions, it would probably be to increase them. Therefore greater numbers of citizens would probably be drawn into voluntary compliance thereby making the certainty of punishment less relevant.

Finally, plan C would not generate any greater criminal incentives among those convicted than are now produced. Offenders would experience no more deprivation after release than they do now. In addition, connecting the prison experience directly to compensation of the victim might well give meaning to incarceration. The prison experience could conceivably then draw inmates into a meaningful relationship with conventional society whereas it now tends to alienate them.[21] To the extent that this happened, this particular restitutive plan might actually reduce criminal incentives.

Overall, then, plan C would appear to have no negative consequences for the deterrent goals of criminal justice and, if anything, would seem to enhance slightly the deterrent possibility. It would not increase penalties, it would not reduce conviction rates, and it would not generate greater criminal incentives. It would probably lead to greater feelings of justice and perhaps to heightened sense of social responsibility by convicted offenders, both of which would make certainty of punishment less relevant for producing conformity.

Restitution Instead of Punishment

Although the simplest restitutive plans would make compensation additional to normal sentencing, other restorative schemes would involve more radical departures from current practice. These plans would substitute reparations for punishment and would operate on the premise that as long as the offender cooperated in the restitutive process, no punishment (such as incarceration) would be required. In fact, in a legal system based on this approach the whole concept of punishment or sanction would be abandoned in favor of a concept of "responsibility for harm." Denial of the right of social participation (through incarceration, execution, or banishment) would follow from unwillingness of an offender to fulfill the obligations of social participation implied by restitutive mandates. It would not be intended as punishment for the original deviant act, but rather as a declaration of social rejection because of the person's refusal to make reparations. Four basic patterns of this general approach will illustrate variations relevant to the deterrence issue.

The first (plan D) would require that convicted offenders repay all expenses associated with the crime either from their own resources or through regulated labor until the obligation was met. Thus if a person burgled a house and took various household goods worth two thousand dollars, he would have to compensate the state (which had already compensated the victim) the two thousand dollars plus compensatory damages to cover the inconvenience and expense to the homeowner of testifying or doing other things associated with the legalities of the case and perhaps for any trauma he might have experienced. Moreover, there would be additional charges for the cost of police investigation, trial, and administration of the restitutive plan. The full obligation might total as much as ten thousand dollars for a crime that netted the thief only five hundred dollars. This amount could be paid from the offender's own resources or by regulated labor.

A second variation of this basic plan (E) would require a convicted offender to meet a full restitutive obligation (ancillary and direct costs) through regulated labor, regardless of his personal means. For instance, a man might be convicted of murder and be required to pay a total of two hundred and fifty thousand dollars (most of which would go to support a widow and children). Even though he might be wealthy, he would have to work at a designated job under state supervision until his forfeited pay equalled his compensatory obligation.

The third alternative (F) would require only that the offender restore the direct damage to a victim, either by his own resources or through regulated labor, while a fourth (G) pattern would mandate reparations equal to the direct damage to a victim, but payable only through regulated labor. For instance, an individual convicted of embezzlement would be required to replace the actual amount stolen. Under plan F he could do this by simply returning the money, replacing it with money of his own, or by regulated work. Under plan G he would have to perform regulated work until the debt was repaid.

Effects of Plan D. Plan D bypasses standard penalties and instead calls for full reparation of all direct and indirect costs by personal means or regulated labor. Therefore, estimating whether this would constitute more or less severe sanction is not easy. There is no question that for many offenders full restoration would be difficult and unpleasant. A restitutive obligation would always far exceed any financial profit from a crime, and in cases of injury or property destruction it would almost certainly be large, requiring of most offenders a considerable period of regulated labor. But whether this would be perceived by the recipients or by the general population as more unpleasant than penalties now likely to be imposed depends upon a number of variables. Considering that the vast majority of prison inmates would prefer parole, even though it means restricted freedom and supervision, we can probably assume that most people would find the prospect of freedom, even with regulated labor, more pleasant than incarceration. And, of course, offenders or potential offenders with private means would certainly see it as less severe, since they would neither have to lose their freedom nor engage in regulated labor.

But many offenders are not sent to prison anyway, and most of those who are incarcerated are soon paroled.[22] In fact, offenders in the United States actually serve very little time despite relatively severe statutory provisions. Surely regulated labor would be interpreted as more unpleasant than simple probation or parole, and since the actual length of time that most would be obligated to for compensation would very likely exceed current sentences, it is probable that the majority of offenders would perceive the requirements of plan D as more severe than punishments now imposed. Of course, the effect on other potential lawbreakers is hard to assess. For those with no prison experience and no awareness that actual time spent in prison is short, incarceration may appear far more undesirable than regulated labor. But there is reason to believe that ordinary citizens make few distinctions in the magnitude of penalties. The simple possibility of experiencing any penalty may be more important than the exact nature of the penalty.[23]

Effects of this plan on the certainty of sanction would actually appear to be positive. On one hand the necessity of linking compensation to specific criminal acts would make plea bargaining practically impossible, particularly since there would be no possibility of a sentence that could be reduced in exchange for guilty pleas. But on the other hand, there would be good reason for defendants to avoid trial. The amount of assessed compensation would reflect the costs of criminal justice processing as well as victim damage. Therefor a defendant who insisted upon a trial would risk greater restorative obligation in case of conviction. Moreover, since conviction would not mandate punishment per se, but rather simple reparation for damage done, juries would probably have little reluctance to convict, except in extremely serious cases. But, more important, a system of justice that makes victim harm the focus of attention will not have to deal with "victimless" or "moralistic" crimes. This would mean that the enormous police resources now used to combat vice could be concentrated on victim-related crimes. Consequently more offenders should be arrested and evidence could be more effectively and thoroughly compiled. The net effect would be an increase in arrest probability and a greater likelihood that conviction will result.

Implications of plan D for criminal incentives involve contradictory elements. Although many convicted individuals would experience extended periods of deprivation—some of them of interminable length—they would also avoid many of the criminal and antideterrent influences of prison. Incarceration often undermines the deterrent threat by showing the individual that doing time is easier than he thought and by exposing him to an inmate subculture that minimizes the threat of punishment while glorifying the criminal life.[24] There is no way to determine how these two factors might balance, but I would guess that the net effect of these contrary forces would be negligible.

Plan D would probably have its most adverse effect on the deterrent function through a decrease in voluntary compliance. Making the victim the center of the justice process would certainly inspire greater confidence among some citizens, and it is possible that emphasis on responsibility for harm would integrate offenders rather than alienate them as punishment often does. But the elimination of the possibility of incarceration would no doubt neutralize some of these effects. After all, many citizens believe that offenders deserve to be punished, and that retribution is an essential element in justice. Therefore any plan that denies that premise is likely to alienate a lot of people. Moreover, a plan that allows the rich directly and ostensibly to use their wealth to avoid consequences that others suffer is likely to engender hard feelings. This restitutive scheme would very likely undermine some voluntary compliance without a concomitant increase in sanction characteristics that could deter the increased numbers who would contemplate illegal behavior.

The overall effect of plan D, then, would appear to be some decrease in perceived severity of penalties and in voluntary compliance, some increase in conviction rate, and little effect on criminal incentives. The decline in voluntary compliance would make sanction characteristics more important, but there would be accompanying ameliorative change in certainty of sanction that would counter the decline in severity. Thus the deterrent function would probably be increased by the use of plan D.

Effects of Plan E. The forecast for plan E would be similar to that for plan D except that the deterioration of voluntary compliance would be less. Plan E would not permit convicted offenders to fulfill their obligations from personal resources. This should make the system seem somewhat more just, but the absence of a retributive element would still undermine support. Hence the net effect of plan E would appear to be some increase in deterrence.

Effects of Plan F. Alternative F, on the other hand, would probably seriously erode the deterrent function. Under that plan a convicted offender would restore only direct damage to the victim, and he could do that with his own resources or through regulated labor. Rather obviously the magnitude of sanctions would decrease in most cases. Only where the damage was unusually large would the time of regulated labor exceed current sentences. In the majority of instances, the proceeds from property crime would probably be restored in much less time than is now standard in sentencing, and even many crimes of violence would not require long periods to compensate for damage. And, of course, the magnitude of penalty for those of means would be minimal for any type of crime.

Moreover, the certainty of conviction and perhaps even of arrest would decline sharply. The necessity of connecting compensation to a specific criminal act, and the absence of sentences to use in negotiation, would completely eliminate plea bargaining. In addition, there would be little incentive for guilty pleas since the magnitude of compensation would in no way depend upon the length of judicial proceedings as it would in plans D and E. Of course, there should be no reluctance by juries to convict, but the necessity for proof would still mean that many cases now disposed of through bargained pleas would never be tried. Furthermore, given low conviction rates and lenient sanctions, the impact upon police morale would probably be devastating, offsetting somewhat the increase in police resources that would result from the elimination of victimless crime.

Third, plan F would probably severely undermine confidence in justice, producing less voluntary compliance at the very time that sanction characteristics were losing their potency. Plan F would offend some because of an absence of retribution, it would bother others because it does not even demand full compensation, and it would be considered unfair by many because the wealthy could escape.

It probably wouldn't have much effect on criminal incentives, however. Although offenders would be personally deprived and in positions of temptation, the length of time they were so deprived would not be excessive except in a small proportion of cases. Moreover, they would escape the consequences of incarceration. But with reduction in penalties, reduced conviction rates, and lessened confidence in justice, the deterrent function is likely to be erased regardless.

Effects of Plan G. Projected consequences of plan G are similar to those of plan F, except that the former would elicit more voluntary compliance with the law, thereby making sanction characteristics less relevant. Certainly most people would think it more just to require offenders of all levels of wealth to fulfill compensatory obligations through regulated labor than to allow personal resources to be used. But even so, this scheme would still be faulted by many because of the absence of a retributive element and because it relieves the offender of responsibility for all the damage his violation caused. And, of course, like plan F, it would still reduce the magnitude of sanctions and the probability of conviction. Thus the effect would be considerable deterioration of the deterrent effect.

Summary of Effects. If my assumptions are correct and if current evidence concerning deterrence is valid, four of the seven restitutive plans considered here would induce less compliance through fear than does the current criminal justice process: plans A and F, and to a lesser extent, G and B. But three of the schemes, D, E, and C, promise some increase in deterrence by fear. Thus from a deterrent point of view (where deterrence is defined in terms of constraint through fear), only three of these schemes are feasible. Either plan C, D, or E could probably be implemented with minimal negative consequences for deterrence. Although plan E would be preferable, the others would not be far behind. This is especially interesting since plan C involves only slight modification of existing practice while plans D and E represent drastic departures from what is now done. The fact that they are fairly close together in potential outcomes suggests that a deterrent system has no inherent incompatibility with a restitutive system. The key factor appears to be the way in which restitutive plans are organized.

Deterrence Broadly Conceived

Mechanisms

Although some scholars think that deterrence occurs only when illegal behavior is prevented by the mechanism of individual fear, others believe that deterrence encompasses any situation in which illegal behavior is curtailed by sanctions or sanction threats, no matter what the intervening variable. In the previous section the potential effect of various restitutive plans on deterrence by fear were considered. In this section I shall examine the probable effects of various restitutive schemes on deterrence through nine other mechanisms.[25]

Incapacitation. Incapacitation refers to the prevention of illegal behavior by denying potential offenders the opportunity to commit crimes. Sanctions can deter by incapacitation if they involve incarceration, exile, maiming, or execution of those who are likely to be frequent offenders; that is, those who have already been guilty of crimes. It is not known how much criminal behavior is deterred by incapacitation, but at least some scholars believe it is a substantial amount. Thus evaluation of the deterrent consequences of restitutive plans must take into account the possible effects on incapacitation.

Increased Surveillance. It is also possible that punishment causes increased surveillance of those who are sanctioned as well as generally increased security measures. When somebody is punished, citizens and law enforcement personnel are alerted to the potential for future crime by the one sanctioned and to the possibility of criminal activity generally. As a result those who come in contact with the former offender may take added precautions not to allow opportunity for victimization and they may impose tighter security on their property so that other potential deviants are prevented from breaking the law. In a similar way police may watch former offenders more closely. The net effect of these responses may be considerable deterrence, particularly if the probability of further crime is greater among ex-convicts. Of course, it is also possible that stigmatization may produce more deviance by closing off legitimate opportunities, forcing ex-offenders into association with others like themselves, and leading to the development of deviant identities.[26] Nevertheless a complete analysis of the consequences of restitution must deal with the potential effects on increased surveillance.

Education. Another theoretical effect of sanctions is to make more people aware of the norms and the limits of permissible behavior. Many theorists point out that even when citizens are inclined toward obedience, they are often ignorant of the laws. Sanctions are said to serve an educative purpose by dramatizing the laws and their requirements. By this means they deter crime that would occur as a result of ignorance. Thus we must contemplate whether restitutive approaches would add to or detract from this effort.

Reformation. It is also possible that sanctions can change the personality, identity, or thinking of a person so that he no longer desires to perform the crime, or if he does contemplate it is restrained by moral commitments developed during his period of punishment. Indeed, the rehabilitative ideal has served as a foundation for many prison systems. Although the general efficacy of rehabilitative efforts is questionable, it is at least plausible that in some cases sanctions may deter by this means.[27] Therefore the impact of restitutive reforms on deterrence by rehabilitation must be given some attention.

Norm Reinforcement. Probably the most frequently expounded theoretical effect of sanctions or sanction threats is that of normative reinforcement.[28] Punishment is thought to strengthen the imperatives of the law in three ways. First, it reminds citizens that the rules are important. Those who observe or become aware of punishment of violations are made conscious of the fact that the collectivity considers the laws essential. Second, punishment draws the members of a social group together in reaction against the deviant. This strengthening of social bonds presumably renews commitments to uphold those rules that define the integrity of the group.[29] And third, punishment of violators helps build and strengthen individual moral commitment. Many theorists believe that morality is intimately linked to negative reactions from others. The threat of punishment is thought to be essential in formation of moral beliefs and its continued possibility is necessary for the maintenance of moral commitments.[30] And it follows that the greater the magnitude of penalty, the greater the ability to strengthen moral feelings.

When people believe the norms are important and that they represent the ethos of collective identity, and when they have personal moral belief in the wrongness of the acts prohibited by the law, they are likely to avoid violation. Therefore, sanctions may deter much deviance by reinforcing normative standards, and to the extent that restitutive schemes would erode that function, one could project serious negative consequences.

Vengeance Defusion. A less often recognized effect of sanctions, but one that nevertheless needs attention, is the defusion of motives for illegal behavior that stem from desires for vengeance. A legal process of sanctioning that causes suffering to the perpetrator of a crime is thought by some to dissipate the anger of victims or their associates and friends. Without provision for retribution, those angered by an offense might well engage in destructive behavior themselves. Restitutive plans that overlook this element of sanctions may lead to unanticipated social costs.

Preventive Insulation. This process makes it less likely that deviant individuals will influence others to break the law. When sanctions are imposed on an individual, that person is often denied opportunities for full participation in social life. When incarcerated he is cut off from interaction with conventional persons, and if he is stigmatized by the judicial process others often shun association with him long after formal punishment is complete. Therefore to the extent that offenders are "bad apples" who may spoil the barrel, sanctioning deters crime by separating them from full contact with others. There is no way to gauge the actual effect of this factor, but at least it must be taken into account if the full potential of restitutive schemes is to be assessed.

Associational Response. Sanctions or sanction threats may have no direct effects on individuals, but they may inspire associates or family members to exercise personal influence in persuading a person to satisfy his needs through legal means. Parents no doubt train their children to obey the law at least partly because they fear punishment for them. And in like manner peers probably persuade their friends to seek legal alternatives when they know they are contemplating illegal behavior. Again the overall deterrent effect produced by this process is impossible to demonstrate empirically, but a complete evaluation of restitution must at least take note of it.

Habituation. Finally, sanctions may also deter by creating law-abiding habits among citizens. At first the threat of punishment may induce conformity through fear of consequences, by normative education and reinforcement, or via associational response. But then, if such conformity continues, it may become habitual. Sanctions therefore forestall illegal behavior by molding habits that reduce contemplation of deviant acts. Although the evidence concerning the operation of this process in social life is meagre, we do know that the role of punishment in conditioning animals is well established. Furthermore, the plausibility of the argument makes it especially important that the effect of restitutive schemes on this deterrent effect be given careful thought.

Effects of Restitution

Table 3-1 summarizes projections of the effects of the various restitutive approaches described earlier on the deterrent function as it might occur via each of ten mechanisms. I have used pluses to indicate some increase in deterrent effect, with the number of pluses symbolizing degree of positive change. Zeroes are used to show no expected consequences. And minuses are indicative of negative influence, with the number of minuses again symbolizing degree of negative influence. In some cases some of the symbols are used in combination to show that the effects are problematic, with some influences in one direction and some in another. Consider row one, for example. Forecasts of effects on deterrence by fear were made earlier, and here plans A and F are shown to have serious eroding effects on fear. This is noted by the presence of three minuses in columns A and F. Plan C, which is projected to have some salutary effect, is described by the plus in column C.

Incapacitation. First, the potential consequences for deterrence by incapacitation are fairly obvious. The three plans that combine standard penalties with

Table 3-1
Projected Consequences of Various Restitutive Plans Upon Deterrence through Different Mechanisms

Deterrent mechanisms	Restitutive plans						
	A	B	C	D	E	F	G
Fear	− − −[a]	− −	+[c]	+	+ +	− − −	− −
Incapacitation	0[b]	0	0	− − −	− − −	− − −	− − −
Surveillance	+	+	0	+	+	±	±
Education	+	+	0	+	+	±	±
Reformation	+	+	+	±[d]	±	±	±
Norm validation	+ +	+ +	0	−	−	− −	− −
Vengeance	+ +	+ +	+	−	−	− −	− −
Insulation	0	0	0	−	−	−	−
Associational response	+	+	0	0	0	−	−
Habituation	0	0	+	+ +	+ +	−	−

[a]More than one symbol indicates intensity

[b]Indicates no change over present system

[c]Indicates increased deterrent effect

[d]Indicates some increase and some decrease

restitution would continue to incapacitate just as much as current practice does. However, the four schemes that substitute restitution for punishment would completely eliminate deterrence through incapacitation.

Surveillance. The effects of the various plans on deterrence by surveillance would be mixed, although most of the schemes promise salutary influence. Plans A, B, D, and E would all require many offenders to engage in regulated labor for considerable periods beyond the normal sentence. The necessity for some form of government supervision for regulated laborers would of itself mandate increased surveillance by officials. But in addition, the administrative apparatus that would be required would probably alert citizens to the status of the offender. These four restitutive systems imply normal surveillance that now comes from conviction alone, as well as increased amounts stemming from the visible presence in the community of offenders who are under restorative obligation.

Plans F and G, on the other hand, are problematic. Since offenders would be obligated only for restoration of direct damage to victims, many would engage in regulated labor only for short periods of time—often much less than present periods of parole. For such offenders levels of surveillance would actually decrease. Other offenders who had inflicted severe damage would be obligated for much longer periods than they would be under the current system. For them surveillance would increase. Therefore, without more knowledge of the amounts of harm typically perpetrated by lawbreakers, it is impossible to estimate whether the net effect would be positive or negative.

Plan C, however, would not appear to produce any effect on the surveillance variable. Offenders would fulfill their obligations while under sentence just as they do now. From a point of view of deterrence by surveillance, plan C would offer no advantage, but it would involve no disadvantage either.

Education. The effects on deterrence by education would follow these same patterns; as surveillance increases with sanctions so does the likelihood that people will become conscious of the law. Thus where a restitutive scheme is expected to enhance deterrence by surveillance, it is also expected to enhance by education as well. This means that plans A, B, D, and E would have positive effects while plans F and G would have mixed results, and plan C would have no effect.

Reformation. Proponents of restitutive schemes argue that the sanctions imposed under such plans may have more beneficial effects for the offender than those imposed under punitive schemes. This is because the sanction is connected to a concrete situation rather than to an abstraction. Restitution makes the sanction directly relevant to some tangible harm caused by the crime. This means that the suffering of a specific victim becomes a central focus of attention. By contrast, harm in a punitive system is measured in abstract terms. It is not the specific suffering of a victim that is of concern, but rather the violation of a legal rule. This makes restitution potentially more rehabilitative because it is easier to identify with specifics than with generalities. Hence it is more likely that offenders will feel remorse, sorrow, or guilt for their crime where they are required to make compensation. And to the extent that such feelings lead to determination to avoid criminal actions in the future, restitutive plans add an element not present in punitive systems of justice.

If this is true, we can project that those schemes that combine restitution with punishment will offer an increase in deterrence by reformation. Offenders would continue to experience the same reformative influences that they now do, whatever they might be. But in addition they would benefit from the reformative influences of restitution. Those plans that substitute restitution for punishment would seem to have mixed possibilities. On one hand they would add the reformative capabilities of reparation but they would take away many of those institutional influences now thought to be rehabilitative, such as psychotherapy and education.

Yet some would maintain that institutional experience is inherently anti-rehabilitative so that those plans that eliminate it would actually be more reformative. It is plausible, therefore, to rate each of the restitutive plans positively with the four "substitution" plans being even more rehabilitative than the "punishment plus" schemes. But since the actual effect of imprisonment is debatable,[31] it is probably safer to assume that the effects of the "substitution" schemes are problematic as far as the effect on deterrence by reformation is concerned.

Norm Validation. Consequences of the different restitutive schemes for deterrence through norm validation are varied. Plans A and B would likely lead to some increase. The same processes that now operate would continue, but there would be additional factors. Since a lot of offenders would be in the community working off restorative obligations even after the usual sentences were complete, there ought to be some increase in consciousness of the importance of the law because more people will become aware of the imposition of sanctions through their interaction with those individuals. And since in general the severity of sanctions will be increased, beliefs in the moral rightness of the law should be strengthened.

Plans F and G, on the other hand, portend some decline in deterrence by normative validation. Neither of these approaches involves punishment and both would imply sanctions less severe than currently imposed. Therefore citizens could not unite around the sanction in opposition to the deviant, and the weakness of sanctions would undermine moral commitments. Moreover, there would be no long-term presence of large numbers of compensating offenders in the community to remind citizens of the importance of rules.

Alternatives D and E would also probably forfeit some of the deterrent effect that ordinarily stems from norm validation by sanctions, but certainly much less than plans F and G. Like those plans, D and E would not permit solidarity through uniting against the deviant, and the relative leniency of sanctions would affect morality. (But each of these effects would be less than for plans F and G, since the sanctions in plans D and E are at least more severe than the ones projected by the former.) Unlike them, however, plans D and E would place large numbers of supervised offenders in the community. But in the absence of severe punishment, it is unlikely that this factor would add much. So it seems probable that the overall effect would be some erosion of deterrence.

Finally, forecasts for variation C specify no effect for deterrence by normative validation. Plan C would continue to make citizens aware of norms by punishing violations as now, and it would allow renewal of social solidarity just as it presently does. In addition, the magnitude of penalties would not decrease, so the effect on moral commitments would be unchanged.

Vengeance. As with incapacitation, the "punishment plus" schemes are clearly demarcated from the "substitution" schemes in terms of their potential effects on deterrence by the defusion of vengeance motives. Obviously those plans that add some penalty or obligation to current sanctions will come closer to satisfying the desire of victims or their friends and relatives for revenge. And the more obligation or penalty that is added on, the greater the probability of defusion. Therefore those schemes that substitute restitution for punishment are likely to lose some deterrent effect simply because they cannot satisfy these motives. In particular the "substitute" plans that require less than complete compensation would produce serious loss of deterrence by this mechanism.

Preventive Insulation. Preventive insulation would appear to be unaffected under the "punishment plus" schemes. Those who are presently isolated through incarceration would continue to be isolated, and insulation stemming from stigma would remain. But "substituion" plans do suggest some decline in deterrence by preventive insulation. Justice under each of those plans would not involve incarceration. Therefore, offenders would almost never be isolated from interaction with conventional persons. Perhaps stigmatization would increase since more citizens would be aware of conviction because of the supervision that would accompany regulated labor, but it is unlikely that this would be enough to compensate for the loss of preventive insulation from incarceration.

Associational Response. The assumption of deterrence by association is that friends and associates influence individuals to obey the law because they vicariously fear the consequences of disobedience for them. Vicarious fear would seem to be based on the possible severity of sanction. If an individual warns his child not to go into the street for fear of the child's being hit by an automobile, he no doubt thinks of the dreadfulness of what can happen, not how likely it is to happen. Thus when a restitutive plan suggests a change toward greater severity of sanction, it will also probably mean greater deterrence by associational influence. Therefore, plans A and B, which portend increases in the magnitude of penalties, should increase deterrence by association. Plans C, D, and E promise little change in severity of sanctions and should produce little change in associational response. But plans F and G involve less severe sanctions so they should also lead to declines in associational influence.

Habituation. The extent to which citizens develop law-abiding habits as a result of sanctioning is a function of the effectiveness of four of the deterrent mechanisms already discussed—fear of consequences, normative education and reinforcement, and associational response—although fear is probably the most important of the four. We can estimate the consequences for deterrence by habituation of each of the restorative plans by considering these four variables in combination, giving more weight to fear. The results of this combination suggest that habituation would be unaffected by plans A and B. They would lead to serious declines in fear, some increase in deterrence by education, large enhancement of normative reinforcement, and increases in associational response, but since fear is more important than the others its strong negative rating would probably balance out the other positives. But plans F and G suggest decreases in deterrence by habituation since the four mechanisms include three strong negative effects with one problematic rating. Plan C, on the other hand, appears to have positive possibilities. It combines a positive deterrent effect for fear with three neutral effects. And since fear is the most important of the four, plan C would seem to warrant a positive rating in terms of its potential effect on deterrence by habituation. However, plans D and E promise the greatest improvement in deterrence by habituation because they would increase deterrence by fear and by education; they would have neutral effects on associational response and negative effects for norm validation.

Summary of Effects. Summarizing the overall effects of the restitutive approaches on deterrence broadly conceived is difficult because we do not know the relative importance of each of the ten deterrent mechanisms. For example, if we knew that deterrence by fear was relatively unimportant compared with such mechanisms as surveillance or norm validation, we might easily conclude that plans A and B were clearly superior since they promise positive changes in surveillance and norm validation. But we cannot rank the deterrent processes. Therefore, the best we can do is to assume that those plans that offer increases by means of the greatest number of deterrent mechanisms and that suggest decreases through the fewest deterrent processes are the most desirable.

Following that logic it appears that plan C is superior to the others. It promises to enhance four deterrent processes and to reduce none. The next most advantageous plans are A and B. Each of them is projected to bolster deterrence in six different ways, but they are expected to reduce deterrence through fear. Plans D and E suggest increases in four deterrent processes but decreases in four others, so they would appear less desirable. And finally, plans F and G are completely unacceptable because they offer no deterrent increases at all although they would probably erode seven different deterrent functions.

Conclusions

First, it is abundantly clear that knowledge about deterrence is far too meagre to permit any firm projections of what might happen under different systems of justice. We are just not in a position to estimate the consequences of restitution. But, then, we also don't know the deterrent consequences of current practice. So the various schemes that might be justified by the projections set forth in this paper have as much claim to credence as does the present criminal justice system.

Second, application of extant knowledge and assumptions about deterrence suggest that there is no inherent conflict between deterrence and restitution. Indeed, for one concept of deterrence, the most radical restitutive plans are precisely the ones that have the greatest potential for increasing deterrence. It seems very likely that restitution, at least under some implementation plans, would be highly compatible with the deterrent goals of the law, no matter how narrowly or broadly deterrence is conceived.

Third, one can conceptualize deterrence in more than one way, and depending upon the conceptualization one chooses, draw different conclusions about the particular implementation scheme that would be most compatible with deterrent objectives. If deterrence is taken to mean curtailment of law violation by fear of sanctions, then a plan that substitutes full restitution (all costs associated with the crime) through regulated labor would seem to offer the best alternative. But thinking of deterrence as curtailment of illegal behavior by sanctions or sanction threats through any means would lead to the conclusion that the best plan is one that requires partial restitution equivalent to that which could be provided through regulated labor for the period of an ordinary sentence.

To avoid choosing one approach or the other it seems safest to suggest that the most appropriate plan would be one that has the most advantage and the least disadvantage from both points of view. Plan C, the combination of partial restitution and ordinary sentences, would appear to fill the bill. It does not promise the greatest increase in deterrence by fear nor does it promise increases in deterrence by the greatest number of mechanisms, but it does suggest some increase in fear deterrence and it probably will increase deterrence in three other ways. And, in addition, it alone entails no reduction in deterrence by any mechanism. This is not to say that other plans are not workable. Indeed, it appears that two of them offer more advantage than disadvantage and two more promise at least as much advantage as disadvantage. And one who is willing to make some assumptions about relative importance of deterrent mechanisms might conclude that all but two of the plans are not only feasible, but positively desirable.

Notes

1. Jack P. Gibbs, *Crime, Punishment, and Deterrence* (New York: Elsevier Scientific Publishing, 1975).
2. Johannes Andenaes, "The Moral or Educative Influence of Criminal

Law," *Journal of Social Issues*, 27 (2): 17-31; John Finley Scott, *Internalization of Norms: A Sociological Theory of Moral Commitment* (Englewood Cliffs, New Jersey: Prentice-Hall, 1971); and Matthew Silberman, "Toward a Theory of Criminal Deterrence," *American Sociological Review*, 41 (June, 1976): 442-461.

3. See Gibbs; Daniel Nagin, *General Deterrence: A Review of the Eimprical Evidence* (Pittsburgh: Urban Systems Institute, Carnegie-Mellon University, 1975); and Charles R. Tittle and Charles H. Logan, "Sanctions and Deviance: Evidence and Remaining Questions," *Law and Society Review* 7 (Spring, 1973): 372-392 for reviews of the state of knowledge.

4. Charles R. Tittle, "Deterrents or Labeling?" *Social Forces*, 53 (March, 1975): 399-410.

5. Gibbs, pp. 58-64.

6. See David F. Greenberg, "The Incapacitative Effects of Imprisonment: Some Estimates," *Law and Society Review*, 9 (Summer, 1975): 541-580; and Shlomo Shinnar and Reuel Shinnar, "The Effects of the Criminal Justice System on the Control of Crime: A Quantitative Approach," *Law and Society Review*, 9 (Summer, 1975): 581-611 for conflicting interpretations of data.

7. Throughout this paper regulated labor will refer to any form of work arranged by the state and/or in which the state claims a proportion of earnings specifically to compensate for damages associated with a criminal act. Different forms might include work in prison industries, contracted labor for those incarcerated or under state supervision on probation or parole, and personally arranged employment in private industry or governmental organizations.

8. Donald J. Newman, "Pleading Guilty for Considerations: A Study of Bargain Justice," *Journal of Criminal Law, Criminology and Police Science*, 46 (March-April, 1956): 780-790.

9. William J. Chambliss and Robert B. Seidman, *Law, Order and Power* (Reading, Massachusetts: Addison-Wesley, 1971), pp. 447-472; and Frederic Suffet, "Bail Setting: A Study of Courtroom Interaction," *Crime and Delinquency*, 12 (October, 1966): 318-331.

10. Abraham S. Blumberg, "The Practice of Law as a Confidence Game: Organizational Cooptation of a Profession," *Law and Society Review*, 1 (June, 1967): 15-39.

11. H. Laurence Ross, "The Neutralization of Severe Penalities: Some Traffic Law Studies," *Law and Society Review*, 10 (Spring, 1976): 403-413.

12. Jack P. Gibbs, "Crime, Punishment and Deterrence," *Southwestern Social Science Quarterly*, 48 (March, 1968): 515-530.

13. Charles R. Tittle, "Crime Rates and Legal Sanctions," *Social Problems* 16 (Spring, 1969): 409-423; William C. Bailey and Donald W. Smith, "Punishment: Its Severity and Certainty," *Journal of Criminal Law, Criminology, and Police Science*, 63 (December, 1972): 530-539; and Charles H. Logan, "General Deterrent Effects of Imprisonment," *Social Forces*, 51 (September, 1972): 64-73.

14. Jackson Toby, "Is Punishment Necessary?" *Journal of Criminal Law, Criminology, and Police Science*, 55 (September, 1964): 332-337; and Franklin E. Zimring and Gordon J. Hawkins, *Deterrence: The Legal Threat in Crime Control* (Chicago: The University of Chicago Press, 1973).

15. Leslie Stephen, *The English Utilitarians* (3 vols) (New York: G. P. Putnam's Sons, 1900).

16. William J. Chambliss, "Types of Deviance and the Effectiveness of Legal Sanctions," *Wisconsin Law Review* (Summer, 1967): 703-719; Zimring and Hawkins, *Deterrence: The Legal Threat*; and Franklin E. Zimring, "Of Doctors, Deterrence, and the Dark Figure of Crime—A Note on Abortion in Hawaii," *University of Chicago Law Review*, 39 (Summer, 1972): 699-721.

17. Charles R. Tittle, "Sanction Fear and the Maintenance of Social Order," *Social Forces*, 55 (March, 1977): 579-596; and Solomon Kobrin, Steven G. Lubeck, E. Wayne Hansen, and Robert L. Yeaman, *The Deterrent Effectiveness of Criminal Justice Sanction Strategies* (Los Angeles: Public Systems Research Institute, 1972).

18. William J. Chambliss, *Criminal Law in Action* (Santa Barbara, California: Hamilton Publishing Company, 1975), p. 166.

19. Don W. Brown and Stephen L. McDougal, "Arrest Rates and Crime Rates: When Does a Tipping Effect Occur?" *Social Forces* (forthcoming).

20. Franklin E. Zimring and Gordon J. Hawkins, "Deterrence and Marginal Groups," *Journal of Research in Crime and Delinquency* (July, 1968): 100-114; and Toby.

21. John Irwin, *The Felon* (Englewood Cliffs, New Jersey: Prentice-Hall, 1970); and Charles R. Tittle, "Institutional Living and Rehabilitation," *Journal of Health and Social Behavior*, 13 (September, 1972): 263-275.

22. Leonard Orland, *Justice, Punishment, Treatment* (New York: The Free Press, 1973), pp. 53-54.

23. Maynard L. Erickson and Jack P. Gibbs, "Specific Versus General Properties of Legal Punishment and Deterrence," *Social Science Quarterly*, 56 (December, 1975): 380-391; and Silberman.

24. Gresham M. Sykes, *The Society of Captives* (Princeton: Princeton University Press, 1958); and Charles R. Tittle, "Prisons and Rehabilitation: The Inevitability of Disfavor," *Social Problems*, 21 (3): 385-395.

25. See Gibbs, *Crime, Punishment, and Deterrence* for fuller discussions of these processes.

26. Charles R. Tittle, "Labelling and Crime: An Empirical Evaluation," in Walter Gove (ed.), *Societal Reaction and Deviant Behavior: The Evaluation of a Theory* (New York: Halsted Press, 1975).

27. Tittle, "Prisons and Rehabilitation."

28. Herbert L. Packer, *The Limits of the Criminal Sanction* (Stanford: Stanford University Press, 1968).

29. Emile Durkheim, *The Division of Labor in Society* (New York: The Free Press, 1949).

30. Scott; and Silberman.
31. Tittle, "Prisons and Rehabilitation."

4

The Therapeutic Uses
of Restitution
Paul W. Keve

In this day of general skepticism about the effectiveness of any kind of treatment effort in any kind of correctional setting one is certain to feel a bit self-conscious in making assertions about the rehabilitative effect of restitution—or any other treatment procedure. Any such assertions should be backed by convincing reports of competent research in order to be truly satisfying. But this cannot be, for the evaluations are not yet done, and when they are done and the reports duly filed they are most certain to be inconclusive on the question of rehabilitative effect.

It may be that this is one reason why the planners of restitution projects are reluctant even to suggest rehabilitation of the offender as one of the purposes of the programs. Currently, six major restitution projects are being started and are subject to a thorough evaluation to be conducted by the Criminal Justice Research Center, Albany, New York. The projects are in California, Colorado, Connecticut, Georgia, Maine, Massachusetts, and Oregon. In their statements of purpose only one of these clearly asserts that one goal is the rehabilitation of the involved offenders. Another speaks of a desired corrective effect, but the accompanying phrases in the statement indicate that improved attitudes and social functioning are not quite what the author had in mind.

One senses that all the project managers are hopeful that their restitution programs will do good for the offenders as well as for their victims but that as a matter of their own honesty they are reluctant to claim a purpose that is so uncertain of achievement and so nearly impossible to demonstrate.

Of course we could get some inkling of rehabilitative effectiveness if we were to limit ourselves to a very narrow definition of rehabilitation; a simple counting up of new offenses on the premise that a low recidivism rate is correlated with rehabilitation. We may have to content ourselves with that as a research definition, but it would be regrettable if we were in fact and practice to content ourselves with no greater accomplishment than a lowered rearrest rate. Our real goal should be the intangible one of helping people, no matter how few, to be more mature, more responsible, less selfish, more socially competent. And for the purposes of this paper the latter sense of rehabilitation will be intended.

If it were to be found that there is no rehabilitative effect in restitution there would still be more than adequate justification for it in the political and economic benefits it brings. If it also has treatment value this presumably relates to certain characteristics that are regularly observed in our clients, such as low self-esteem, and its close relatives, a preponderance of failure experiences,

59

and a lack of experience in being useful to others in socially approved ways. Most people would probably agree that those whom we consider normal, happy, and law abiding do have a generally good feeling about themselves; they know that in certain chosen endeavors they can be successful, and they enjoy the very essential satisfaction of being able to be useful to others in some modest way.

These observations lead quite naturally to several assumptions about how we can best achieve rehabilitative effect in restitution programs. These will be listed and discussed here; but first some explanation should be made of the breadth of the restitution concept as used in this discussion.

In its narrowest sense restitution may refer only to those programs that permit a victim to receive a monetary restoration of his loss directly from the offender. But any study of the rehabilitative effect almost forces attention to a wider concept that includes so-called symbolic restitution. This may mean programs that serve persons other than the victims—programs that serve individuals, or those that serve groups (perhaps whole communities). And this brings within the area of restitution the community service programs.

From the earliest beginnings of penology the penalities were adjusted for rich and poor offenders to provide that those who were rich would be punished in their purses, while those without purses would instead have to be punished in their bodies. But now we are perhaps coming to the view that both the affluent and the indigent could be subject to similar kinds of restitutional penalities: personal involvement in the giving of service. It might be too easy for an affluent offender to pay back a monetary loss to a victim; that act for him might be no more than a casual business transaction with no therapeutic effect. But both the affluent and the indigent offender are appropriate subjects for a restitutional penalty that involves them emotionally in giving of personal time and effort to some restorative help to either the victim or the larger community.

The Effective Elements of Treatment

In looking at criteria for rehabilitative quality, the major points should probably be such as the following.

The Payment Should Truly Be an Extra Effort, a Sacrifice of Time or Convenience. Probably no improvement in self-awareness or raising of self-esteem will derive from the writing of a check or any other casual restitutional act that does not interrupt accustomed activities or diminish personal resources in a felt way. It might be argued that this distinction is of more political value than therapeutic value. Politically it is useful to assure the public that the clients are being "punished" by having to spend their free time on weekends in some unpaid labor in order to pay back either a victim or the full community. In fact, an emphasis upon this point may have much to do with the public's willingness to accept restitution programs when they are used as sole sanctions.

Whether this element of inconvenience and sacrifice also has therapeutic effect is a conjectural matter. Very likely it contributes to the rehabilitative effect in certain fortunate applications, but no doubt there are many other cases in which the useful effect is minimal or absent.

The Assigned Restitutional Effort Should Be Clearly Defined, Measurable, and, Without Being Easy, it Should Be Achievable. This principle is in tune with the current emphasis on more explicitly stated sentences and release dates, and for the same reason: the client is likely to perform better if he has a clearly stated goal to accomplish. He will most certainly be more benefited if he knows that the goal is achieved.

This speaks to one of the most basic principles of treatment and it deals with one of the most pervading reasons for maladjustment among our clients. To a very large degree they are people who have had more than their share of failure experiences. The reasons are not so important as is the fact that a person who is accustomed to failure is also to some degree resigned to it. Translate this to mean that the consequences of crime—consequences such as arrest, trial, and prison—are accepted in his mind as likely, perhaps even certain, and so they have little or no deterrent value.

For such a person, simply to remain unarrested, unincarcerated, may be an achievement, and an unexpected one. If he is going to achieve in this respect it is important and essential that he believe that he can achieve. And if he is to gain this faith in his ability to achieve continued avoidance of crime and arrest we must give him actual experience at it. It does not matter so much what he succeeds at, as long as we insure that it is a constructive kind of endeavor and that he does in fact recognize that he was able to achieve the goal that was set.

The monumental significance of this is seen in contrast to the all too usual talent of the correctional system for setting up clients for failure. Rules of probation, institutional rules, parole rules, have all been structured according to what well-adjusted, middle-class people consider appropriate and attainable. Goals and rules have been set for correctional clients that are so unrealistic in terms of their living habits and capabilities that often they are virtually certain to fail.

So the restitution requirements must be attainable. If the money to be repaid is far too much for the client's earning capacity, a realistic compromise sum must be set. If a service is to be performed, it is fine if the service interferes with the client's free time on weekends, but it must not require the person, for example, to get to a distant worksite without a car, to lose time from his paid employment, or to compromise essential duties to the family at home.

The Restitution Effort Should Be Meaningful. One of the well-organized restitutional programs has been the Community Service Program operated by the Inner London Probation and After-Care Service. This can properly be classed as a symbolic restitution program, and its type is now being implemented in other areas in the United Kingdom. One of the lessons quickly learned by the London staff was that the assigned service needed to be meaningful if the individual case was to have the best chance of success. Judge Leenhouts, who started one of the earlier community service programs in this country, also found this to be true. In his program conducted in Royal Oak it was found that clients would stay with the assigned work better if the work was something truly needed, if it benefitted a person or the community in some important way, and if tangible, visible results were being achieved. By the same token, any work that seemed like busy work or any contrived sort of token work usually failed to produce good performance or good attitudes.

Having some impact on one's environment, and doing so in a way that brings recognition, is essential to development of a mature personality. As a group, the clients we deal with tend to have lacked this experience. Too often they have grown up in the constant knowledge that they and their families are people who seem always to be in the demeaning position of being helped instead of helping; instead of being contributing people they are the subjects of other people's help, control, restraint, admonitions, or correction.

If we are going to have any therapeutic effect upon our restitution program clients we must at least not reinforce the factors that have contributed to their maladjustment. Admittedly, no amount of therapy that we build into these programs can possibly guarantee a rehabilitative outcome, but we might well remember and apply an observation that is imputed to Florence Nightingale, that the first requirement of a hospital is that it not make its patients any worse!

Unfortunately, there was ample need for Miss Nightingale to make this elementary point. The early hospitals, with imperfect understanding of the basic principles of sanitation and bacteria control, often introduced new sources of infection to their patients and so jeopardized their chances of recovery. In social and psychological terms the correctional systems have fostered the same problem. A person whose criminal conduct stems partly from anger and resentment toward the social system in which he has been unable to succeed comes into our prisons and the regimenting, boring "put-down" of the custodial operation adds to that anger. A person handicapped by his poor self-image comes into prison and its heavy stigmatic effect further depresses his self-image. Not the least of the negative elements in institutionalization is the loss of opportunity to do meaningful things that will be of usefulness to anyone. Imprisonment itself cuts off almost all opportunities to perform useful and meaningful service, and, worse, the system tends to say to the prisoner, however unintentionally, that his service is not really wanted. The fact that he is called upon to do jobs around the prison is no contradiction of this principle. Washing sheets in a prison laundry does not qualify as meaningful work for the purposes of therapy.

If, then, an offender is put in a restitution program in lieu of incarceration, it should be an essential and elementary principle that this be a chance to exploit the restorative potential in a meaningful, satisfying giving of oneself to help another. A good example was a Minneapolis program a few years ago in which girls on juvenile court probation worked weekends with senile psychotic patients in a state hospital. In that setting, where staff was short and the attention to the basic needs of these pathetic patients was minimal on the weekends, the girls had the very rewarding experience of being able to brighten the lives, quite visibly, of the elderly and incompetent women.

The Restitutional Assignment Should Be Designed to Produce Rewards. It seems an altogether accepted view that human behavior is shaped by the twin forces of painful consequences for mischievious acts and rewarding, pleasurable consequences for approved acts; and it just might be that the truly normal, well-adjusted person is shaped more by rewards than by punishments. But here again the correctional institutions have a talent for reinforcing the wrong approach. In a typical prison there is paucity of available rewards; the principal tool for controlling behavior is the use of punishments.

Accordingly, an advantage to exploit in the restitutional program is the opportunity to give the correctional client an assignment that can have a rewarding outcome. This may seem a contradictory idea to some persons who see restitution in more or less punitive terms. Of course there is a punitive quality to the idea of requiring an offender to pay a monetary claim to his victim; and there is a punitive quality in the requirement of symbolic restitution through unpaid community service. But this does not interfere in the slightest with the goal of designing the restitutional assignment so that the offender has a sense of reward at the conclusion of it.

In the community service type of programs the best therapeutic artistry would be the assignment of a client to a task that would use certain talents that he may have; and, second, a task in which his individual talent could be used to help some person or persons who are in a worse position than himself. Restitution programs that are designed more for the direct paying back of monetary losses suffered by a victim can and do reach for this same sense of achievement and reward, although the experience has been that this kind of accomplishment is uncertain and sometimes just not possible. Logic suggests that it is desirable to bring victim and offender together in a constructive context that may create in the victim a better feeling about the justice system. Equally good logic suggests that the experience may be good for the offender by making him see his victim as a real person, and the victim's losses as a real hurt. This would also give the offender a rewarding feeling of having done something to help a person whom he had wronged.

The latter is a fine idea if it works. If the contact between victim and offender goes smoothly and produces for the offender a good feeling that his restitution was needed, was helpful, and was warmly appreciated, then the feeling of reward is there and with it some degree of therapy. Such complex human feelings would be involved, however, in such contacts that they cannot be designed so much on a program basis as on a case-by-case basis. Here the skill of staff is in constant demand.

Indirect Benefits of the Program

Throughout the field of corrections there are always many different types of programs being tried at any time. But all of them, including any type of restitution program, probably have value only to the extent that they are effective in bringing people together in constructive relationships. Program design is important, but it is a vehicle for the delivery of a therapeutic encounter rather than itself being the therapy. As a vehicle the restitution program can be designed to have different sorts of therapeutic thrusts.

It is quite possible and appropriate, for instance, for some restitution programs to have educational value, particularly in a program for juveniles. Over the past few years several juvenile courts have operated programs for boys or girls in which they could work in groups, making restitution to the whole community. In one instance a group of boys was helping to develop a new public park and their responsibility required them to make some study of landscaping, of horticulture, and of other aspects of park design. When they finished their work and walked away from a spot of beauty that would not have been there but for their efforts, they had their reward in the visible, publicly approved product, and they had had a good educational experience, too.

The basic idea behind this program can often be employed in any variation of the restitution program, that is, requiring the offender himself to carry all the responsibility he can for the planning and development of the restitution project. This principle must be applied skillfully, of course, so that success is virtually guaranteed. If the client is required to do some planning that he is unable and unprepared to do, then we are just setting him up for one more failure experience and defeating our therapeutic goals. But to the extent that he is capable, let him do the planning and arranging. We thus encourage the possibility that he will learn something and that he will have more commitment to the endeavor because he has had a part in shaping it.

Part II: Psychological Perspectives on Restitution

5

Applications and Limitations of Restitution
O. Hobart Mowrer

In this paper, I propose to approach the phenomenon of restitution from the vantage point of common childhood discipline. In principle, the management methods used with children and with legally convicted persons are often not very different. That is, in both instances they involve punishment of a more or less retaliatory nature. The object is to inflict some type of discomfort or pain that cancels out the gratification derived from a disapproved or illegal form of behavior and that will, it is hoped, have the effect of preventing the future recurrence of such behavior. Although we continue to use this approach, both with children and with other persons, we know that it often does not work well, and may indeed only make bad matters worse.

The person who, in my opinion, has written most perceptively about childhood discipline is the late Rudolph Dreikurs (d. 1964), a Chicago psychiatrist and exponent of the psychology of Alfred Adler. Repeatedly, Dreikurs wrote and was heard to say: "Don't ever get into a power struggle with your children. You can't win." And he saw discipline of a retaliatory nature as necessarily involving the exercise of power. Thus, he was opposed to the use of punishment in the common sense of the term with children, and advocated instead reliance upon what he referred to as *natural and logical consequences*. Whenever feasible, Dreikurs urged parents to allow natural consequences to operate. If, for example, a child was doing something that might involve a somewhat painful but not seriously injurious fall, he counseled parents to caution the child with respect to what might happen but not forcibly to remove him or her from the situation. In other words, the child was allowed to learn, on his or her own, to come to terms with the laws of gravity; and the same strategy applied to confrontation with hot objects and other potentially pain-producing situations. Here the parent shows concern but keeps his or her "cool" and the child comes to see the warnings as useful instead of arbitrary and restrictive.

Sometimes, of course, trusting to natural consequences, for one reason or another, is not practical; it is in these cases that Dreikurs recommended the use of what he called logical consequences. For example, if at mealtime a child is allowed to serve him or herself and then doesn't eat all the food taken, a parent can either precipitate a fight with the child or can, in a calm, matter-of-fact way, withhold dessert or put the uneaten food away, to be eaten at the next meal. It often seems better in such situations not to say very much and just act, thus avoiding the possibility of an argument. Similarly, there can be an understanding that the child doesn't play on Saturday mornings until his or her room is tidied up; and there are numerous other circumstances in which privileges of various kinds can be withheld until certain tasks are performed. Behavior modification psychologists call this "contingent reinforcement." And it can usually be practiced in a rather low-key fashion, and quite effectively, if the parent is consistent and fair.

It has been my privilege to spend considerable time in several therapeutic communities for drug addicts; and although this particular language is not used there, it is obvious that much use is made of natural and logical consequences as disciplinary measures. Once when I was at the Swan Lake, New York, Daytop facility, I heard the then director, David Dietch, say to a group of relatively new members something like this: "In the past you have been in an assortment of cages that were easy to get into and hard to get out of. Where you are now is just the reverse, hard to get into and easy to get out of. There are no bars on the windows or locks on the doors, and you can leave, day or night, anytime you decide to do so. But we would like you to talk it over with us first before you split. We may be able to say something to you out of our own experience that will change your mind. However tough it may seem to you here, you know what is waiting for you out there: the possibility of arrest and a prison sentence or ending up in the morgue from an overdose. Here, in the Daytop family, there is hope for you; out there, there are only dead-ends."

There is very little talk of restitution for acts committed before one came into a therapeutic drug community. Perhaps learning to "stay clean" and "go straight" is regarded as a reasonable trade-off in this connection, but infraction of rules and obligations here and now is dealt with promptly and often very effectively. I am not sure what legal penology has to learn from places like Daytop Village, but the two institutions certainly stand in sharp contrast in terms of both spirit and action (Sugarman, p. 187).

The organization which, I suppose, has been directly or indirectly responsible for radically transforming more lives than any other contemporary institution is Alcoholics Anonymous. And although the term *restitution*—which literally means putting something back in place—is rarely used, much emphasis is put on an equivalent concept, namely, *making amends*. The only "punishment" that AA members are likely to receive is being laughed at for some of their naive and immature attitudes, but they are earnestly enjoined to take a searching inventory of the harm they have done to others and, whenever feasible, to make amends. Steps eight and nine of the twelve-step Recovery Program read as follows: "Made a list of all persons we had harmed, and became willing to make amends to them all;" and "Made direct amends to such people whenever possible, except when to do so would injure them or others."

And it is fair to say, I think, that those who really "make" the program in AA work at these two steps very diligently. Recently I heard an AA member who is a photographer say that some years ago there was a fire in his studio and most of his equipment was destroyed but that he did manage to salvage a camera that had a particularly valuable lens on it. However, he reported this camera as a loss to the insurance company and was compensated for it, because he was deeply in debt at the time and desperately needed the money. When he joined AA he began "working the steps," his action in this connection preyed on his mind to such an extent that, in the presence of a fellow AA member, he destroyed the camera and prized lens. And he added when he told me the story, "You know I have never for a moment regretted it." As is well known, Alcoholics Anonymous has been so successful in helping its members achieve sobriety and a new life style that persons with other addictive tendencies have formed similar organizations and found restitution a potent factor in effecting personal change.

The only psychologist I know has been seriously interested for a long time in the use of restitution instead of retribution in the management of persons convicted of felonies and lesser crimes is Dr. Albert Eblash. Some twenty years ago he sent me a paper entitled, "Restitution vs. retribution in the treatment of legal offenders." This, I think, was the first such treatise I had ever read, and it made a deep and favorable impression on me, as have other materials that Dr. Eblash has subsequently published or privately circulated. But he has been a voice crying in the wilderness, with little impact upon either his own profession or legal practice. A decade or more ago, a judge in Cleveland made national headlines by imposing a restitutive rather than retributive penalty upon some careless young people who had left a beach badly littered after a party. The sentence passed upon them was not a conventional one, but the rare assignment that they go to the beach and carefully clean up the mess they had made. This could have hardly seemed arbitrary or unfair to the young people involved in this escapade, and it was almost certainly less expensive than "due process of law," as usually conceived, would have been.

Although the Cleveland judge's decision seems to have met with widespread approval, it was not generally emulated. One wonders why. The littering of a public beach, while a nuisance, did not particularly frighten the local citizenery. Where public safety is threatened, people get jittery. An individual who has committed a crime of violence, if left at large, is seen as a public menace and the public cries out for protection, which can be most obviously assured by arrest or incarceration of some sort. But this response is not necessarily incompatible with restitution. If prisons had successful work programs and reasonable remuneration for participation therein, an inmate, instead of "doing time" idly and at great state expense, could make at least token restitution to those who had suffered from his crime and contribute to the support of his otherwise often destitute family.

Prison-operated shops are by no means unheard of, as are farming and public works such as road building. But, somehow, the atmosphere in such cases has been more one of punishment than of productive work. Also, private enterprise has objected to the competition offered by prison-made products; and there has been pressure on prisons to purchase commodities, including food, from the "outside" instead of producing it themselves. Half a century ago, most state-operated mental hospitals had their own dairies, vegetable gardens, and bakeries, but outside economic pressures have operated here, too, to eliminate largely this type of self-sufficiency and the opportunity for lucrative, and therapeutic, employment of inmates. How can a man or woman convicted of a "serious" crime make restitution, and regain self-esteem instead of becoming increasingly bitter and resentful, unless allowed to spend much of his or her time productively, either in or outside prison walls?

One wonders if the restitutive route has been given a fair shake, or even if, for societal reasons, it can be. It is generally admitted that retributive justice is not working, from either a preventative or rehabilitative standpoint. We have briefly examined child-rearing practices that involve punishment and seen that there are promising and practical alternatives. But is there not a larger problem, namely, that in a highly technological society the goal is to make factories and industries ever *more efficient*, which, in the final analysis, means using more machinery and employing fewer people? Indeed it is now taken for granted that such a society is going to have a growing number of unneeded, unemployed citizens. Idle incarceration might be hard to oppose since it cuts down on the size of the so-called labor market as well as creating a multibillion-dollar industry known as our penal system. Of course the other side of the coin is that unemployment is not only demoralizing but also breeds desperation and behavior that would not otherwise occur. Unemployed persons who have been interviewed by the news media are often frank in saying that they would prefer to work and earn a decent wage, but that if they cannot get work they will resort to whatever other activities may net enough money for them and their families to get along. The products of our advanced technology—food, household conveniences, automobiles, and so on—are attractively advertised through multimedia, and this advertising impinges upon the unemployed as well as the employed and only serves to heighten the latter's discontent and anger. For this reason, too, restitution, while vastly superior to retribution in theory, faces monumental obstacles when it comes to implementation in our society.

In conclusion, I wish to repeat my belief that Rudolph Dreikurs is profoundly right in his contention that parents "can't win" if they permit themselves to become involved in a power struggle with their children—and that such power struggles are a common and potent source of marital disruption as well. Extrapolating from these observations, we find further justification for distrust of a system of criminal justice that is basically retributive, vengeful, and vindictive. However, no alternative has been found that is very different in its approach and yet has widespread public approval and support. Restitution has many attractive aspects, but it also seems in practice to have some rather serious limitations. Since it is an uncomplicated and rather obvious concept, we can be sure it would otherwise have long since become a universal policy and practice.

It goes without saying, I hope, that I am deeply sympathetic with such efforts as are currently being made to still find a way in which it can be made to work, broadly and effectively; and it would be marvelous if these efforts should yet prove successful. But my attitude remains one of skepticism, which seems to be widely shared and empirically grounded.

References

Dreikurs, R. *Children the Challenge*. New York: Hawthorne Books, 1964.
Mowrer, O.H. *The Crises in Psychiatry and Religion*. Princeton, N.J.: D. Van Nostrand Co., 1961.
Mowrer, O.H. *The New Group Therapy*. Princeton, N.J.: D. Van Nostrand Co., 1964.
Sugarman, B. *Daytop Village: A Therapeutic Community*. New York: Holt, Rinehart and Winston, 1974.

6

Equity Theory and Restitution Programming
Mary K. Utne and Elaine Hatfield

Kurt Lewin once observed that "there is nothing so practical as a good theory." We've found Equity theory (a general theory of social exchange) to be an eminently "practical" theory.[1] It gives a framework for sorting out the complex issues connected with restitution programming.

In theory, the idea of collaboration among experts from a variety of disciplines—social psychology, law enforcement, and corrections—in pursuit of a broader understanding of an issue, always sounds exciting. *In reality*, such collaborative enterprises rarely work out. First, the experts soon find that they do not share a common language. Psychologists' definitions of "wrongdoers" turn out to be vastly different from lawyers' definitions. Then the experts discover they do not agree as to what constitutes "strong evidence." For psychologists, a laboratory experiment is the essence of "proof." For correction officers, natural field observations are more compelling. For lawyers, precedent is what counts. When, finally, theorists suggest some practical recommendations, practitioners scoff. They can recite a dozen practical reasons why theorists' recommendations are useless. It is our hope, however, that Equity theory propositions are basic and general enough that they can provide a theoretical framework for some of the complex questions surrounding restitution programming in a way that all will find useful.

Overview. In Section I, we will review Equity theory—a general theory of human behavior. In Section II we will see what Equity theory has to say about the probable impact of current procedures of the U.S. legal system for restoring equity to the offender-victim relationship. In Section III, we will point out several things that Equity theory suggests restitution programmers should probably consider when designing any restitution program. Finally in Section IV we will offer some caveats and qualifiers to an Equity approach to restitution programming.

This research was supported, in part, by NIMH grant MH 26681.

73

Section I: The Equity Formulation

Equity theory is a strikingly simple theory. It views social interaction as a process of reciprocal exchange, governed by a norm of distributive fairness. The theory comprises four propositions.

The Equity Propositions

Proposition I. Individuals will try to maximize their outcomes (where outcomes equal rewards minus costs).

Proposition IIA. Groups can maximize collective reward by evolving accepted systems for equitably apportioning resources among members. Thus, groups will evolve such systems of Equity, and will attempt to induce members to accept and adhere to these systems.

Proposition IIB. Groups will generally reward members who treat others equitably, and generally punish (increase the cost of) members who treat others inequitably.

Proposition III. When individuals find themselves participating in inequitable relationships, they will become distressed. The more inequitable the relationship, the more distress individuals will feel.

Proposition IV. Individuals who discover they are in an inequitable relationship will attempt to eliminate their distress by restoring equity. The greater the inequity that exists, the more distress they will feel, and the harder they will try to restore equity.

How Do Social Psychologists Define Equity?

According to Equity theory, a relationship is "fair" if people are getting exactly what they deserve in their relationship with others—no more and certainly no less. What do people "deserve"? Equity theorists say people deserve equal relative benefits or gains from their interactions with one another. Psychologists have found the following *formal* definition of Equity to be a useful one.

Definitional Formula. An equitable relationship exists if the person *scrutinizing* the relationship believes that all participants are receiving equal *Relative Gains* from the relationship; i.e., where

$$\frac{(O_A - I_A)}{(|I_A|)^{k_A}} = \frac{(O_B - I_B)}{(|I_B|)^{k_B}}$$

What does this mean?

Definition of Terms. The *scrutineer* is simply the person who is examining the relationship, to determine if it is fair or unfair. The scrutineer may be an outside observer (such as the public, a social work agency, a judge, or a jury) or either of the participants.

Inputs (I_A or I_B) are defined as "the participant's contributions to the exchange, which are seen (by a scrutineer) as entitling him to reward *or* costs." In different settings, people consider different inputs to be relevant. For example, in industrial settings, businessmen assume that such hard assets as capital or manual labor entitle a person to reward. Such liabilities as incompetence or disloyalty entitle him to cost. In a legal setting, such inputs as intent, fault, and negligence may be of primary importance.

Outcomes (O_A or O_B) are defined as "the positive *and* negative consequences that a scrutineer perceives a participant has received in the course of his relationship with another." The participant's outcomes are equal to the *rewards* he obtains from the relationship, minus the *costs* he incurs.[2]

Scrutineers will often disagree about what constitutes "equity" or "inequity" in any particular relationship. Different observers may judge different inputs and outcomes to be relevant. And even when inputs and outcomes are agreed upon, the value or weights accorded them may not be the same. For example, we may tend to value a contribution of our own more highly than a similar one made by another because of a keener awareness of our own exertions to produce the input. Similarly, our own negative outcomes may "hurt more" than do others'. But in many other instances scrutineers *will* agree, as when the inputs and outcomes involved have values broadly agreed upon (for example, dollars of pay or hours of labor at particular tasks).

By convention, the person who intentionally takes larger relative outcomes than he deserves is an "exploiter" or a "harmdoer"; the person who gets less than he deserves is the "victim."

The Psychological Consequences of Inequity

As stated in Equity theory's Proposition III, both the exploiter and his victim find an exploitative encounter at least somewhat distressful. Theorists have labeled such distress reactions in various ways: guilt, empathy, fear of retaliation, dissonance, conditioned anxiety, shame, anger, and so on. Most agree, however, that exploiters' and victims' distress arises from two sources.

Retaliation Distress. When children exploit others (or allow themselves to be exploited) they are sometimes punished. Soon the realization that an injustice has occurred comes to arouse conditioned anxiety. This distress may have cognitive correlates. Harmdoers may attribute their distress to a fear that the victim, the victim's sympathizers, legal agencies, or even God, will retaliate against them. Victims may attribute their distress to a fear that their friends will ridicule them or consider them "fair game" or a "pushover."

Self-concept Distress. There is a second reason why exploitation is upsetting. In our society there is an almost universally accepted (if not followed) norm that one should be fair and equitable in his dealings with others. (See Fromm for an interesting discussion of the pervasiveness of the fairness principle.)[3]

Of course, when we say that "individuals accept a code of fairness" we do not mean that everyone internalizes exactly the same moral principles, accepts them to the same extent, and follows them without deviation. Juvenile delinquents and confidence men, for example, often *seem* to act as if it is completely consistent with their self-concept to exploit others. However, the evidence suggests that everyone internalizes some primitive norms of fairness. It is true that they may repeatedly violate such norms for financial or social gain (as Proposition I suggests they might), but such violations do seem to cause at least some distress. Anecdotal evidence on these points comes from interviews with confidence men[4] and delinquents.[5]

When a normal person participates in a profoundly inequitable relationship, then, he should feel at least some glimmerings of distress. Presumably, people are motivated to reduce their distress by restoring equity to their relationships.

Techniques to Reduce Distress

Restoration of Actual Equity. One way participants can restore equity is by including a person who has reaped far more profit than he deserves to compensate his victim, thus raising his victim's outcomes. For example, large retailers often have a policy of "money cheerfully refunded" if a customer is not satisfied with his purchase. A variety of studies make it clear that exploiters do often exert considerable effort to make such restitution.[6] Parallel evidence indicates that a victim's first response is to seek restitution.[7] Of course, if this fails (the exploiter may refuse or lack the means to help the victim) the victim may choose to "get even" by retaliating,[8] that is, restoring equity by reducing the exploiter's outcomes.

Restoration of Psychological Equity. Participants can reduce their distress in a second way. They can return the "fairness equation" to equality by distorting reality and convincing themselves (and perhaps others) that their seemingly inequitable relationship is, in fact, "perfectly" fair. That is, they can change their perceptions of the values of various inputs and/or outcomes. Individuals have been found to be very adept at rationalizing exploitation and even their own status as victims in order to restore equity.[9]

Exploiters have been found to denigrate their victims ("He was a bad/weak/dumb person [negative inputs] and deserved it!") and to deny responsibility for their acts ("He made me do it").[10] Others have restored equity by minimizing their victim's suffering ("Oh, it didn't hurt her *that* much—she makes such a fuss").[11]

Fascinatingly, there is even some sparse experimental evidence that under the right circumstances, victims will justify their own exploitation.[12] Everyday observation adds to this evidence ("I'm so dull and shy, no wonder she took advantage of me").

Reactions of Outside Agencies

The preceding discussion has focused upon the ways that participants react to inequity. Participants are not the only possible agents of equity restoration, however. The courts, the police, social workers, the participants' friends, and so on, may all observe inequity, become distressed by it, and intervene to right existing wrongs. Are there any data on how such "impartial" observers respond to inequity?

According to Equity theorists, impartial observers should react to injustice in much the same way that participants do, with one qualification: observers should react less passionately than do participants. The discovery that observers' reactions are only a pale reflection of the participants' vivid ones should come as little surprise. An observer who empathizes with an exploiter may well share his embarrassment and rationalizations. An observer who empathizes with a victim may well share *his* anger and indignation. If, as seems likely, the feelings we empathize with are less intense than the ones we experience, it is understandable that observers react less passionately to inequity than do the harmdoers and victims themselves.

Strong evidence that participants and impartial observers react to injustice in much the same way comes from a number of researchers.[13] On the basis of the existing evidence, theorists have concluded that even the most aloof of "impartial" observers are motivated to right existing wrongs, and failing that, at least to convince themselves that this a just world, a place where exploiters are somehow entitled to their benefits and the deprived somehow deserve to suffer.

As a theory of justice, concerned with behaviors of actors as well as third-party agents, Equity theory is particularly applicable to issues in the judicial system. In this system the relationships between victim and offender, and judge and jury and defendant, involve fundamental issues of equity. In any particular legal case, the salient relationship is between the offender and society (as embodied by the victim). The victim's outcomes are established by the magnitude of the crime, with inputs presumably constant. The inputs of the offender are many and diversified, including magnitude of offense, heinousness of act, personal characteristics, and prior record.

Operating with the assumption that relevant inputs and outcomes can be roughly measured and scaled quantitatively, the Equity formula has provided researchers a valuable heuristic tool with which to describe judicial decisions vis-à-vis a criterion of justice. The number of studies using Equity-derived hypotheses in the legal arena is growing rapidly.[14] Austin and Utne,[15] for example, examined the possible equity-restoring effects on jurors' sentencing behavior of the extralegal input of offender suffering. In each of three studies, the salient comparison was between how much the defendant suffered during commission of the crime and how much the victim suffered. Each study used a different crime, increasing in severity: simple robbery, robbery and felonious assault, or robbery and rape. The offender was depicted as suffering excessively relative to his victim, about the same, or not at all. Austin and Utne found that Equity-maintaining responses predominated in the case of robbery, where jurors assigned significantly less punishment for each successive level of offender suffering. But for the personal injury crimes of assault and rape only excessive offender suffering was effective in lowering sentences. In a fourth experiment[16] the effect of the "relevance" of the offender's suffering was studied. The results were identical to those of the first three studies, and whether the offender suffered "in the act" of committing the crime or later, while out on bail, was irrelevant. These results may simply indicate that crimes involving personal injury and trauma are seen as far more severe than the material crime of robbery, and thus demand a tremendous amount of offender suffering to "even the score" and restore equity. Or they may instead reveal that as crimes increase in severity or shift from material to personal loss the motive for retribution takes precedence over the motive for equity or proportional justice.

Section II: Equity and the Current U.S. System

Macaulay and Walster[17] surveyed the American legal system with two questions in mind: to what extent do existing laws and informal legal procedures encourage restitution and reconciliation? and to what extent do existing legal procedures foster self-justification—derogation, denial, and minimization of the victim's suffering? They observed that

On its face, American law is consistent with the goal of supporting compensation . . . For example, the common law of torts consists of rules which say that a wrong-doer must compensate his victim. In addition, the legal system in operation provides more avenues to restitution than are available in its formal rules. A wide variety of informal procedures encourage compensation. For example, criminal sanctions are sometimes used as a leverage to induce restitution. A police officer may decide not to arrest a shoplifter if the wrong-doer is not a professional thief and if the stolen items are returned; a district attorney may decide not to prosecute if the amount embezzled is returned.[18]

However, they also noted that some informal procedures and formal rules discourage legal harmdoers from making equity-restoring compensation. In our society, probably the most common case in which one individual does serious physical or economic harm to another is the automobile "accident." Let us use this case as an example of how common law civil litigation may actually discourage participants from making exact compensation.

The Necessity of Determining Who Is at Fault. In the law, the first step is to determine who did what under what circumstances—who is at fault.[19] This requirement may dilute the harmdoer's incentive to restore equity: often, it is unclear who is at fault. The law requires judges and juries to make a series of difficult judgments. For example, the trier of fact must decide whether the defendant was driving at an appropriate speed for the conditions and was paying attention. But what is an "appropriate" speed in a residential neighborhood on an overcast afternoon? Can someone who has the car radio on and is flirting with a passenger be said to be paying "proper attention" to driving? Although we can all agree that some kind of conduct while driving a car involve fault and some do not, there are numerous in-between situations. The harmdoer and the victim are likely to have very different perceptions as to who is at fault. This makes the harmdoer reluctant to make and exact compensation.

In most states, substantive tort law also gives the harmdoer an incentive to denigrate his victim. The victim who is himself contributorily negligent cannot recover from an injury partially caused by another's negligence. If the driver can convince others that the victim was partially responsible for his own injury, he can avoid the possibility of having to make what he would deem an inequitably large settlement.

Effects of Delay in Judgment. Usually a long time elapses between commission of the accident and the possibility of compensating. In time, memory dims. It becomes easier for the harmdoer psychologically to restore equity and distort reality—either consciously or unconsciously. It becomes easier for the harmdoer to say, "I'm not really at fault. I really didn't cause the accident. I'm legally right, and if we went to court, I'd win."

Pressures Toward Bargaining. In practice, litigants must pay high cost to bring and defend lawsuits. Also, the courts are not adequately staffed to respond quickly. Both these factors predispose individuals to bargain rather than to seek the exact restoration of equity: indeed some injuries are so small as to fall beneath the economic barriers to litigation. The plaintiff's inability to wait for months or years for the legal system to process his case may force him to accept a grossly inadequate settlement. In short, costs and delay join fault and fact to push for bargaining and compromise rather than reestablishment of equity.

Most drivers own car insurance. Insurance companies are naturally more concerned with getting off as cheaply as possible than with seeing to it that exact compensation is made. The plaintiff's attorney, who specializes in personal injury litigation and negotiation with adjusters, and who often is paid a percentage of any recovery he can obtain, has the opposite concern—he wants to get as much money as possible for his client. He, too, is relatively less concerned with equity. The result is a system of institutionalized bargaining, which is impersonal. The adjuster and the plaintiff's attorney play the game. Both the harmdoer and the injured stand at the sidelines.

In addition to impersonal delegation, another facet of the typical insurance policy tends to blunt the harmdoer's urge to compensate. One who attempts to help his victim obtain compensation from the insurance company could lose his rights under the policy. Insurers typically suggest that policyholders say and do more than that which is necessary after an accident, and they must cooperate with the defense against the victim's claims.

Exact compensation is rarely the result of this bargaining between adjuster and plaintiff's attorney. Sometimes plaintiffs get excessive settlements because of their skill in manipulating the facts. More often, they are inadequately compensated. Bargaining tends to give people with good cases less than their loss and those with weak cases more than they would have received in court.[20]

In theory, the common law is designed to encourage wrongdoers to compensate their victims. In practice, bargaining occurs. The law, then, supports the ideal of best balance of self-interest possible between harmdoer and victim in light of bargaining skill and position. Rather than develop the harmdoer's best motives, the system tends to guard against his worst.[21]

The automobile accident case just examined provides a somewhat limited example for review, as it involves a situation usually outside the purview of the broader criminal justice system. For more serious offenses society often takes a different tack, restoring equity to the harmdoer/victim relationship by forcing a harmdoer to undergo punishment.

Legal philosophers have long discussed the various *reasons* that society punishes wrongdoers. They note that we punish people to restore equity, rehabilitate wrongdoers, protect society, set a deterrent example for other potential wrongdoers, and express a sense of moral outrage.[22]

The punishing response no doubt is meant to serve all these ends to some extent. Historical and experimental evidence exists to suggest that a significant portion of our desire to punish a wrongdoer derives from equity-restoring motives; most people seem to feel that to *some* extent, wrongdoers should expiate their crimes by suffering. For example, the Code of Hammurabi (about 2250 B.C.) was predicated on the philosophy that things should be "set right" via *exact* punishment: "If one break a man's bone, they shall break his bone."[23]

Durkheim observed

And in truth, punishment has remained, at least in part, a work of vengeance. It is said that we do not make the culpable suffer in order to make him suffer; it is nonetheless true that we find it just that he suffer.

In supposing that punishment can really serve to protect us in the future, we think that it ought to be above all an *expiation* of the past. The proof of this lies in the minute precautions we take to proportion punishment as exactly as possible to the severity of the crime; they would be inexplicable if we did not believe that the culpable ought to suffer because he has done evil and in the same degree.[24]

And, today, people *still* feel the punishment should fit the crime.[25]

Section III: An Equity Analysis of Restitution Programs

There is no doubt that punishment functions to restore Equity. If we view the relevant relationship as one in which the offender's relative outcomes are greater than his victim's, then decreasing his positive outcomes (for example, physical freedom, esteem in his community, voting rights) and increasing his negative outcomes (for example, public censure), restores equity.

For some time now, however, criminal law theorists have been arguing that there is a better way to "set things right." Society can restore Equity by punishing the harmdoer, but one can also "even the score" by having him make restitution. Legal agencies can subtly prod—or force—wrongdoers to make restitution to their victims. If that fails—because the criminals are unknown, or unable or unwilling to make restitution—social welfare agencies can compensate the disadvantaged. The wrongdoers will still have gotten away with more than they deserve, but at least the victim will be compensated. The relative inequity will be less.

The psychological impacts of such interventions will probably depend on whether the agency prods the exploiter to compensate, forces him to compensate, or simply provides backup compensation to his neglected victim.

Prodding the Wrongdoer to Make Restitution. Society's first intervention attempts are usually directed toward persuading wrongdoers voluntarily to compensate their victims. For example, through its street-level representative, the beat police officer, society keeps many illegal inequities from entering the formal legal system. The beat officer's broad discretion is often exercised in urging parties to settle things between themselves. Although there are no figures available, undoubtedly a great number of certain types of criminal inequities are handled this way.

If wrongdoers can be thus induced to compensate those they have injured, everyone benefits. The repentant harmdoers should become stauncher adherents of the Equity norm.[26] They serve as behavioral models for others; when observers find themselves in similar situations they tend to imitate the models they have, in this case, equitable models.[27]

Forcing the Harmdoer to Make Restitution. Once it becomes evident that a social agent is not going to be able to prod the wrongdoers to make restitution, legal agencies may intervene and force them to make amends.

Societies have tried to force wrongdoers to make restitution via a variety of techniques. For example, Shafer[28] observes that the ancient Germanic laws (*leges barbarorum*) stipulated how much wrongdoers must compensate all types of victims for all types of crimes. In Germanic law, freeborn man was worth more than a slave, an adult more than a child, a man more than a woman, and a person of rank more than a freeman. Every kind of blow or wound had its price. Part of the "compensation" was paid to the victim and part to the community or king. The Germanic tribes exerted intense pressure on the wrongdoer to make restitution. If the wrong doer paid up he was protected. If he was reluctant to pay, or could not raise the necessary sum, he was declared an outlaw; he was ostracized and anyone might kill him with impunity.[29]

Today in almost every country, legal agencies try to force harmdoers to make restitution. In most countries, a victim can sue a harmdoer for psychic or physical injury, or for loss of potential income. (In the German Federal Republic one can recover a *solatium* for one's injured feelings; in Holland one can sue an insulting person for damage to one's honor and reputation.)

These systems have worked out a variety of procedures for forcing wrongdoers to pay the damages they owe. The Danish, Hungarian, and Norwegian legal systems take the wrongdoer's willingness to make restitution into account when determining sentences or granting paroles. In Finland, Italy, Canada, and Cuba, the state often turns a portion of the prisoners' earnings over to their victims.

There is some wisdom in *this* approach to restitution. Wrongdoers who are forced to compensate at least are dissuaded from justifying their inequitable behavior. The actions of the enforcing agency also prevent the offender from serving as an unsettling model for others. The norm of Equity is reinforced in the perpetrator and in the observing public.

Providing Compensation to the Victim. Sometimes an agency must admit defeat: there is no way to elicit restitution. For example, criminals may be unknown or indigent. Some theorists and practitioners argue that in such cases, the community should reconcile itself to the fact that an injustice has occurred and simply intervene to alleviate the victim's suffering. Such intervention is consistent with our notions of fairness (the innocent victim is recompensed) and is expedient (society affirms the legitimacy of Equity norms).

Some legal theorists have even proposed that, in the interests of justice and efficiency, the state should *routinely* assume responsibility for compensating victims of criminal violence.[30] They argue that the state could save time and money if, instead of tracking down harmdoers and prodding them into making restitution, the state simply provided automatic compensation to the disadvantaged.

Equity theorists would warn that society should be wary of eroding an individual's feeling of responsibility for restoring Equity. Even worse, it is probable that an agency set up to "right all wrongs" would soon be unable to fulfill its mandate. Funds for social justice are always meager. (Although citizens may agree that victims should be compensated, they are seldom willing to pay the price.) Social welfare agencies thus soon evolve from agencies of perfect "social justice" into agencies of "social compromise."

For these reasons, most policymakers view public compensation as a source of residual restitution, to be resorted to only when agencies have totally failed to induce the exploiter to make restitution.

Practical Considerations

Regardless of the particular form a restitution program may take, there are potential problems in implementation that Equity theory alerts us to. From the Equity perspective, those who attempt to develop effective restitution programming are likely to have to hammer out solutions to the following problems:

1. Equity is always in the eye of the beholder. Any program's first problem, then, is to settle on procedures for deciding who is "the harmdoer" and who is "the victim." This is rarely an easy task. The lines between the two are often hazy. For example, in his classic study of violent crime, Wolfgang found that 26 percent of homicide cases were victim-precipitated.[31] Charging an offender with complete responsibility for restoring the victim's loss in such cases would no doubt arouse new feelings of injustice on the part of the legally defined offender.

2. Because equity is in the eye of the beholder it is not always apparent whose scale of justice to use in calculating costs and adequate restitution. When losses are strictly material, with monetary equivalents, the task is not so formidable. The fact that restitution programs of victim compensation are for the most part limited to property crimes reflects legislators' and administrators' awareness of this. But should we ignore the losses of the physically and emotionally harmed because it is hard to administer restitution to them? Such a

policy would not seem just. Yet, how much should pain and suffering "count"? And what kind of restitutive efforts could possibly restore equity to these victims? In the future, it will probably become possible at least to arrive at consistent answers to such questions. In the past, some standards have existed. Workmen's compensation scales, for example, have been used in industry for years. Similar scales could be adapted for use in the restitution arena. And although in cases of personal loss it may never be possible to restore perfect equity to the victim, there is no doubt that some help and official recognition of his plight is better, in the victim's eyes, than no system response at all.

3. How much should the wrongdoer's "inputs" count in deciding how much compensation victims deserve? For example, it is obvious that we care very much whether or not the harmdoer *intended* to harm the victim, when deciding how much he should be punished. It is less clear that intent should count when determining how much restitution the victim is to receive. On one hand, the person who doesn't really intend to do harm shouldn't have to pay quite so much as one who intentionally harmed another. On the other hand, the victim may have suffered equally in every case. Should the harmdoer's compensation be supplemented by society?

4. If a harmdoer is rich it is easy to force him to make compensation, but criminal offenders rarely are. The offender can rarely afford to make amends. What if he is poor? It is usually futile for courts to award plaintiffs heavy damages—should the harmdoer's prison wages be allocated? Restoration of the victim to his status quo position may create a new inequity because of the unequal hardships restitution can create for offenders. When one offender is relatively far wealthier than another, a new sense of inequity may be created when equal monetary restitution is demanded of them, because the relative costs of restitution are so different. A possible solution to this problem might be the giving of personal time and effort rather than money.

Section IV: Concluding Remarks

Equity theorists would argue that society must closely examine its goals in instituting any restitution program. This is essential because any one program can have markedly different impacts on the various actors it affects. Is the primary goal of a restitution program to help the victim, and restore his faith in the equitableness of the system? Is it to help the offender, restore his self-esteem, rehabilitate him and reinforce his adherence to society's norms? Or is it to help the system, to ease its financial and prison maintenance expenses in a strictly practical way? Or, finally, is the restitution program to be a public relations vehicle, instituted in response to and in service of public demands that the system "work better?" Some of these goals may act in competition with others, although each may work to promote equity in a particular way. For example, perfect justice to victims (actual and total equity restoration) may seriously drain public funds and anger the majority of taxpayers who are never victmized. This resentment (actually a response to a newly felt inequity) may lead to citizens' dissociation from and denigration of victims, and withholding of future funds. In another case, the amount of restitution from offenders that is sufficient to reinforce adherence to the equity norm and augment rehabilitation may be completely inadequate from the point of view of the underbenefited victim. Articulation of target groups and goals of restitution programming may help to circumvent administrators' frustrations that restitution is *too* complicated in its implications and thus not worth implementing.

It may be that restitution will never *supplant* punishment in the criminal justice system, although the two are theoretically equivalent as means of equity restoration. To the extent that restitution can fulfill the other-than-equity-restoring functions that punishment provides, it may indeed be adopted more broadly. There appears to be a great amount of compatibility between restitution and other of the goals of the criminal justice system, such as deterrence, retribution, and rehabilitation.

Notes

1. For a complete overview of Equity theory, see Walster et al., *Equity: Theory and Research* (Boston: Allyn and Bacon, 1978).

2. (The exponents k_A and k_B take on the value of +1 or −1, depending on the sign of A and B's inputs and A and B's gains (Outcomes − Inputs).)

$$k_A = \text{sign}\,(I_A) \times \text{sign}\,(O_A - I_A) \text{ and}$$

$$k_B = \text{sign}\,(I_B) \times \text{sign}\,(O_B - I_B)$$

The exponent's effect is simply to change the way Relative Gains are computed: If $k = +1$ then we have $(O - I/|I|)$, but if $k = -1$ then we have $|I|.\times(O - I)$. Without the exponent k, the formula would yield meaningless results when $I < O$ and $(O - I) > O$ or $I > O$ and $(O - I) < O$.

Reprinted, in part, from Walster et al., *Equity*.

3. Eric Fromm, *The Art of Loving* (New York: Harper and Row, 1956).

4. Erving Goffman, "On Cooling the Mark Out: Some Aspects of Adaptation to Failure," *Psychiatry* 15 (1952): 451-463.

5. Gresham Sykes and David Matza, "Techniques of Neutralization: A Theory of Delinquency," *American Sociological Review* 22 (1957): 664-670.

6. Ellen Berscheid and Elaine Walster, "When Does a Harmdoer Compensate a Victim?" *Journal of Personality and Social Psychology* 6 (1967):

435-441; Elaine Walster and Perry Prestholdt, "The Effect on Liking of Misjudging Another: Overcompensation or Dissonance Reduction?" *Journal of Experimental Social Psychology* 2 (1966): 85-97; J.L. Freedman, Sue Ann Wallington, and Evelyn Bless, "Compliance Without Pressure: The Effect of Guilt," *Journal of Personality and Social Psychology* 7 (1967): 117-124.

7. Gerald Leventhal and J.T. Bergman, "Self-depriving Behavior as a Response to Unprofitable Inequity," *Journal of Experimental Social Psychology* 5 (1969): 153-171; David Schmitt and Gerald Marwell, "Withdrawal and Reward Allocations as Responses to Inequity," *Journal of Experimental Social Psychology* 8 (1972): 207-221.

8. Ellen Berscheid, David Boye, and Elaine Walster, "Retaliation as a Means of Restoring Equity," *Journal of Personality and Social Psychology* 10 (1968): 370-376.

9. David C. Glass, "Changes in Liking as a Means of Reducing Cognitive Discrepancies Between Self-esteem and Aggression," *Journal of Personality* 32 (1964): 520-549.

10. Gresham Sykes and David Matza, "Techniques of Neutralization: A Theory of Delinquency," *American Sociological Review* 22 (1957): 664-670; Timothy C. Brock and Arnold H. Buss, "Dissonance, Aggression, and Evaluation of Pain," *Journal of Abnormal and Social Psychology* 65 (1962): 197-202.

11. Brock and Buss, "Dissonance, Aggression, and Evaluation of Pain."

12. William G. Austin and Elaine Walster, "Participants' Reactions to 'Equity with the World,' " *Journal of Experimental Social Psychology* 10 (1974): 528-548.

13. Stephen Schafer, *Restitution to Victims of Crime* (London: Stevens & Son Ltd., 1960); Melvin J. Lerner, "The Desire for Justice and Reactions to Victims," in Jacqueline Macaulay and Leonard Berkowitz (eds.), *Altruism and Helping Behavior* (New York: Academic Press, 1970), pp. 205-229; Alan L. Chaikin and John M. Darley, "Victim or Perpetrator: Defensive Attribution and the Need for Order and Justice," *Journal of Personality and Social Psychology* 25 (1973): 268-276.

14. V. Lee Hamilton and Steven Rytina, "Fitting the Punishment to the Crime," in *Equity, Retribution, and Other Factors in Legal Justice Reactions,* symposium submitted to Eastern Psychological Association annual meeting, 1978; Ellen Cohn, Louise Kidder, and Philip Brickman, "The Relative Virtues of Restitution, Rehabilitation, and Retribution," in ibid.; William Austin and Mary K. Utne, "Simulated Jurors' Responses to a Defendant's Suffering: How Much is Enough?" Paper presented at the American Psychology-Law Society meetings, Chicago, 1975; William Austin and Mary K. Utne, "The Differential Impact of an Offender's Suffering on Jurors' Conviction and Sentencing Behavior" (unpublished manuscript, University of Virginia, 1976).

15. Austin and Utne, "Simulated Jurors' Responses."

16. Austin and Utne, "The Differential Impact of an Offender's Suffering."

17. Stuart Macaulay and Elaine Walster, "Legal Structures and Restoring Equity," *Journal of Social Issues* 27 (1971): 173-188.

18. Ibid., p. 179.

19. R.L. Rabin, "Some Thoughts on Tort Law from a Sociopolitical Perspective," *Wisconsin Law Review* 51 (1969): 65-80.

20. A.F. Conrad, J.F. Morgan, R.W. Pratt, Jr., C.E. Voltz, and R.L. Bombaugh, *Automobile Accident Costs and Payments* (Ann Arbor: University of Michigan Press, 1964).

21. L.M. Friedman and Stuart Macaulay, *Law and the Behavioral Sciences* (Indianapolis: Bobbs-Merrill & Co., 1969).

22. William Austin and Mary K. Utne, "Sentencing: Discretion and Justice in Judicial Decision-making," in Bruce Dennis Sales (ed.), *Psychology in the Legal Process* (Englewood Cliffs, N.J.: Spectrum, 1977), pp. 163-194.

23. R.F. Harper, *The Code of Hammurabi: King of Babylon About 2250 B.C.* (Chicago: The University of Chicago Press, 1904), p. 73.

24. Emil Durkheim (Translated by George Simpson), *The Division of Labor in Society* (New York: The Free Press, 1933), p. 88.

25. F.C. Sharp and M.C. Otto, "A Study of the Popular Attitude Toward Retributive Punishment," *International Journal of Ethics*, 20 (1910): 341-357; A.M. Rose and A.F. Prell, "Does the Punishment Fit the Crime?" *The American Journal of Sociology*, 61 (1955): 247-259; M. Fry, "Justice for Victims," *Journal of Public Law*, 8 (1956): 155-253; William Austin, Elaine Walster, and Mary K. Utne, "Equity and the Law: The Effect of a Harmdoer's 'Suffering in the Act' on Assigned Punishment and Liking," in Leonard Berkowitz and Elaine Walster (eds.), *Advances in Experimental Social Psychology* (New York: Academic Press, 1976), pp. 163-190; Austin and Utne, "Simulated Jurors' Responses;" Austin and Utne, "The Differential Impact of an Offender's Suffering."

26. Judson Mills, "Changes in Moral Attitudes Following Temptation," *Journal of Personality* 26 (1958): 517-531.

27. Albert Bandura, "Vicarious Processes: A Case of No-trial Learning," in Leonard Berkowitz (ed.), *Advances in Experimental Social Psychology* (New York: Academic Press, 1965), pp. 3-48.

28. Schafer, *Restitution to Victims.*

29. F. Pollock and F.W. Maitland, *The History of English Law*, 2nd ed. (Cambridge, 1898), vol. 2, p. 451.

30. For example, see M. Fry, "Justice for Victims."

31. Marion Wolfgang, *Patterns in Criminal Homicide* (Philadelphia: University of Pennsylvania Press, 1958).

Part III: Restitution and the Crime Victim

7

Victims, Offenders, and the Criminal Justice System: Is Restitution an Answer?
Emilio C. Viano

This nation's decade-long search for more effective means to control crime has carefully explored every aspect of the criminal justice system. The role of every performer has been scrutinized. But the victim has been the forgotten party in the criminal justice system. The system focuses first on the crime itself, and thereafter on the offender. Who is he? Was he arrested? Are the police doing their job? Were the offender's rights protected? Does he have a lawyer? What is happening in the courts? The criminal justice system is under more public scrutiny than ever before. How can we speed up trials, improve sentencing, incarceration, prisons, probation, parole training, rehabilitation? But this increasing attention and reform still ignores the victim.

The victim's needs are not the single concern of any agency in the criminal justice system. When attention is directed to victims, it is offender- and offense-oriented. The police come and leave with as many answers as a victim can provide, and the evidence. The victim's possessions may be taken for evidence and returned months, or even years, later. The police and prosecutor may ask the victim to make statements, look over mugshots, or attend a lineup. The victim/witness may have to repeat the story, confront the attacker, relive the crime, spend days in court, or simply wonder what happened if the case never comes to trial. All of this asks a great deal of the victim, and offers very little in return. Yet, it is the evidence provided by the victim that makes it possible to identify, apprehend, prosecute, and convict the offender. Thus, one should consider victim/witness an important public figure having critical responsibilities for the welfare of others.

Victim's Needs and Problems

In reality, very little data are currently available on victim's needs or their responses to services. Recent research has attempted to determine, for the first time, how much victimization there actually is, and who the victims and offenders are. These surveys show that far more crimes occur than we knew—or were willing to admit. For each unreported crime, there is a silent victim.

When individuals do report crimes, victim service agencies must make a basic decision: who will they regard as a "first priority victim"? Financial restraints will make the answer almost inevitably "victims of violent crimes." But, property crimes can also create serious personal emergencies. Very few inner-city residents, for example, have checking accounts; many elderly citizens are unwilling to use banks. For these citizens, an apartment robbery can mean the loss of rent or food money. Food-stamp thefts create real problems for those who have absolutely nothing to spare. Defining the kinds of victims will be one of the fundamentals in structuring any program. The problems that result from some types of victimization are more obvious than from others.[1]

Homicide

Homicide leaves the victim's family in disarray. If the victim provided family support, there is sudden financial hardship as well as the shock of loss. Family members are often unaware of available assistance for funeral expenses. Insurance, job-related benefits, and Social Security may be a complete mystery for the relatives of an intermittently employed victim.

If a homicide is the outcome of a family quarrel—and this is often the case—there may be serious, continuing family problems as well as immediate legal ones. If the perpetrator is at large, fear becomes another immediate problem for the family.

Sexual Assault

This presents particular problems for the victim—so much so that rape is disproportionately underreported. Besides the immediate shock of assault, which itself requires sensitive professional handling, there is the ordeal of giving testimony and dealing with family and public reaction. Despite efforts to improve the attitudes of law enforcement and medical personnel, as well as the public, the rape victim is almost inevitably revictimized by the treatment she receives. Unless the victim is a child, or elderly, she herself is often blamed.

Studies of rape victims show a tendency to deferred reaction and long-term emotional problems. For many women, the circumstances of rape mean they must find new, safer housing, change employment, or completely alter their lifestyles, and these changes may be difficult to arrange. If a victim does want to prosecute, she may need support during the legal process. Victim services must help provide a new security without further setting the victim apart.

There is a strong movement toward creating specialized rape crisis centers. A few hospitals have established highly professional and responsible medical and counseling services. Such centers have tested victim service approaches. Whether these centers should be absorbed into general victim services is a subject for debate.

Assault

Assault, like rape, leaves a victim with serious ongoing problems. Rape victims may be lucky enough to find themselves in a supportive environment, but assault victims are rarely helped to deal with the fear and hostility reactions that accompany their physical injuries. Little data are kept on the compound costs of assault, but they can be overwhelming, even for injuries that are not permanently disabling. Ambulence service, emergency room treatment, followup medical care, job time sacrificed both at the time of injury and during the prosecution process, all add up to make even a relatively minor injury a serious financial blow, especially to a low-income victim. Access to emergency assistance and Medicaid or Medicare, vocational rehabilitation if an injury dictates a job change, problems of housing security, and chances of repeat victimization are serious problems facing the victims.

Recidivism is, in fact, a particular problem in assault situations. A survey of victims by the National Crime Panel shows that of those who had been robbed or assaulted once, 15 percent had been victimized a second time, and fully a third of those twice-victimized were subjected to one or more incidents subsequently.[2] Assault victims are frequently elderly, an easy target for stronger, younger attackers, particularly when low incomes and insufficient local housing make it impossible to move out of high-risk areas. Victim counseling in apartment security, relocation, or escort services would help.

Family assaults are also frequently repeated. Active family crisis intervention, counseling, and support are rarely available. Child abuse is a particularly handicapping and poignant aspect of intrafamily assault. In many jurisdictions, a child victim is taken from his parents. But more is needed here—professional help for the child victim and his family.

The third group of repeater victims will be even harder for supportive services to reach. There are the young victims of street and bar encounters who end up late at night in emergency wards with gun and knife wounds. These victims often refuse services and are much more likely to identify with their attackers than with a victim service program. Although they are a relatively less sympathetic target of crime, services provided for these people could reduce the chance that the next opportunity for services will be in a pretrial or probation context—or that the next encounter will be fatal.

Additional Offenses

These may seem unimportant by comparison. But even minor property crimes can make drastic inroads on the means and security of those who are only marginally able to support themselves.

In each offense category and with every victim, the impact of the crime will vary. Some victims are, of course, cushioned by highly supportive family situations, insurance, and the ability to purchase private medical care and counseling. But those most often and most easily victimized are rarely so lucky. Victims are predominantly the young and old. They are likely to be poor, and undereducated. The victim of crime is often the very person *least able to cope* with the problems of crime, to identify or utilize existing services.

Victim Definition

Victim definition is not as obvious a task as it sounds. The criminal justice system has set the inner boundaries by defining crimes. Many of those who will appear at victim service centers as legitimate victims of crime are also long-term victims of all the social problems that put one in the path of a criminal act.

A commonly used term is *bona fide victim*. For victim centers with a strong police or court tie, that includes only victims who report the crime to the police and cooperate in prosecution of the offender. In rape cases, it means that the police believe the victim's story. In assault situations, if the victim and offender were fighting or the victim provoked the attack, either party may be the victim.

Crime victims' characteristics have an important impact on case outcomes. An INSLAW study[3] utilizing PROMIS data indicates that certain victim attributes, such as opiate use, alcohol abuse, and criminal record did affect the prosecutor's decision to dismiss cases. In addition, the perception of the prosecutor at case intake and screening that the victim had either provoked the defendant or participated in the crime increased the likelihood that the case would not be filed with the court. Very young and very old victims were less likely to have their cases dismissed than others; female victims of assault had their cases pursued at higher rates than did male victims.

In general, when a close social or family relationship existed between the victim and defendant, a dismissal was more likely. The critical relationships appeared to be spouse or lover; in these cases dismissals were most likely. Some of these dismissals occurred because the victims, at some point, refused to cooperate with the prosecution; others, however, seemed to be the result of the prosecutor's anticipation of problems that had not yet developed.

Victims and the Criminal Justice System

How well do victims meet their responsibility vis-à-vis the criminal justice system? The evidence is not encouraging. Every citizen is expected to call police when victimized. But we are told that only one in every three does so.[4] Victims are expected to report the crime quickly so that the chances of catching the perpetrator are better. But victims often wait for a period of time before calling the police—half-hour and at times longer.[5] Victims are supposed to cooperate fully with the prosecutor. In one city, however, it has been shown that for every four prosecutions brought, one is abandoned because of "witness noncooperation."[6] The noncooperation rate may even be higher.[7]

Victims are expected to behave more prudently, some as a result of their own misfortune, and others as a result of having learned about someone else's. But this is not so. Some who are victimized once are victimized again, at times in the same manner.[8] Many who would like to, cannot readily escape from a victimization situation. Some people read about someone else's victimization but dismiss any thought that it may happen to them as well as and continue to behave as usual.

Why is it that citizens who are victimized or called upon to cooperate with criminal justice agencies do not meet expectations? Some reasons are the following:

Inconvenience. Getting involved with the law takes up too much of one's time and effort.

Safety Concerns/Intimidation. People are afraid that the offender will retaliate against them.

Reputation. Some people do not want to get themselves or others into trouble or to be embarrassed.

Cultural Reasons. Some people think that crime should be handled as a private matter, or that they would lose face or be ostracized if their victimization were known.

Anonymity. There were other witnesses and no one else reported it. The person feels, "Why should I?"

Financial Reasons. People fear insurance cancellations or increased rates.

Distrust of the System. People feel the police are not interested; do not care about them; are not on "their side"; are not that effective anyway; that if the offender were caught he would not get the punishment deserved.

Influence of Others. Someone talks the victim/witness out of reporting, of prosecuting, and so on.

Bad Experience. The victim/witness has had a bad experience (individually or as member of a group, perhaps a minority group) with the police or the system.

Uncertainty. The victim/witness is not certain that a crime has been committed.

Shared Culpability. The victim/witness is not completely innocent.

Role Reversals. Today's victim is tomorrow's offender and vice versa.

Financial Losses. Getting involved means having to take time off to go to court later on without compensation and/or the risk of losing one's job.

Feeling Like an "Outsider". The criminal justice system is highly structured and lay people feel ill at ease, lost, ambivalent, used, when they become involved with it. Going to court is for many an uncomfortable, distressing, even fearful, situation.

Bureaucratic Convenience. The "insiders" are seen as operating for their own convenience without taking the victim/witness' needs into account. The victim/witness has "no status."

Emotional Damage. The psychological repercussions of being victimized can discourage a person from pursuing the case further.

Lack of Personal Satisfaction. The routine handling of criminal cases rarely offers the victim/witness a sense of personal vindication or participation in the course of justice.

Frustration/Anger. The willing victim/witness finally drops out because of the slowness, impersonality, expense, delays of the system.

Different Priorities/Agenda. What the victim wants done is not necessarily what the system wants to do.

In the aftermath of their victimization, victims rate income and property loss highest. Time loss and physical-emotional suffering are among the most serious problems for the greatest number of people. Yet, these are not the priorities of the criminal justice system when it comes to pursuing the case. These are, rather, the quality of evidence, high clearance rates, efficient calendaring, speedy trials, keeping the cases moving through the courts, conviction rates, and so on. This conflict of goals, priorities, and expectations results in a lack of incentive to cooperation with the criminal justice system and in strained relations between victim/witnesses and the system.

If one keeps in mind the problems we have listed, it should not be difficult to understand why victim/witnesses are uncooperative, drop out, do not show, are sullen or angry, and the like. The frustration, the anger, the disillusionment, the cynicism of the victim/witness towards the system are often reflected by the police and the prosecution. Locked into such negative feelings, these actors—whose performance is crucial to the success of the criminal justice system—fail to cooperate, coordinate, and work together for the success of their case. It should be a definite priority of any police or prosecutor's office to break this vicious cycle.

The Role of Restitution Programs

Because the disregard for the victims' rights and needs may very well be one of the major reasons for their reluctance to report their victimization and/or to testify, it is essential that steps be taken to ensure that the criminal justice system focus more on the victim. Restitution is definitely one of the major types of redress that can be offered to satisfy the claims of the victim. Since victims rate income loss, property damage, and property loss as "very serious" crime-related problems (see table 7-1), a system of effective and meaningful restitution could have an important positive impact on the victims' perceptions of the criminal justice system and of society in general.

Table 7-1
Summary of Crime-Related Victim Problems

Problem	Victims experiencing problem		Victims rating problem as "very serious"	
	N	Percent	N	Percent
Physical injury	470	27	240	51
Property loss	768	45	432	56
Property damage	658	39	355	54
Lost time	835	49	389	47
Lost income	446	26	278	62
Lost job	39	2	35	90
Insurance cancelled	13	1	9	69
Mental or emotional suffering	1,001	57	495	49
Reputation damaged	251	12	110	44
Problems with family	358	25	182	51
Problems with friends	215	12	83	39

Source: *A Guide for Community Service: A Prescriptive Package.* Center for Criminal Justice and Social Policy. Milwaukee, Wisconsin: Marquette University, 1976.

Several alternatives are open to someone who has been victimized, although few are meaningful and practical. The individual has the right to initiate civil action to recover losses from the offender. The victim may seek indemnification from a private or public insurance agency. Compensation may be offered by the state. In certain jurisdictions, as in Europe, criminal and civil proceedings can be combined to make it easier and less costly for the victim to present a claim.

Restitution appears to be one of the more attractice and realistic alternatives, although its success depends on several factors being present and working in unison: the willingness of the offender to make restitution; the offender's possession of useful and marketable skills; a favorable employment situation; the absence of other crushing financial obligations; appropriate encouragement and supervision on the part of the probation officer; and the open-mindedness of the employer and of fellow workers. Under the right conditions, restitution can serve the victim, the offender, and ultimately society by restoring the victim to a previous condition, by forcing the offender to face his responsibilities and remedy the damage done, and by strengthening societal ties. The major benefit to be derived would be greater public confidence and participation in the criminal justice system and more support for enlightened correctional reform.

Too often, however, the focus of restitution has remained the offender and the benefits to be derived by the correctional system. The victim is again treated as incidental to the plan and in the long run is vastly shortchanged. It is essential to explore how restitution programs address the victim's needs, to solicit and take into account the victim's input, and to make the victim's concerns a central element in the planning and delivery of any restitution plan. Otherwise restitution would be more of a convenience for the system and the offender than a genuine benefit to the victim.

It is time to break "the penal couple"—to stop talking about the victim only in reference to the offender, the offender's needs, or the needs of the criminal justice system. It is the victim's needs that should be taken first and foremost into account, independently of arrest, prosecution, conviction, crowding in prison, or whether we know what to do with juvenile offenders.

Seen in this light, restitution constitutes a serious challenge to the vision and the imagination of social activists, concerned citizens, and correctional reformers. The difficulties surrounding the design and the implementation of an equitable restitution plan should not be seen as an excuse to shelve the idea and avoid its implementation; rather they should be considered as a challenge to our system of values and institutions and to the skills, competence, and compassion of those charged with representing society in the eyes of the victim, the offender, and their fellow citizens.

Notes

1. Mary E. Baluss, *Integrated Services for Victims of Crime: A County-*

Based Approach (National Association of Counties, 1975).

2. U.S. Department of Justice, Law Enforcement Assistance Administration, National Criminal Justice Information and Statistics Service, *Crimes and Victims: A Report on the Dayton-San Jose Pilot Survey of Victimization* (Washington, D.C.: U.S. Government Printing Office, 1974), p. 21.

3. *Highlights of Interim Findings and Implications.* (PROMIS Research Project) (Washington, D.C.: INSLAW, 1977).

4. National Crime Panel Survey Report, *Criminal Victimization in the United States: A Comparison of the 1973 and 1974 Findings* (Washington, D.C.: U.S. Department of Justice, Law Enforcement Assistance Administration, May 1976), pp. 40-41.

5. The magnitude of this problem is still uncertain, although the *existence* of the problem is not, as has been indicated by preliminary, unpublished data prepared in a Kansas City, Missouri, "response time" study, an LEAA-funded research project which, as of this writing, is still underway.

6. The finding, in Washington, D.C., that one prosecution in four was dropped because of "witness noncooperation" was later found to be somewhat misleading. A followup study, to examine the cause of this dropout rate, found that 205 of the 215 witnesses labeled as dropouts (in a sample of 922) disagreed with the conclusion. The researchers speculated that the true rate was perhaps 1 in 5 or 1 in 6, which is still an unacceptably high figure. Still, if the 1 in 4 calculation was in error, the error was not a clerical one: each recorded instance of noncooperation evidently related to significant actions or inaction on the part of the witness, or it represented the prosecutor's judgment of what the witness's *future* behavior would entail. See generally, Frank J. Cannavale, Jr. and William D. Falcon, *Witness Cooperation* (Lexington, Massachusetts: D.C. Heath & Co., 1976), or the LEAA/NILECJ publication, *Improving Witness Cooperation.*

7. Few jurisdictions take a careful measurement of the proportion of cases that are dropped, and of these, which are dropped because of witness noncooperation. But there are indications that noncooperation is endemic and of severe magnitude. In Brooklyn, for example, nearly 55 percent of all witnesses expected in court on a given day do not show up–a "no-show" rate that is obviously hard on the prosecutors and, ultimately, on the just disposition of their cases.

8. The "recidivistic victim" problem is at times a serious one, particularly in cases like domestic violence.

8

Expanding the Victim's Role in the Disposition Decision: Reform in Search of a Rationale
William F. McDonald

The recent wave of interest in the victim's role in the administration of justice has raised many issues, suggested several reforms and, in doing so, has forced people to reexamine some basic principles. This paper will address the question of what role the victim should play in the final disposition of cases, including cases in which restitution is not an issue. For purposes of this discussion final disposition will refer primarily to the plea negotiation and the sentencing decisions.

There are several important cross-currents in criminal justice today. One is the increased interest in victims. Another is the renewed interest in restitution programs. A third is the current decline of the rehabilitative ideal. Each of these has significance for the other and each forces one back to first principles.

The attack on the rehabilitative ideal has gained momentun and prestige. It is grounded on two facts that are not easy to ignore: the cumulative lack of empirical evidence that existing therapeutic techniques succeed in bringing about rehabilitation, and the cumulative empirical evidence that the rehabilitative ideal with its emphasis on individualized justice has led to gross disparities in the sentencing of similarly situated defendants.[1] For the foreseeable future rehabilitation will not enjoy the position of unquestioned dominance among alternative penal philosophies that it has had in the past. During this period of retrenchment one can expect that other penal philosophies will be given greater consideration. Already a shift toward an emphasis on deterrence seems evident. Also, one can expect that as is usually the case in times of change, there will be a greater opportunity for the introduction of new ideas.

This current shift in the relative dominance of various penal philosophies holds implications for developments in the area of restitution programs that are different from those for reforms relating to the victim's role in disposition decision making. The current theory behind restitution programs is threatened by the change but the idea of restitution itself is not. The current programs of restitution are tied to the rehabilitative ideal. They arose out of a search for new and more successful ways to rehabilitative offenders.[2] They operate on the assumption that by paying restitution and participating in the associated program an offender's prospects of real rehabilitation are enhanced. However, if rehabilitation as a correctional goal were replaced tomorrow by either one of the two major alternative penal theories—namely, deterrence or retribution—restitution programs could continue but with a different underlying rationale. After all, historically and in primitive cultures it is these latter two objectives—deterrence and retribution—that appear to have been the rationale for the practice of restitution. The rehabilitative rationale is a modern invention.[3]

The implications of the current reassessment of penal philosophies for reforming the victim's role in final disposition decision making are less clear. At the outset, two points should be noted. First, when any reform is proposed it is usually assumed that the situation to be reformed is thoroughly understood by the reformers and found unacceptable. In the case at hand, however, the victim's present role has not been systematically studied and described. What little information there is suggests that the victim's role is indeed minimal and that there is ample room for expansion. But the studies also indicate that in some jurisdictions under certain circumstances the victim does play an important role in the disposition decision. It is unfortunate that more is not known about this role. The proposals for expanding the victim's role might seem less radical if it could be shown that they accord with actual practice.

Second, it is relevant to examine the sentencing and the plea bargaining decisions together as if they were almost the same thing. These two processes are closely interrelated and in some jurisdictions are in fact virtually synonymous. In most jurisdictions plea bargaining consists of sentence bargaining as well as charge bargaining.[4] In many instances the sentence determined by the plea negotiations will be the sentence that is imposed. Therefore any discussion of sentencing that ignores the relationship between sentencing and plea negotiations is naive and incomplete. If the victim is to have a role in setting the sentence, then it may be that his input will have to come at the time of plea negotiations. Thus, both processing points are considered in the following analysis.

With regard to the issue of the victim's having control over or veto power over the sentence imposed, none of the three major rationales of punishment provides any theoretical support for such a proposal. From the point of view of rehabilitative theory, the victim should not be given such power on the grounds that the purpose of the sentencing decision should be the rehabilitation of the defendant. Therefore, the basis for the decision should be a scientific assessment of the needs of the defendant and the suitability of alternative treatment techniques. Short of having the ideal person to make this decision (such as a behavioral scientist), the rehabilitationist is likely to argue, the system as it exists would be better than turning the matter over to individual victims, most of whom possess no knowledge or experience in applying a rehabilitative perspective to the decision.

The deterrence theorist would also oppose giving the victim control over the sentencing decision. In fact this very point was made over two hundred years ago by Caesare Beccaria in his famous *Essay on Crimes and Punishment.*[5] He argued that victim control of the final disposition decision could not be tolerated because it reduced the certainty and uniformity of punishment, which in turn reduced the deterrent value of punishment.

The retributionist would also be opposed to letting the victim control the sentence. The theory of retribution is based on the notion that a defendant should be punished according to "just deserts"—regardless of whether this would serve any rehabilitative or deterrent interest. For over a century this theory of punishment has been disdained by correctional leaders because of their belief in the superior value of rehabilitation.[6] There has been a tendency to try to discredit this theory as primitive and unenlightened. There has also been a tendency to misunderstand it and to identify it with the idea of satisfying the vengeance of individual victims.[7] This, in turn, may have fostered the view that retribution is a victim-oriented theory of punishment and that the theory would support individual victims controlling sentences. Such a conclusion is incorrect. The theory of retribution believes that punishment is an end in itself.[8] It further holds that punishment should be proportionate to the crime.[9] The retributionist would argue that some victims may be inclined to seek more or less punishment than the defendant "deserves."

It is possible to construct a fourth theory of punishment that is not listed among the major philosophies of punishment except implicitly, either by mistaken interpretation of retributive theory or by way of reference to historical practices. This theory might be referred to as the personal revenge theory of punishment. It incorporates the ideas which, as noted above, seem to have been mistakenly associated with retributive theory. According to this theory the purpose of punishment should be to satisfy the individual victim's demand for vengeance. Clearly under such a theory the victim's desires regarding case dispositions would be controlling.

Although this theory is not among the recognized theories of punishment, it is not without some support in theory and in practice. Oliver Wendell Holmes argued that vengeance is a justifiable purpose of the criminal law,[10] which suggests that he would support the proposition that the victim's desires should at least be among the factors considered at sentencing (although not given exclusive consideration).

The strongest support for this theory comes from the actual practices of judges and prosecutors. Although the information on this point is sketchy, my observations in ten jurisdictions suggest that the victim is presently being given either actual control over or a heavy influence on the sentencing and plea bargaining decisions. But this practice occurs on a sub rosa, informal, nonroutine basis, depending upon the prosecutor or judge and what type of crime is involved.

Some judges want to know the victim's opinion of a disposition decision. Sometimes this is done with the idea that if the victim is not satisfied or cannot be persuaded to accept the terms of the disposition, then the terms will be altered. An extreme form of this latter approach was exemplified by the practice of a judge in Delaware County, Pennsylvania, several years ago. He engaged in what one local attorney called "reverse plea bargaining." In one instance the judge was sentencing a youth for stealing and destroying an automobile. The judge turned to the owner of the car (who was attending the sentencing hearing) and asked, "What would you say to six months in jail?" The victim was upset and protested that he thought that the crime was worth more than that. So the judge suggested a year to which the victim agreed and the sentence was imposed.

In my experience this form of blatant bargaining with the victim is atypical. But a somewhat more subtle form of the same practice seems to be fairly common. In these cases the judge or the prosecutor is willing to impose a lower sentence or agree to a plea to a lower charge provided that the victim does not object. When the District Attorney of Los Angeles was considering plea bargaining with Sirhan Sirhan for the assassination of Senator Robert F. Kennedy, he wrote the Kennedy family and asked for their opinion of what a suitable sentence would be.[11] When the state's attorney in Chicago was considering a plea bargain in a case involving the murder of a policeman, he enlisted support from the family of the slain officer, the man's fellow officers, and even some of the people in the neighborhood where the victim had grown up.[12]

In both these examples it may be that the prosecutor's decision would have remained even if the victim's relatives had objected. But in many other less celebrated cases it is clear that if the victim does not agree to the plea bargain then it will not be accepted. Usually this rule begins as the personal policy of an individual judge but is quickly recognized and adopted by prosecutors and defense attorneys who practice before that judge. In plea bargaining the prosecutor will pass the word along to the defense attorney that if he can get the victim to agree then the deal will go through.

But it is unlikely that this practice will be permitted to continue when it comes to the attention of the higher courts. The Minnesota Supreme Court, for example, recently went out of its way to condemn the practice. The court's remarks came in a case in which it found no reversible error but took the opportunity to criticize the trial judge's insistence at the time when negotiations about a possible second degree murder plea were going on that the parents of the fourteen-year old victim consent to the plea agreement. The court said this "was an invalid condition."[13]

Denying the victim this kind of power is not so much a denial of the worthiness of the personal vengeance theory of punishment as it is a reassertion of the distinction between criminal and civil law. Theoretically criminal matters are solely between the state and the accused. The victim has no interest in the matter other than to serve as a witness as the state sees fit. This position was stated in unvarnished terms by a Connecticut court in a decision opposing private prosecution. The court stated:

In all criminal cases in Connecticut, the state is the prosecutor. The offenses are against the state. The victim of the offense is not a party to the prosecution, nor does he occupy any relation to it other than that of a witness, an interested witness mayhaps, but none the less, only a witness.

It is not necessary for the injured party to make complaint nor is he re-quired to give bond or prosecute. He is in no sense a relator. He cannot in any way control the prosecution and whether reluctant or no, he can be compelled like any other witness to appear and testify.

The Peace is that state and sense of safety which is necessary to the com-fort and happiness of every citizen and which government is instituted to secure.[14]

By contrast, the victim does have a controlling interest in any civil suit.

That this distinction is simple and clear is usually taken for granted, but it should not be. In the actual day-to-day operation of the criminal justice system it easily becomes blurred at the edges. Allowing victims to control the sentencing decision is just one example. Others include the practice of allowing victims to use the criminal justice system to collect on bad checks or on nonsupport pay-ments; for that matter restitution programs (especially as part of diversion pro-grams but also in cases where offenders are sentenced to probation on the condi-tion of payment of restitution) make the criminal justice system more like a civil justice system. But most telling in this regard is the large extent to which the workload of the criminal justice system involves cases in which defendants and victims are not strangers to each other. In the course of their disputes they com-mit acts that are technically crimes but usually do not constitute matters that are appropriate for conviction and imprisonment. A "burglary," for example, may be a boyfriend breaking down his girlfriend's door so he can talk to her about a recent quarrel. A "robbery" may be one drunk "rolling" another. In a recent study of the New York City courts, Vera Institute of Justice found that in half the felony arrests for crimes against the person the victim had a prior relationship with the defendant.[15] This was true not only of homicide and as-sault but, of robbery as well. Even in property crimes, prior relationships figured in over one-third of the cases. Moreover, the presence of such a relationship had a significant impact on the outcome of the cases, in particular, leading prosecu-tors to offer reduced charges and light sentences in return for guilty pleas and even more commonly leading to case dismissals.[16]

The Vera findings point out the extent to which we have forced our sys-tem of criminal justice to do double-duty. It is the instrument we use to deal with "real," predatory crime. But we also use it to deal with a large volume of matters that might better be conceived of and handled as civil disputes be-tween private parties. As Vera notes, this double-duty arrangement is the result of the fact that "our society has not found any adequate alternatives to arrest and adjudication for coping with inter-personal anger publicly expressed.[17] Other scholars have reached the same conclusion and have already begun to re-commend the establishment of alternative means of dispute resolution, such as arbitration and mediation programs.[18] The available information on such pro-grams, however, is at this time quite limited. It remains to be seen what pro-portion of those quasi-civil disputes that are now being handled by the criminal justice system could be successfully transferred to a civil system.

Meanwhile, it is important to recognize this significant discrepancy between the law in theory and the law in reality. A substantial proportion of violations of criminal law are in actuality more like civil matters than like real crimes. What is more, they are treated like civil matters by prosecutors, judges, and defense attorneys, which in turn adds to the confusion about the goals the criminal justice system is and should be pursuing and the roles that various parties including the victim should be allowed to play. In actual practice the victim appears to be given considerable influence over the disposition of the quasi-civil cases. If the victim chooses to have the case dismissed, for example, many prosecutors will defer to the victim's wishes unless the prosecutor believes that there is an overriding societal interest in the case.

In my observations, when the case is no longer a private matter between the victim and the defendant, prosecutors may distinguish those cases in which they are willing to let the victim's wishes heavily influence the case disposition from those in which they are not.

There seems to be operating on a de facto basis in our country a system for determining when the victim should be allowed to control the prosecution of cases which is similar to the system established by law in West Germany.[19] The German Code of Criminal Procedure provides for the private prosecution of certain cases (breaching domestic peace, insult, causing bodily harm, threatening with a serious crime, violating the secrecy of the mails, causing damage to property, and violating copyright laws and laws against unfair competition). Ordinarily these cases can be prosecuted only if the victim chooses to file the charges. But the public prosecutor is authorized to file charges if the particular violation affected people in addition to the victim and if the prosecution is of public concern because of the severe, brutal, or dangerous character of the offense, the motives of the offender, or his position in public life. Moreover, if the victim requests that the public prosecutor assume responsibility for a case of private prosecution and if the public prosecutor decides there is no public interest at stake, he is not required to assume the burden of prosecuting the case.[20]

For purposes of reconciling our own practices in this regard with our theoretical pronouncements about the separation of civil and criminal law, we may do well to consider adopting something like the German model. That is, we should establish at law what we do in practice. This would not only bring greater uniformity to our current practice but could become the basis for a system that could serve as a supplement or an alternative to arbitration and mediation programs. And, the change would not be on paper only because it would mean that some portion of those quasi-civil cases now clogging the courts would not be filed.

So far the discussion has focused on the question of victim control of the disposition decision. Now let us examine a less drastic proposal, namely, victim input into the disposition decision. In particular, we shall discuss the proposition that victims should be given notice and should be allowed to appear and allocute at the relevant proceedings. When I have suggested to judges, prosecutors, defense counsel, and legal scholars that the victim should be allowed to allocute at sentencing, the response has generally been negative. The usual concern (aside from the administrative problems that the proposal entails) is that the victim's involvement may affect the impartiality of the judge. But this argument is easily blunted by pointing out that much of what the defendant can say or has said on his own behalf may affect the impartiality of the judge. The question then becomes, why should we go to the additional bother?

Here there seem to be two sound answers. One has to do with the benefit to the victim (and ultimately to the public). The possible benefit to the victim would be the satisfaction of having one's say in the matter even though one's wishes may not ultimately prevail. It is this kind of satisfaction that, I believe, Holmes felt the criminal justice system should try to provide.

The second reason has to do with the quality of information available to the criminal justice decision maker and the system of checks and balances in our legal system. A key ingredient to rational decision making is adequate information. The first chapter of a well-respected book on sentencing deals with obtaining information.[21] The second chapter deals with assuring the accuracy of the information. Whether it is the sentencing decision or the plea bargaining decision or the dismissal decision, the adequacy of the information on which the decision is made is critical. It is for this reason that the victim should be allowed to allocute at disposition hearings. The victim can supply relevant information that might not otherwise be conveyed. He can also serve as a check on the integrity of the plea bargaining process. To appreciate the importance of these two functions, one has to understand certain aspects of plea bargaining.

One of the purposes served by plea bargaining is to hide the victim from the judge. Defense counsel frequently note that they will accept almost any plea deal in some cases just to keep the victim away from the judge. They explain that if the judge were to see the victim and the injury done, the sentence would undoubtedly be more severe. Judges corroborate this point in explaining why they sentence defendants more severely when they go to trial than when they plead guilty. The justification often given is that more negative information comes out about the defendant at trial. In our study of plea bargaining we have found that the information given to the judge at the time a plea of guilty is entered has frequently been modified to make the deal more palatable to the judge. Police officers and prosecutors will tone down their description of the seriousness of the crime.

No matter which theory of punishment one subscribes to there is no quarrel with one point. The information about the crime committed should be accurate. If the victim would assure this accuracy, then each theory would support his presence. What is more, if the involvement of the victim would enhance the prospects of rehabilitation as was mentioned above, then the proposal to involve victims would find yet another support.

Notes

1. Herbert S. Miller, "Current Perspectives in Corrections: A Cacophony," *Law and Contemporary Problems* 41 (1977).

2. Stephen Schafer, "The Victim and Correctional Theory: Integrating Victim Reparation with Offender Rehabilitation," in *Criminal Justice and the Victim*, William F. McDonald (ed.) (Beverly Hills, Calif.: Sage, 1976), pp. 227-235.

3. Edward Ziegenhagen, *Victims, Crime, and Social Control* (New York: Praeger, 1977).

4. Herbert S. Miller, William F. McDonald, and James A. Cramer, "Plea Bargaining in the United States: Phase I Report" (U.S. Law Enforcement Assistance Administration, 1977).

5. Caesare Beccaria, *An Essay on Crimes and Punishment* (Philadelphia: P.H. Nicklin, 1919).

6. Typical of this attitude is Principle II in the Declaration of Principles of the National Congress on Penitentiary and Reformatory Discipline convened in 1870, which stated in part "[t]he supressed aim of prison discipline is the reformation of criminals, not the infliction of vindictive suffering." (National Prison Association, *Transactions of the National Congress on Penitentiary and Reformatory Discipline* (Albany: Weed, Parsens, 1871), p. 541. A hundred years later these principles were reaffirmed in somewhat modified language at the Centennial Congress of Correction. Principle II of the 1970 Declaration of Principles describes the conflict between the retributive view and rehabilitation. The "punitive sentence" should be commensurate with the seriousness of the offense and the extent of the offender's participation. But, the length of the "correctional treatment given the offender for purposes of rehabilitation depends on the circumstances and characteristics of the particular offender and may have little relationship to the seriousness of the crime committed." (American Correctional Association, "Declaration of Principles of 1970." (Author, 1970).

7. See, for example, Robert G. Caldwell, *Criminology* (2d ed.) (New York: Ronald Press, 1965), pp. 420-423.

8. A.C. Ewing, *The Morality of Punishment* (Montclair, N.J.: Patterson Smith, 1970), p. 13.

9. Ibid., p. 15.

10. Oliver W. Holmes, *The Common Law* (Boston: Little, Brown, 1881), pp. 39-42.

11. Robert G. Gaiser, *RFK Must Die* (New York: Grove Press, 1971), p. 519.

12. Albert Alschuler, "The Prosecutor's Role in Plea Bargaining," *University of Chicago Law Review* 36 (1968): 50-112.

13. *State* v. *Nelson*, Minn. Sp. Ct., 8/5/77.

14. *Mallery* v. *Lane*, 97 Conn. 132, 138.

15. Vera Institute of Justice, *Felony Arrests: Their Prosecution and Disposition in New York City's Courts* (New York: Author, 1977), p. xiv.

16. Ibid., p. 20.

17. Ibid., p. xv.

18. John Greacen, "Arbitration: A tool for Criminal Cases?" *Barrister Magazine* 2 (1975): 10-14; and Gilbert M. Cantor, "An End to Crime and Punishment," *The Shingle* 39 (1976): 99-114. See also, William L.F. Felsteiner and Ann Barthelmes Drew, "European Alternatives to Criminal Trial and Their Applicability in the United States" (Monograph, Social Science Research Institute, University of Southern California, 1977).

19. Joachim Herrmann, "The German Prosecutor," in *Discretionary Justice in Europe and America*, in Kenneth C. Davis (ed.) (Urbana, Ill.: University of Illinois Press, 1976), pp. 16-74.

20. Ibid., pp. 28-31.

21. Robert O. Dawson, *Sentencing* (Boston: Little, Brown, 1969).

Part IV: Restitution Research

9

Evaluation of Recent Developments in Restitution Programming
Marguerite Q. Warren

The National Evaluation of Adult Restitution Programs is funded by the National Institute of Law Enforcement and Criminal Justice (NILECJ) of the Law Enforcement Assistance Administration (LEAA). The sponsoring agency is the Criminal Justice Research Center of Albany, New York. The project began in October, 1976. At the same time, the Office of Regional Operations of LEAA funded restitution programs in a variety of criminal justice settings in seven states. This collaboration on the part of the two divisions to develop and evaluate the seven programs is an innovation on the part of LEAA aimed at maximizing the payoff from the support of new programs.

Aims of the National Evaluation

The mandate of the national evaluation is to study, describe, and evaluate seven restitution programs. Project staff aims to assure the clear conceptualization of program goals in the various sites, to describe in detail the program components and procedures as they actually operate, and to assess the program impacts in ways relevant both to the individual projects and to the national effort. An attempt is being made to produce a body of scientifically derived knowledge, analyzed and presented in such a way as to provide reliable information and guidance for ongoing and future research and planning in the restitution area.

Specifically, the questions being asked in the National Evaluation include the following:

1. For what kinds of *offenders* is restitution planned or ordered? The types of data used in answering this question include demographics; prior record; attitudes toward self, others, and the criminal justice system; and social and personal characteristics. And, even more importantly, how are these characteristics related to success on restitution? Are some offenders more appropriate for restitution programs than others?

2. For what kinds of *victims* is restitution planned or ordered? The types of data used in answering this question include demographics, attitudes, and social

Some of the issues discussed in this paper are further detailed in Harland, A.T. and Warren, M.Q., Research Report No. 1 of the National Evaluation of Adult Restitution Projects. Data collection instruments are presented in Brown, E.J., Harland, A.T., Rosen, R.A., Warren, M.Q., and Way, B.B., Research Report No. 2, 1977.

113

characteristics. And, again, how are these characteristics related to success of restitution? Are some victims more appropriately involved in restitution programs than others?

3. For what kinds of *incidents* is restitution ordered? Incident characteristics include offense, where committed, offender role, victim precipitation, and victim/offender relationship. How are these incident characteristics related to success of restitution? Are some incidents more restitutionable than others?

4. How are restitution plans formulated, monitored, terminated? What are the program components and procedures? What incentives and sanctions are used? What community supports are available?

5. How does the extent and type of restitution (financial or service) ordered, as well as the collateral services offered in the restitution program, relate to characteristics of offenders, victims, and incidents?

6. To what extent are restitution orders met? Problems considered include late payments, partial payments, no payments, and the counterparts for service restitution.

7. Compared with a similar group of offenders (randomly chosen) not participating in the restitution program, how do offenders ordered to make restitution do in the following areas:

a. subsequent law violations/technical violations and criminal justice processing;
b. subsequent employment, residence, and family stability;
c. pre/post-restitution change in attitudes toward crime, victims, and the criminal justice system;
d. pre/post-restitution change in personality characteristics.

8. How do victims whose offenders were ordered to pay restitution compare with a comparable group in postrestitution attitudes toward crime, offenders, and the criminal justice system?

9. How does restitution affect criminal justice processing? Such dimensions as processing time, proportion of offenders incarcerated, proportion of offenders sent to various program alternatives, and decision making, are considered in looking at the impact of instituting restitution programs.

10. Does restitution work better at some points in the criminal justice system than in others, for example, better as a sentencing alternative than as a component of a work release program?

11. What are the cost/effectiveness implications of restitution versus alternative programming?

Questions 1 through 3 above focus on the components used in making the restitution decision, that is, the characteristics of the offender, victim, and incident. Questions 4 and 5 focus on how the restitution programs operate. Questions 6 through 11 are concerned with the effectiveness of the restitution programs, that is, their impact on offenders, victims, criminal justice processing, restitution commitments met, and costs.

One of the most important goals of the evaluation is an assessment of the interaction among the various data sets. The interest here is in the *differential* effectiveness depending upon type of offender, type of victim, type of program, and the stage in the criminal process at which restitution arises. Do certain types of offenders do better in repaying certain types of victims? Are certain types of offenders more willing to repay with service than with money? Are certain kinds of victims more satisfied with a restitution program that involves repayment close to the time of the offense (for example, a court-based program) rather than with a program that locates repayment at a more distant point in time (for example, a work release program)? Answers to these and other questions of differential impact are being sought by systematically studying outcome variation within programs (and the offender/victim/system variables associated with this variation) and to some extent variation among the programs.

Evaluation of the various programs is our mission, but our interests are theoretical as well. Thus we will keep our eye on such broader questions as: what are the advantages, if any, of viewing restitution as an offender treatment technique rather than a victim compensation mechanism? Is restitution another way of securing civil damages for the victim? and, if so, what are the legal issues involved? How many and what types of victims should be selected for restitution, to assure maximum fairness for all involved? How can the rationality of the penalty for the offender be maintained when using a community service type of restitution? Does restitution act as a deterrent? and if so, how? Is restitution a punishment? and, if so, can it serve as the sole punishment or must other sanctions be added? Because the sites vary considerably in their assumptions about restitution, their primary goals, the form of restitution used, as well as their procedures, we can examine some of these broader issues.

Evaluation Design

In each of the sites, a target population, eligible for restitution, was defined. Selection criteria were established at each site and offenders screened with respect to these. The design calls for the random allocation of the eligible group of offenders into two subgroups, an experimental group and a comparison group. The advantage of this design is to increase our confidence that any differences discovered between the two groups at a later stage can be attributed to the experimental treatment (restitution), rather than any initial differences between the groups. What happens to the comparison cases depends on the particular program, but ideally these offenders are assigned to a nonrestitution condition or to the program that existed before this experimental program began.

The remaining part of the design consists of following the offenders in both experimental and comparison groups to the point of further penetration into the criminal justice system, satisfactory completion of disposition conditions, or until the offender is otherwise out of the system. In addition, for those offenders who may be discharged during the course of the evaluation, a follow-up will check for later contacts with the criminal justice system.

Anticipated Progress During 1978

The national evaluation, like the restitution programs, was funded for two years. By the end of that time, considerable descriptive information concerning offenders, victims, and criminal justice processing will be reported. In addition, the steps in program processing in each site should be well detailed. The impact assessment (experimental versus comparison pre/post measures), however, will at that time involve low numbers of cases. Even though the sites that started taking cases earliest are those with the largest numbers of offenders involved, restitution payments are rarely completed in a year and may be extended over a several-year period. To maximize the comparability of assessment conditions for the experimental and comparison cases, as well as to maximize the number of cases on which some pre/post data are available, offenders and victims in both groups will be reinterviewed and the offenders tested at a six-month point. Beyond this, an extension of the national evaluation would be necessary to continue collecting postprogram assessments and other follow-up data.

Problems and Issues

In a way, few unexpected problems have arisen in connection with the evaluation. That is to say, most research projects that take place in action settings face similar problems. For example, when in project development do the evaluators begin to participate? If the evaluator role includes working with action staffs toward the clearest possible definitions of goals, populations, and procedures, there is an advantage in bringing on the research team before program proposals are accepted. It is possible that the long delays in the start-up time of action programs could be shortened by exploring or negotiating clearer definitions and procedural approvals before funding occurs.

Furthermore, there is the fact that research activities create a broad range of strains in an operating agency. Much has been written on this subject. If a program is to be evaluated, the program staff will be forced to engage in some conceptualizing activities and perhaps some procedural modifications which—in a nonevaluated program—would not have occurred. These changes would occur to some extent in the most simple evaluation design. Adding a random assignment design creates tension and opposition in many, if not most, agencies.

By and large the objection is not to the merit of the experimental design but rather to issues of feasibility and procedural complication. A variety of concerns with an experimental/control design are raised but behind the objections are often the strong belief that, since the experimental program is a good thing for the clients, the comparison cases are being unfairly deprived. It is understandably difficult for program staff to be openminded with respect to the beneficial aspects of the innovative program. A commitment to the value of the intervention seems crucial to the morale and best efforts of the action staff.

At the same time, the research staff is committed to conducting the best possible test of the restitution concept, trying to maintain the high level of research validity attainable through the experimental design. Considering these areas of potentially strong disagreement, it is impressive that the seven restitution programs have begun operating within an experimental framework. The willingness of the agency administrators to do so means that some of the confusion over the purposes and the effects of restitution programming will decrease. And program expansion and improvement can be based on knowledge rather than intuition. Acceptance of this principle by the program staff may not resolve all the tension and ambivalence they may feel for the research or the researchers, but the strain may be reduced to a manageable level.

Another example of the problems that arise in any action research project involves factors over which neither program nor research staffs have any control. Changing legislation, political decisions, changing decision-makers, budget modifications—all of these can represent serious program delays, program revisions, or cancellations. There is little one can say about these difficulties except to note them.

Perhaps the greatest challenge to the National Evaluators has been the requirement of conducting "action research across the miles." A major principle of action research is that frequent, ongoing interaction will occur between the program and research staffs. This ongoing dialogue will provide program staff with input regarding similar program development and research findings from other settings, improve conceptualization of problems as they arise (thus anticipating crises), and make possible considerable feedback that can serve a training function. These transactions are equally useful to researchers, providing them with the truest possible picture of how the program is actually operating.

The national evaluators find themselves feeling that they catch up with issues too late to be maximally helpful, that they are not up on all that is happening in the various sites, and that they are unable to serve as enablers in the way that they would like. On the other hand, at least one position seems easier from a distance: maintaining a tough stance with respect to the experimental design. Over the miles it is somewhat more difficult to become so identified with each agency that the agency's difficulties in operationalizing the design become defined as impossibilities.

Ideally, research will be seen as an asset rather than a liability by the action agency, both in the short run and the long run: the strains created will more than be made up for by the payoff available. A number of paths to this end are being considered, at least in the form of suggestions that may be useful in the next National Evaluation.

10 Attitudes Toward the Use of Restitution
John T. Gandy

The purpose of the present paper is twofold: first, to discuss research findings regarding the attitudes of citizens and criminal justice officials toward the use of restitution and, second, to discuss the implications of these attitudes toward the further development of restitution programming. Although the number of research studies regarding attitudes toward restitution is extremely limited, the studies do provide adequate data to identify implications.[1]

Attitudes Toward Creative Restitution

A rather detailed research undertaking, "Community Attitudes Toward Creative Restitution and Punishment,"[2] provides a rich source of data. A primary purpose of the study was to determine community attitudes toward creative restitution. It was assumed that community attitudes would differ according to the various subsamples used including police, social work students, members of a women's community service organization, probation officers, adult parole agents, and juvenile parole officers. A significant question related to the study purpose and variety of community groups was: are there differential attitude patterns present among the various study subsamples with regard to creative restitution and the traditional concepts of punishment?

The second purpose of the research was to explore empirically the interrelationship in terms of attitudes between creative restitution and punishment. Punishment was conceptualized in relation to the traditional concepts of punishment, that is, retribution, deterrence, rehabilitation, social defense, and the impact of imprisonment. Thus, an important question was: what is the relationship between the traditional concepts of punishment and creative restitution?

A final purpose of the study was to determine attitudes and perceptions that would support or impede programmatic approaches to creative restitution. For the purposes of the study creative restitution "is a process in which an offender, under appropriate supervision, is helped to find some way to make amends to those he has hurt by his offense."[3] It refers to "payments in either goods, services, or money, made by offenders to the victims of their crimes."[4] Creative restitution, as it was conceptualized, also refers to services provided by the offender to the community and to the general "community good." Thus, it may take three forms: monetary payments to the victim, service to the victim, and service to the general community.

Punishment was conceptualized as retribution, deterrence, rehabilitation, social defense, and the impact of imprisonment.[5] Several agruments have been presented concerning the relationship of creative restitution and punishment. It has been suggested that "spiritual satisfaction" is inherent in punishment and corrections itself and is, in part, restitution, which thus is an objective of punishment.[6] The research study assumed that punishment and creative restitution have a relationship theoretically, as punishment confronts the offender with the fact that he has violated the criminal law and creative restitution provides him the opportunity, both for himself and the victim, to make amends for that violation.[7]

Methodology

Data collection instruments were distributed to 705 individuals in the study sample; 60.5 percent (427) were returned and utilized in the study. The rates of responses received and utilized were as follows: police, 34 percent (58); second-year social work graduate students, 76 percent (58); members of a women's community service organization, 75 percent (79); juvenile probation and parole officers, 67 percent (10); and adult probation and parole officers, 65 percent (60).

Pilot tests and a pretest were utilized in the development of the data collections instruments. The punishment scale contained twenty items and consisted of five subscales, which measured retribution, deterrence, rehabilitation, social defense, and impact of imprisonment. An eleven-point Likert scale ranging from "strongly agree" to "strongly disagree" was used. The creative restitution questionnaire was developed as an operational measure of creative restitution and incorporated various aspects of the concept including its potential value use as a rehabilitative approach, appropriateness with various offender types, the concept as a substitute for imprisonment, the contractual relationship, reactions to types or forms of creative restitution, use in phases of the criminal justice process, level of interest in the concept; and an open-ended question relating to comments regarding creative restitution. Reliability and validity measures were conducted in the development of the scales with the test-retest method of reliability incorporating the Spearman rank-order correlation test. Coefficients in measuring the test-retest scores for each of the scales ranged from .56 to .75. Validity measures used included logical validation and predictive validity of the concurrent type.

For the purposes of the present analysis, two of the hypotheses are of interest.

Hypothesis I. Attitudes toward creative restitution and traditional concepts of punishment will vary according to specific community groups.

Hypothesis II. Attitudes toward creative restitution will be conditioned by attitudes toward the traditional concepts of punishment.

Findings

The study sample was relatively young, with the majority being thirty-five years of age or younger. Fifty-nine percent of the respondents were male. The sample was predominantly married, Protestant, Caucasian, and ranked high in educational level. Table 10-1 displays median score values for each of the attitudinal scales.[8] One important finding of the present study was the strong support of the concept of creative restitution. All six of the study populations reflected such support, although it was lower for the police. The rehabilitation concept was supported by the study sample with the exception of the police.

Hypothesis I suggested that the community groups would respond differentially to the six attitudinal variables. Kruskal-Wallis one-way analysis of variance was utilized to test this nondirectional hypothesis; Table 10-2 presents the results. The average rank scores indicated significant difference at the .001 level among the six community groups. The six populations responded differentially to creative restitution and the five dimensions of punishment. Another finding concerned the patterns of association among the six study populations. Social work graduate students, the women's community service organization, juvenile parole officers, and probation officers, respectively, tended to represent response patterns in opposition to the police and adult parole officers.

Spearman correlation coefficients were computed to test hypothesis II. The test results are presented in table 10-3. The correlation coefficients of the retribution, deterrence, rehabilitation, social defense, and impact of imprisonment scales with creative restitution were significant at or beyond the .001 level. Significant relationships were found to exist between the punishment scales and creative restitution. All the punishment scales, with the exception of rehabilitation, were negatively correlated with creative restitution. The rehabilitation scale was positively correlated with restitution. Although negative correlations existed between the punishment scales and creative restitution, positive support for creative restitution was indicated by previous findings. A related finding was that people supporting the traditional concepts of punishment, except rehabilitation, responded positively toward creative restitution but less positively than people holding favorable attitudes toward rehabilitation. This clustering of attitudinal patterns appears to have significant implications and will be discussed later.

A primary finding of the study was the overwhelming support for the concept of creative restitution. Community support as represented by the community service organization was at a high level and exceeded the support

Table 10-1
Median Statistics for Attitudinal Study Variables for Subsamples and Overall Study Sample

	Police	Second year social work graduate students	Members of a women's community service organization	Juvenile parole officers	Adult parole officers	Probation officers	Overall study sample
Retribution	28.10	13.83	17.00	14.00	23.50	20.28	20.59
Deterrence	23.50	14.00	14.00	17.50	24.00	20.59	18.53
Rehabilitation	19.17	35.00	34.88	31.50	27.30	31.17	30.43
Social defense	32.36	20.30	26.56	19.50	30.50	28.50	27.41
Impact of imprisonment	22.50	12.00	12.25	13.50	20.00	18.50	17.29
Creative restitution	61.50	72.75	72.58	72.17	69.00	70.79	70.14

Table 10-2
Study Populations and Attitudinal Variables by Average Rank Scores

	Retribution[a]	Deterrence[b]	Rehabilitation[c]	Social defense[d]	Impact of imprisonment[e]	Creative restitution[f]
Police	122.66	179.94	341.00	150.75	153.67	316.99
Second year social work graduate students	282.45	276.75	131.70	306.44	291.22	180.19
Juvenile parole officers	276.15	265.50	170.30	276.75	255.50	177.95
Parole officers	192.47	168.82	262.22	167.04	171.91	232.61
Probation officers	212.93	189.69	205.99	205.93	194.97	204.97
Members of a women's community service organization	241.49	270.58	166.52	236.84	267.35	172.16

[a] $H = 58.11$; 5 d.f.; $p < .001$, significant
[b] $H = 52.88$; 5 d.f.; $p < .001$, significant
[c] $H = 100.43$; 5 d.f.; $p < .001$, significant
[d] $H = 62.72$; 5 d.f.; $p < .001$, significant
[e] $H = 63.55$; 5 d.f.; $p < .001$, significant
[f] $H = 572.0$; 5 d.f.; $p < .001$, significant

Table 10-3
Correlational Matrix for Relationships between Attitudinal
Study Variables for the Study Samples of 427

	Deterrence	Rehabilitation	Social defense	Impact of imprisonment	Creative restitution
Retribution					
Correlation coefficient	.408	−.629	.512	.512	−.273
Level of significance[a]	.000	.000	.000	.000	.001
Deterrence		−.449	.353	.713	−.166
		.000	.000	.000	.001
Rehabilitation			−.516	−.546	.381
			.000	.000	.000
Social defense				.395	−.252
				.000	.001
Impact of imprisonment					−.228
					.001

[a]Two-tailed.

of the criminal justice personnel. Although individual items were not the focus of analysis, several findings were of interest. The vast majority of the study sample indicated that creative restitution is of potential value to the criminal justice system and would be quite useful as a rehabilitative approach. The respondents thought that restitution would be most appropriate with property offenses, such as auto theft, shoplifting, income tax evasion, and possibly drunk driving and burglary. Conversely, restitution was viewed as inappropriate for offenses against persons, such as rape, manslaughter, armed robbery, and assault. The study sample indicated that restitution could be a substitute for imprisonment with some types of offenders. In general the respondents viewed the development of a contractual relationship between an offender and victim as realistic, although there was some question. Monetary payments and service to the general community were considered to have somewhat greater potential than service to the victim. The vast majority of the respondents were interested in the concept of restitution.

Perceptions of the Legal Community

Based on one of the recommendations of my own study (1975) a related research endeavor was undertaken, to study "Attitudes of the Legal Community Toward Creative Restitution, Victim Compensation, and Related Social Work

Involvement."[9] Utilizing the findings of the previously discussed study, the research sought to analyze the attitudes of the legal community in South Carolina toward creative restitution. In addition, attitudes toward victim compensation were of interest.

Methodology

The purpose of this study was twofold: first, to describe the attitudes of the legal community toward creative restitution and victim compensation; second, to describe the differences in the attitudes of the three subsamples—judges, lawyers in private practice, and solicitors. The study population was the legal community of South Carolina.

Data collection instruments were mailed to 250 members of the legal community including 57 judges, 51 solicitors, and 142 practicing attorneys. One hundred data collection instruments were returned, ten of which were unusable, yielding a response rate of 38 percent. Usable returns were received from 57 percent of the lawyers, 22 percent of the solicitors, and 21 percent of the judges.

Study Findings

The study sample was in general married, white, and male. Median statistics were computed for each attitudinal variable and are presented in table 10-4. Restitution scores were well above but victim compensation scores were well below the theoretical median level of acceptance of creative restitution and the general nonacceptance of victim compensation. The total sample as well as all three of the subsamples reflected strong support for restitution. Lawyers in private practice were highly supportive of restitution with judges ranking closely behind. Age was found to be significantly associated with restitution scores at the .05 level. Respondents between the ages of thirty-six and fifty had a more positive attitude toward restitution than younger or older respondents.

The second question was concerned with implementation and support by legal community of programs of victim compensation and creative restitution.

Table 10-4
Median Scores of Attitudinal Variables

Scale	Solicitor	Judge	Lawyer	Total sample
Creative restitution	24.5	26.0	27.0	26.0
Victim compensation	13.5	12.5	12.5	13.0
Social work environment	15.0	16.0	16.0	16.0

A very important finding of the present study was the perceived potential value of restitutional programs. Eighty-nine percent of the respondents indicated that there was potential value for the use of creative restitution programs with the criminal offender. Only 4 percent of the sample responded negatively. The vast majority, 82 percent, responded favorably or very favorably to restitution as a rehabilitative approach in criminal justice. A large majority, 85 percent, stated that they were interested or very interested in the concept of restitution. This very positive response indicates that the legal community would help implement and support a program of creative restitution if it existed in South Carolina. A majority of respondents, 74 percent, did not think that the state should be obligated to compensate victims of crime. Forty-four percent were disinterested or very disinterested in the concept of victim compensation.

The third question concerned crimes the study sample perceived as appropriate for use with programs of creative restitution and victim compensation. The majority of respondents felt that offenses against property, auto theft, shoplifting, drunk driving, and income tax evasion were appropriate for use with creative restitution. The sample was undecided concerning burglary. Offenses against the person, such as rape and armed robbery, were felt to be inappropriate for use with restitution.

Several individual items were analyzed that were of particular significance for restitution. Eighty-seven percent of the respondents indicated that juveniles were most appropriate for restitution programming, whereas 90 percent viewed restitution programming as most applicable to first offenders. The second item analyzed concerned the type of restitution made to the victim. Forty-seven percent of the respondents indicated monetary payment to be the most appropriate, 13 percent felt service to the victim most suitable, 23 percent indicated service to the community as most appropriate, and 42 percent were of the opinion that any of the above might be appropriate.

Implications of Attitudes Toward Restitution

There are a number of implications of the research studies that have been discussed. The most significant finding was the overwhelming support for restitution. A diversity of groups such as police, probation and parole officers, members of a community service organization, lawyers in private practices, solicitors, judges, defense and prosecuting attorneys, demonstrated strong support for the concept.

An additional finding was that support varied somewhat among the study samples, although strong support was present in each of the groups studied. Of some surprise was the support for restitution found among police, members of a community service group, and lawyers. This is related to a finding in my research that found dual support for the restitutive concept and the concepts of punishment in the groups that supported creative restitution. Police and other groups that might tend to have a retributionist orientation, can, at the same time, support creative restitution. An explanation is that creative restitution may be perceived and conceptualized differentially. Thus, police and other groups may view creative restitution as an element of punishment or containing aspects of punishment. The concept may have great appeal to traditionally conservative elements in the population. Robert Mowatt noted that both liberal and conservative elements in society supported the concept of the Minnesota Restitution Center.[10] Liberals support restitution since it entails more than mere imprisonment; conservatives are attracted to the concept because it forces offenders to be responsible for their actions and pay for their crimes.[11] Restitution may also serve the function of deterrence and rehabilitation.[12] Creative restitution appears to have a broad base of support and is more widespread than was previously believed. The climate thus appears amenable to expansion and a more wide scale employment of restitutional programming. Since the studies found considerably stronger support for restitution with property offenses as opposed to offenses involving persons, further restitution programming, at least initially, should primarily involve property offenders.

There is support for restitution as a substitute for imprisonment with some types of offenders. There is absolutely no question that restitution is viewed as an adjunct crime sanction. The studies demonstrated some hesitancy fully to support the contractual relationship aspect of restitution. Apparently there is some question as to whether it is realistic. Monetary restitution is perceived as most appropriate, at least at the present time. This may be the function of the absence of true creative restitutive programs that incorporate service to the victim and the general community. Both of these avenues for restitution received support, but to lesser degrees than monetary payments. Many respondents felt that all three forms—monetary payments, service to the community, and service to the victim—could be appropriate depending on the individual situation.

An interesting and enlightening finding from the legal community study was the high degree of support for creative restitution accompanying the lack of support for victim compensation. This is of importance to future restitution programming, implying that the respondents were not concerned only with the victim and justice for the victim, but with this combined with concern for the offender and offender benefits from such a program.

A primary product of my study (1975) was the findings that support Schafer's idea that restitution is an element as well as a new concept of punishment.[13] Support for the traditional concepts of punishment was found to co-exist with support for creative restitution. Thus, a punishment orientation, such as retribution or deterrence, also can incorporate support for creative restitution. Several implications are apparent. Politically wise proponents of restitution programs might focus on different aspects of the concept depending on the audience. Police, law enforcement, and traditionally conservative groups will lend their support to restitution, if it is viewed as in harmony with their goals. Those with a nonpunishment orientation would be more receptive to rehabilitative and humane aspects of restitution. Restitution is not a panacea for the ills of the criminal justice system. It is, however, a viable alternative that has a great deal of support and appeal and should be further implemented.

Notes

1. John T. Gandy, "The Application of Creative Restitution to Volunteerism: A Study of Motivations and Contributions," *Proceedings–Roles of Colleges and Universities in Volunteerism* (Blacksburg, Virginia: Virginia Polytechnic Institute and State University, 1977): p. 35.

2. John T. Gandy, "Community Attitudes Toward Creative Restitution and Punishment," (Unpublished doctoral dissertation, University of Denver, 1975).

3. Albert Eglash, "Creative Restitution: Some Suggestions for Prison Rehabilitation Programs," *American Journal of Correction*, XX (November-December, 1958): 20.

4. Joe Hudson and Burt Galaway, "Undoing the Wrong," *Social Work*, XIX no. 3 (May 1974): 313-314.

5. For a more detailed discussion of the punishment dimensions, see Gandy, *Community Attitudes*, 54-63.

6. Stephen Schafer, "Restitution to Victims of Crime—An Old Correctional Aim Modernized," *Minnesota Law Review*, 50, no. 2 (December 1965): 248.

7. For a more detailed discussion of the relationship of creative restitution and punishment, see Gandy, "Community Attitudes," pp. 63-68.

8. The theoretical or hypothesized median is an "idealized" midpoint dividing relative high and low scores on an attitudinal scale. The theoretical or hypothesized median for retribution, deterrence, rehabilitation, social defense, and impact of imprisonment was 24, while the theoretical or hypothesized median for creative restitution was 42.5.

9. Robin Solomon Bluestein et al., "Attitudes of the Legal Community toward Creative Restitution, Victim Compensation, and Related Social Work Involvement," (Unpublished master's thesis, University of South Carolina, 1977).

10. Robert M. Mowatt, "The Minnesota Restitution Center: Paying Off the Ripped Off," Joe Hudson, editor, *Restitution in Criminal Justice* (St. Paul: Minnesota Department of Corrections, 1975): 200.

11. Philip Brickman, "Let the Punishment Fit the Crime," *Psychology Today* (May 1977): 29.

12. Ibid.

13. Stephen Schafer, *Restitution to Victims of Crime* (Chicago: Quadrangle Books, 1960), p. 122; and "Restitution to Victims of Crime—An Old Correctional Aim Modernized," p. 248.

11

Research on Restitution: A Review and Assessment
Joe Hudson and
Steven Chesney

Introduction

The idea of offender restitution to crime victims appears to be receiving renewed consideration as a sanction within the justice systems. The idea, of course, has a long and interesting history in the development of English law and over the past two hundred years intermittent interest in the idea was expressed by a variety of writers. The last ten years, however, have witnessed a different kind of rediscovery of restitution in the form of operational restitution programs and the incorporation of references to restitution in legislation. We recently identified sixteen states in which restitution legislation had been introduced over the past two years.[1] These bills are in addition to legislative references to restitution in most of the state criminal codes.

In addition to and often as a consequence of this legislation, a substantial number of restitution programs have started in the past few years. We recently identified forty formal restitution programs operating at the pretrial level, as a condition of work release, probation, or parole.[2] These restitution programs are characteristically nonresidential, administratively located in state corrections agencies, and are directed at adult male property offenders.

Interest on codifying restitution into statute and implementing the idea within an operational program seems to have far exceeded the commitment to research. Two years ago at the last restitution symposium, Burt Galaway commented that research was being inadequately considered in restitution programming.[3] Since that time, several research studies dealing with restitution have been initiated or completed. While the information generated by these studies is useful in providing some direction for program planning and operation, we still lack an adequate empirical basis for implementing the concept. Our purpose here will be to describe some of the major pieces of descriptive and evaluative research conducted on restitution, discuss some of the major findings, suggest some deficiencies and problems with this research, and propose some directions for further work.

Research Studies on Restitution

The major purpose of the studies to be considered here is either the description of the manner and extent to which restitution is being used as a sanctioning device or the evaluation of the relative effectiveness of specific restitution programs. Five studies aim at description and four at evaluation. While the studies discussed may not exhaust the universe of either descriptive or evaluative research or restitution, they do represent the research studies completed in this country. Most of the studies have been completed since the First National Symposium on Restitution and provide a limited basis for making judgments about some aspects of using restitution as a sanction. The major research studies on restitution, however, are yet to be completed and reported.[4]

Descriptive Studies

Each of the descriptive restitution studies aims at generating information about the manner and extent to which the concept is being used. The studies use different methods and because there is no common sample or population from one study to another, most of the findings have limited generalizability.

Assessment of Restitution in The Minnesota Probation Services.[5] Completed in 1976 by Steven Chesney of the Minnesota Department of Corrections, the major aim of this study was to identify and describe the manner and extent of restitution use in the Minnesota probation systems. In addition, data were gathered on attitudes held toward restitution by probation officers, judges, victims, and offenders. The primary research method involved drawing a stratified random sample of probation dispositions during four months of 1973 to 1974. Counties in the state were stratified on population and seventeen counties were randomly selected from within each of the three strata. In turn, proportionate numbers of probation cases were randomly selected from each of the three levels of courts (District Court for Adult Gross Misdemeanors and Felonies; County Court for Adult Misdemeanants; and Juvenile Court) within each of the sampled counties. A total of 525 cases comprised the final sample. The data sources relied upon were official files and structured interviews. Because of the sample selection procedures, the results of this study were held to be generalizable to the population of probation cases in Minnesota during the twelve months of July, 1973, through June 30, 1974.

An Exploratory Study of the Perceived Fairness of Restitution.[6] Completed by Burt Galaway and William Marsella in 1976, this research aimed at assessing the extent to which restitution is perceived as a fair sanction for juvenile offenders. Juvenile court dispositions involving restitution as a condition of probation in St. Louis County (Duluth, Minnesota) over a four-week period constituted the study sample. A small sample of seventeen juvenile offenders was identified and information obtained from official records and personal interviews with offenders, victims, police, and probation staff.

Restitution Requirements for Juvenile Offenders.[7] Undertaken by the staff at the Institute for Policy Analysis and published in 1977, this is a survey of juvenile court restitution practices. A random sample of juvenile courts in the country was identified and mailed questionnaires used to obtain information on the manner and extent to which restitution was ordered and the attitudes held toward the practice by court officials. Of the total identified population of 3,544 juvenile courts in the country, a random sample of 197 received questionnaires. One hundred and thirty-three responses were received for a 68 percent return rate.

Restitution as Perceived by Legislators and Correctional Administrators.[8] This unpublished study was recently completed by the Minnesota Department of Corrections. The major aim was to assess the way in which restitution is perceived by state legislators and state corrections administrators. Mailed questionnaires were sent to every administrator of state adult or juvenile corrections agencies, and to corrections administrators in major trust territories as well as in the cities of Chicago and New York. In addition, a random sample of 25 states was selected involving the chairperson of the corrections committees in the state legislature as well as three randomly selected committee members. Seventy-three responses were received from the population of 82 corrections administrators (89 percent) and 105 of the population of 271 legislators (39 percent) completed and returned the survey instrument.

Issues in the Use of Restitution.[9] This unpublished survey of parole and probation staff in Minnesota was recently completed by the Minnesota Department of Corrections. The purpose of the study was to assess the extent to which parole and probation officers define different aspects of restitution as problematic. Questionnaires were mailed to all 263 parole and probation officers and supervisors in the state, exclusive of county probation officers in Hennepin (Minneapolis) and Ramsey (St. Paul) counties. One hundred and ninety-seven questionnaires (75 percent) were completed and returned.

Characteristics of Restitution Programs.[10] This survey of operational restitution programs currently operating in the country was undertaken by the Minnesota Department of Corrections. The primary aim was to identify characteristics of operational restitution programs, particularly in relation to significant issues associated with the use of the concept. A mailed questionnaire was sent to state planning agencies and state corrections agencies. Forty-two (76 percent) responses were received from state planning agencies and thirty-eight (46 percent) from corrections agencies.

Extent of Use

Assessing the relative frequency with which a restitution sanction is ordered was a primary concern of three studies. Chesney's research dealt with the use of restitution in a population of probation dispositions in Minnesota counties over a four-month period. He found that out of a total of 508 adult district court probation dispositions, restitution was ordered in 96 (19 percent) of the cases, and in the juvenile courts restitution was obilgated in 225 out of a total of 1,256 (18 percent) cases. In a restricted sample of 7 county courts, 40 cases out of 415 (10 percent) probation dispositions had a restitution condition.

As distinct from Chesney's efforts to assess the actual extent to which restitution was ordered as a probation condition through the examination of official records, the study completed by the Institute For Policy Analysis asked juvenile court officials for an estimation of their use of restitution. Eighty-six percent of the courts reported that restitution was used to some extent. Because of different methods, the two studies are not really comparable, Chesney dealt with actual probation cases in which restitution was ordered while the Institute For Policy Analysis dealt with reported useage as defined by different types of juvenile court officials—judges, probation officers, or other staff.

Offenses for Which Ordered

The Institute for Policy Analysis study estimated that restitution was ordered by juvenile courts in 70 percent of the adjudications for property offenses, 45 percent of the adjudications for robbery, 24 percent of the adjudications for assault, and approximately 11 percent of the adjudications for sex offenses. The Chesney survey found that 96 percent of all ordered restitution cases in Minnesota were for property offenses—53 percent theft-related offenses, 6 percent forgery offenses, 37 percent damage to property. Similarly, all seventeen restitution cases identified by Galaway and Marsella in the St. Louis County, Minnesota study involved property offenses. Quite clearly, then, restitution seems to be predominantly used as a sanction for crimes against property.

The extent to which restitution was perceived by corrections administrators as an appropriate sanction for different types of criminal offenses was addressed in the survey completed by the Minnesota Department of Corrections. Restitution was found to be overwhelmingly supported as a sanction for property offenders by approximately 95 percent of both groups of respondents. Surprisingly, however, a large proportion of both legislators (73 percent) and corrections administrators (70 percent) supported the use of restitution for such person offenses as robbery.

Types of Restitution

Overwhelmingly, the studies show that financial, as opposed to service, restitution is ordered. Chesney found that only approximately 4 percent of restitution obligations involved community services and approximately 2 percent required offender services to the direct victim. Service restitution requirements were found to apply most commonly to the disposition of juveniles. Similar tendencies are reported in the Institute For Policy Analysis Survey: 95 percent of juvenile courts noted the use of financial restitution while 52 percent of the jurisdictions reported using service restitution. The survey of operational restitution programs conducted by the Minnesota Department of Corrections also found that programs serving juveniles characteristically placed greater emphasis on service as compared to financial restitution whereas the opposite was the case with programs serving adults.

Both the Minnesota and Oregon studies found that given that a restitution order is made, full restitution was most commonly obligated to cover the total amount of victim losses sustained. While a number of references in the literature refer to the possible dangers of overburdening offenders by requiring full as opposed to partial restitution, in practice the relatively small amount of damages sustained in typical criminal incidents seems to support a bias toward requiring full restitution. Chesney, for example, found that the mean amount of losses sustained by crime victims was $214 and the mean amount of financial restitution ordered was $167. Studies by both Chesney, and Galaway and Marsella, found that estimates of losses varied between victims and offenders as well as between victims and the courts. Offender estimates of the amount of damages done were found in both studies to be about one-third of overall victim estimates and Chesney found official court estimates to be an average of 20 percent less than those made by victims. Victims may be inflating losses, offenders underestimating them, or some combination of the two.

The Restitution Process

How the amount of restitution is determined, the way in which it is ordered, and the manner in which it is handled once it is ordered are questions that have been addressed to varying extents in the research. For example, the court decision to order restitution appears to be most commonly based upon the perceived ability of the offender to pay. Chesney asked judges to identify factors involved in the decision to order restitution and found that the offender's ability to pay was the only common factor agreed upon. While the Institute for Policy Analysis found that the amount of losses sustained by crime victims was the most important criterion used to determine the amount of restitution to be ordered, the authors note that the ability to pay restitution may be used by judges as a basis for determining a youth's eligibility for a restitution requirement in the first place. In short, the offender's perceived ability to pay may be used as a screening factor for ordering restitution.

A complicating issue here, however, is whether the jurisdiction utilizes partial restitution. For example, Galaway and Marsella concluded that the amount of victim losses and, by implication, the offender's ability to pay were not significant decision criteria because partial restitution was commonly ordered.

Victim-offender involvement in a restitution scheme does not appear to be a common practice. Out of 525 restitution cases studied by Chesney, the direct involvement of victims and offenders in negotiating a formal restitution agreement occurred in only 6 cases. Most commonly, the amount of restitution to be paid was determined by the court and paid by the offender to a third party, such as a probation officer who is then responsible for dealing with the victim. Similarly, in the survey of operational restitution programs, when program managers were asked to report on the extent to which victim-offender interaction was being structured, the overwhelming response was "occasionally," "sometimes," "rarely," or "never."

As distinct from actual practice, however, the survey of corrections administrators found that a majority (59 percent) of respondents were supportive of direct victim-offender involvement in the development and ongoing completion of a restitution scheme. Also, approximately half the surveyed probation and parole officers in Minnesota expressed support for the idea of direct victim-offender involvement. In short, although the idea may be attractive, problems associated with securing and maintaining victim-offender involvement seem to discourage the practice.

The ultimate enforcement of a restitution order usually remains with the court although the type of sanctions imposed may vary considerably between jurisdictions. The Institute For Policy Analysis study, for example, found that in only 16 percent of the juvenile court jurisdictions was probation revoked and the youth incarcerated as a result of not making restitution while 37 percent of the jurisdictions noted that probation was commonly revoked in such cases, and a small number of jurisdictions noted that failure to complete the ordered restitution resulted in the issuance of contempt citations or the attachment of the youth's salary.

Victim and Offender Characteristics

Chesney's research found that restitution was most commonly ordered as a probation condition for white, middle class, first-time offenders. The limited sample in the study by Galaway and Marsella also contained a high proportion of first-time offenders.

To some considerable extent, these characteristics may be the result of screening offenders for restitution on the basis of their perceived ability to pay. The crucial question then concerns the nature of the disposition given to those who are not seen as appropriate candidates for restitution: are they given the same sanction exclusive of the restitution requirement, or do they receive a more severe sanction, such as incarceration?

A further question then concerns the type of victim seen as appropriate to receive restitution. Relatively small proportions of both legislators and corrections administrators favored the payment of restitution to insurance companies or large business firms. In practice, however, Chesney found that the largest proportion of victims represented business firms.

System Implications

Restitution appears to be most commonly ordered as a supplement to probation or parole. A consequence of such a practice can be an increase in the degree of social control exercised over the offender. For example, the Institute For Policy Analysis found that almost half the study sample of juvenile courts reported that requiring restitution increases the offender's length of contact with the justice system. The financial implications of this for the operation of the justice system then become increasingly important. Specifically, do the relative benefits of restitution for the offender, victim, and justice system outweigh the costs involved in supplementing sanctions?

One of the frequently mentioned benefits of restitution is the provision of reparations to crime victims. A derivative benefit, then, is the continued confidence of the victim in the fairness of the justice system. In fact, however, evidence is available to indicate that victims are quite frequently not well informed about ordered restitution. Galaway and Marsella, for example, found that after an average of forty days following court disposition and the restitution order, none of the victims had been informed. Chesney found that after up to two years following court disposition, 12 percent of the victims were unaware that restitution was to be made. It is unlikely that confidence in the justice system will be enhanced by such practices. (One possible reason for victims not being informed about restitution is the belief held by probation and parole officers that restitution causes them a host of problems.)

Evaluation Studies

Each of the studies reported here has tried to evaluate the relative effects of individual restitution programs with outcome effectiveness defined in relation to the dual goals of offender rehabilitation and victim reparation. Because these studies generally tend to be global evaluations of a particular program package and because none of the programs under study uses restitution as the sole sanction, there is little basis for arriving at a determination of the relative effects of restitution as a specific program component. For example, none of the studies deal with questions about the relative outcome effects of restitution as compared with alternative program ingredients. Although these evaluations may have some utility for the respective program managers, the results cannot be generalized to other times or places and do little for the development of a cumulative body of knowledge concerning the effects of ordering restitution as a justice system sanction.

The Minnesota Restitution Center Evaluation.[11] The Minnesota Restitution Center was a community-based residential corrections program established by the Minnesota Department of Corrections in 1972 and operated until the end of 1976. The program involved a contract negotiation phase at the state prison and a restitution implementation phase which occurred upon the offender's release to the center. The major criteria to be met by all inmates considered for the program were these: new court commitment to the state prison for offenses against property; commitment from one of the seven metropolitan counties of Minneapolis and St. Paul; no felony convictions for a crime against persons during the preceding five years of community life; no detainers filed. Inmates meeting these program criteria formed the population pool for the program. From this pool, offenders were randomly assigned to the experimental and control groups. Upon random assignment to the experimental group, offenders had the option of directly participating with their crime victims in the development of restitution agreement. The completed restitution agreement was then reviewed by the paroling authority and, if in agreement, the offender released on parole to the center four months following prison admission.

The research design in effect during the first two years of program operation was an after-only field experiment involving random assignment from within the specified population of prison admissions. A potential contaminating factor was the reservation that the parole authority retain the right to deny parole to any of the selected experimentals. In fact, nine of the seventy-two randomly selected experimentals were subsequently denied release to the center during the first two years. In addition, four experimentals declined the opportunity to participate in the program and as a consequence, the external validity of the research findings was affected.

Offender characteristics in both the experimental and control groups were found to be similar with the largest proportion composed of white offenders under thirty years of age committed for burglary and with an extensive prior felony record. A total of 221 victims were identified for the 62 experimentals actually released to the center. The largest proportion of these victims were private individuals (36 percent) followed by retail sales establishments (19 percent), large sales organizations (15 percent), service establishments (14 percent), entertainment facilities (13 percent), and human service organizations (4 percent). The amount and type of restitution obligations assumed by the 62 experimentals admitted to the center involved relatively small amounts of money: thirty-three (53 percent) of the offenders had restitution obligations of two hundred dollars or less and 44 (72 percent) totalled less than five hundred dollars. In addition, nine (14 percent) of the experimentals had strictly service restitution obligations averaging approximately one hundred and twenty hours per man.

Information on the postrelease status of the experimentals and controls can be presented for the twenty-four period following prison release (see figure 11-1). At least twenty-four months have elapsed since the experimentals were released from the prison to the center and with the exception of three persons in the control groups, similar length of time has elapsed since prison release for offenders on parole status. As of September 1, 1977 these three controls had been on release for twelve, seventeen, and twenty-one months respectively. Consequently, community at risk period is slightly shorter for the controls as compared to the experimentals.

Table 11-1 further summarizes the information.

1. Approximately the same proportion of experimentals (27 percent) as compared to controls (25 percent) *remained under parole supervision* twenty-four months following release.

2. A larger proportion of experimentals (23 percent) as compared to controls (16 percent) had received *parole discharge* twenty-four months following prison release. Considering that eight (12 percent) of the control group had received *flat discharge* from prison as compared to none of the experimentals and including this group with those either discharged from parole or remaining under parole supervision means that a larger proportion of controls (54 percent) as compared to experimentals (50 percent) remained free of any legal sanctions twenty-four months after release.

3. A significantly larger proportion of controls (24 percent) as compared to experimentals (6 percent) had been returned to prison on the basis of *new court commitments*.

4. A significantly larger proportion of experimentals (40 percent) as compared to controls (10 percent) had been returned to prison on the basis of *technical violations of parole*. This substantial difference between groups is likely to have been the function of the relatively more intensive parole supervision provided to members of the experimental group released to the restitution center. At the same time, however, some of these cases may have resulted from the discretion exercised by officials in the criminal justice system. It is reasonable to expect, for example, that some offenders returned to prison and officially classed as "technical parole violators" might otherwise have been classed as "new court commitments" if the offender had been returned to court rather than administratively transferred to prison on violation. In many cases if a parolee admits to an impending charge, the parole may be revoked and the offender returned to prison and officially counted as a parole violator rather than a new court commitment. In such cases, charges may never be officially brought on the grounds that the offender was returned to prison. In other cases, if charges

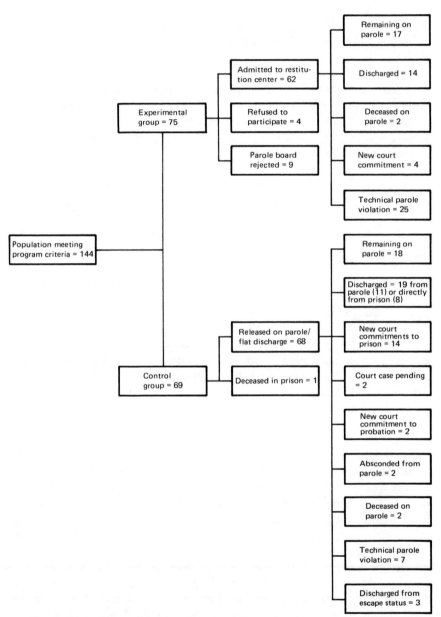

Figure 11-1. Experimental and Control Group Status Twenty-four Months Following Prison Release[a]

[a]In the case of three members of the control group, the actual elapsed time was only 12, 17, and 21 months respectively as of the time data was collected.

Table 11-1

Experimental and Control Group Status Twenty-four Months Following Prison Release

	Experimental	Control
Remaining on parole status	17 (27%)	18 (26%)
Discharged from parole	14 (23%)	11 (16%)
Flat discharge from prison	–	8 (12%)
New court commitment	4 (6%)	16 (24%)
Mechanical violations	25 (40%)	7 (10%)
Absconded	–	1 (1%)
Deceased on parole/flat discharge	2 (3%)	2 (3%)
Discharged while on escape status	–	3 (4%)
Court case pending	–	2 (3%)

are officially brought the offender is likely to negotiate a plea with the sentence to run concurrent with the unexpired portion of the original sentence. In either case, the probability is that the return to prison will be counted as a parole violation rather than as a new court commitment.

5. Grouping together offenders in the experimental and control groups who had received either a *new court commitment* or a *technical parole violation* twenty-four months following prison release, a larger proportion of experimentals (46 percent) as compared to controls (34 percent) had been returned to prison. Including together with such prison returns those offenders convicted of new crimes and placed on probation, or who *absconded,* or who had *court cases* pending, the differences between the groups are narrowed but still tend to favor the controls (40 percent) as compared to the experimentals (46 percent).

Table 11-2 presents information on the length of time under parole supervision for those experimentals and controls released from prison on this status. It should be kept in mind when reviewing this information that a total of eleven controls were not released on parole (eight flat discharges; three escapes) and, further, that as of September 1, 1977, three controls had been under parole supervision for only twelve, seventeen, and twenty-one months respectively. This table shows that while there was some tendency for experimentals to fail on parole at an earlier point, the between-group difference is not substantial.

Table 11-3 presents information on months to prison return from release. It should be emphasized here that two controls were convicted of new offenses and placed on probation status and therefore are not included in the total number of controls returned to prison.

Table 11-2
Length of Time on Parole in Months

	0-3	4-6	7-9	10-12	13-15	16-18	19-21	22-24	No parole	Total
Experimental	12 (19%)	9 (15%)	6 (10%)	7 (11%)	5 (8%)	1 (2%)	—	22 (35%)	—	62 (100%)
Control	5 (7%)	13 (19%)	6 (9%)	9 (13%)	3 (4%)	2 (3%)	5 (7%)	14 (21%)	11 (16%)	68 (100%)

Table 11-3
Months to First Return to Prison from Date of Release

	0-3	4-6	7-12	13-15	16-18	19-21	22-24	Total returning within two years	Total not returning	Grand total
Experimental	9 (15%)	5 (8%)	9 (15%)	4 (6%)	0 —	2 (3%)	0 —	29 (47%)	33 (53%)	62 (100%)
Control	2 (3%)	4 (6%)	7 (10%)	2 (3%)	1 (1%)	1 (1%)	4 (6%)	21 (31%)	47 (69%)	68 (100%)

Inspection of table 11-3 shows a relationship between experimental group status and time to prison return. Experimentals returned to prison much more quickly than controls with approximately half of those returning to prison in the experimental group being returned within the first six months as compared to only 9 percent of the controls. To some considerable extent this would seem to be a function of experimentals being returned for technical parole violations.

The Assessment of Restitution in Probation Experiment.[12] On the basis of 1974 Iowa Legislation requiring restitution as a condition of either deferred prosecution or probation, the Restitution in Probation Experiment was established in the Polk County (Des Moines) Department of Court Services. The program was partially modeled after the Minnesota Restitution Center and included an emphasis on direct victim-offender involvement in the development of restitution plans. In contrast to the Minnesota program, however, this program was nonresidential and operated with offenders on probation or deferred sentence. Regular probation officers carrying both restitution and nonrestitution caseloads comprised the program staff.

Because of difficulties involved in implementing the program and the research, the limited time available for program operation, and the statutory requirement that restitution be ordered in all cases that qualified, the original evaluation plan was altered. No attempt was made to assess the outcome effects of restitution on the offender group. Instead, the research was primarily aimed at describing the nature of the effort expended in the program. Major findings of the study include the following:

Monthly amounts of restitution increased considerably as a result of the experimental program.

As opposed to original program intentions, less than half of the 102 restitution cases involved direct victim-offender negotiations. In such cases, however, staff perceived a greater degree of cooperation among the offenders.

Considerable staff time was required for the development and supervision of restitution agreements and this increased proportionately with the degree of victim involvement. The time needed to establish the restitution plan was much greater with victim involvement but the time needed to monitor and administer the plans was generally less.

The vast majority of victims were business firms and the offenders had been predominantly convicted of crimes against property.

Pima County Adult Diversion Program.[13] While the adult diversion program operated by the Pima County Attorney's Office is not explicitly a restitution program, most of the defendants do make financial restitution and, in addition, are required to perform forty hours of community services restitution. The program operates at the pretrial, postarraignment level and involves primarily property offenders. Direct victim-defendant meetings are structured for the purpose of negotiating the amounts of restitution. Upon the successful completion of the program, charges are dismissed.

The research conducted on this program has been mainly descriptive, aimed at assessing program inputs for the purpose of monitoring program operation. Major findings have been that the vast majority of the defendants had no prior record, were largely composed of white property offenders, and were obligated to make a mean average of $385 in restitution. Victims were largely business firms and direct victim-offender negotiations occurred in 30 percent of the cases.

The Georgia Restitution Shelter Program.[14] With the aim of helping to alleviate prison overcrowding, the Georgia Department of Offender Rehabilitation established four restitution shelters in late 1974 and early 1975. These programs received direct probation referrals from courts as well as parolees from state prisons. Eligibility criteria were quite loose and essentially involved any offender the judiciary or parole board referred to the program. Both financial and community service restitution were used. No emphasis was placed on structuring victim and offender involvement.

The evaluation conducted on the four restitution shelters was an assessment of program inputs and outputs with only limited attention placed on assessing program outcomes. Official records were the sole data sources. Missing data was a serious if not fatal problem, with a large proportion (32 percent) of the population of four hundred offenders admitted to the shelters not followed over time. Major findings of the study can be summarized as follows:

Of the 400 offenders admitted to the four shelters, 80 percent probationers referred by the courts and 20 percent parolees; 57 percent were white and 43 percent black; 78 percent were between seventeen and twenty-seven years of age; 87 percent had been convicted for a felony and 13 percent for misdemeanors; most of these offenses were against property with 18 percent convicted for crimes against persons.

For a one-year period (April 1, 1975 to March 31, 1976), 32 percent of the offenders had no reported income and of those with income, 61 percent had less than $4,732. Most probably as a consequence of restitution obligations totalling $207,567, only $54,828 was repaid.

Approximately one-third of the offenders placed on the program were in-program failures who either absconded, had technical parole or probation violations, or were reconvicted prior to program discharge.

Of the 274 offenders for whom data was available, 31 percent had been re-arrested within six months following program release, 59 percent within twelve months, and 87 percent within eighteen months.

Conviction data was available on only 40 offenders and of these, 45 percent were reconvicted within six months of program release and 75 percent within twelve months. The dispositions received in 22 percent of these cases was probation, in 28 percent of these cases it was incarceration, and in 15 percent of the cases it was a split sentence of jail and probation. The majority of the offenders convicted of new offenses were not committed to prison. This, along with the fact that the vast majority (80 percent) of the offenders admitted to the program were on probation status, would strongly indicate that the program acted as a supplement to probation rather than a diversion from incarceration.

Research Problems and Needs

There are a number of problems with the research completed on restitution as well as a variety of further research needs. Among the major types of problems are the use of an experimental design to assess program outcomes, the validity and reliability of data, and the lack of cumulative findings.

The research conducted on the Minnesota Restitution Center illustrates the problems associated with the use of an experimental design to evaluate new social programs. True randomness in the sample selection procedures, for example, was compromised because of political and administrative constraints. As a result, the internal and external validity of the findings was brought into question. Quite clearly, the realities of political and organizational life will commonly conflict with the idea of random assignment.

A less obvious problem associated with the use of experimental designs in the evaluation of newly implemented social programs is the inability of the program to meet major preconditions of this type of research. Although careful consideration may be given to the methodology to be followed in the research, insufficient attention is likely to be given to the specific character of the program interventions themselves. All too commonly the evaluation places too little emphasis on specifying program interventions with the result that undefined program inputs cause problems in explaining program outcomes. Furthermore, poorly articulated programs will cause external validity problems, especially in terms of attempting to replicate the program in other settings. Frequently compounding poorly articulated interventions are difficulties associated with the changing nature of program efforts over time, and with the use of different client groups.

The requirement that the program as the independent variable remain stable over time may frequently be contradicted in new programs because there may be no set of intervention principles formulated prior to program implementation. As a consequence, the program is left largely free to change in accordance with the changing nature of the external and internal demands placed upon the program manager. Furthermore, freedom to innovate and make alterations in the content of the interventions is likely to be seen by the program manager as a necessary and desirable precondition for the continued existence of the program.

All the evaluation studies reviewed here fail in providing adequate attention to the way in which restitution was used, and especially in relation to the use of a variety of other interventions. As a result, the findings have almost no explanatory power. We are left with little more than speculations about the interventive effects of restitution.

Compounding this problem is the abence of adequate control or comparison groups in most of the studies. When a control group was used, as in the Minnesota Restitution Center, true random assignment was compromised by the releasing authority. The other evaluations failed to provide anything close to a meaningful comparison group.

Several problems having to do with the reliability and validity of the measures used can be found in both the evaluation and descriptive research on restitution. Most of the studies relied upon official records as data sources: the literature is replete with stories of the horrors associated with using such information. Also, a number of studies relied upon program staff to either collect data or act as a primary source for it, and in some cases program staff may have had biases about the program. Additionally, when program staff were used as the data collection source, as in the Institute For Policy Analysis study, different types of staff persons in different jurisdictions acted as respondents. Most of the research does not concern itself with either the development or testing of theory. Only the study completed by Galaway and Marsella attempted to test theoretical propostitions and the small sample and lack of a comparison group receiving alternative sanctions detract from the findings.

One common finding in the research is the predominance of business organizations as victims. Where data were reported, each of the evaluation studies found that business firms were the most common victim type. Little research has been conducted on the variety of questions raised by such a finding. For example, what are the program implications particularly in the terms of the differential impact of making restitution if the victim is a business organization as compared to an individual? Furthermore, what are the implications of paying restitution to business firms relative to the goals of restitution? should the criminal justice system establish programs that in effect subsidize the theft losses of profit firms? The literature on restitution and victimology has generally concentrated on the private citizen as crime victim with little attention paid to differentiating victim types.

Several social policy questions are raised by the findings of these studies. First, several of the studies noted a predominance of white, middle class offenders. Does restitution programming, because of the use of the offender's perceived ability to pay, discriminate against the minority group offender and the poor? The issue of system penetration is also raised by several of these studies. Although restitution is often advocated as an alternative sanction to incarceration, there is evidence to indicate that the reverse is frequently the case. Restitution is commonly used as a supplement to conventional probation and as a consequence tends to increase the offender's involvement with the justice system. A related question concerns the goal or objective of a restitution program: is it one of offender rehabilitation, victim reparation, offender punishment, or some combination of these? Without a clear specification of program objectives, the research is likely to be misdirected.

Notes

1. Joe Hudson, Steven Chesney, John McLagen, "Survey of Recent Restitution Legislation," Minnesota Department of Corrections, St. Paul, September, 1977, unpublished.

2. Joe Hudson, Steven Chesney, John McLagen, "Survey of Operational Restitution Programs," Minnesota Department of Corrections, St. Paul, September, 1977, unpublished.

3. Burt Galaway, "Toward the Rational Development of Restitution Programming," included in Joe Hudson, ed., *Restitution In Criminal Justice,* Minnesota Department of Corrections, pp. 74-87.

4. See paper by Marguerite Q. Warren in this volume, and Peter R. Schneider and Anne L. Schneider, "Evaluating Juvenile Restitution Programs: A Preliminary Design," Institute For Policy Analysis, Eugene, Oregon, August 23, 1976, unpublished.

5. Steven L. Chesney, "The Assessment of Restitution in the Minnesota Probation Services," included in Hudson, ed., *Restitution,* pp. 146-186.

6. Burt Galaway and William Marsella, "An Exploratory Study of the Perceived Fairness of Restitution as a Sanction for Juvenile Offenders," paper presented at the Second International Symposium on Victimology, Boston, Massachusetts, September, 1976.

7. Peter R. Schneider, Anne L. Schneider, Paul D. Reiter, and Colleen M. Cleary, "Restitution Requirements for Juvenile Offenders: A Survey of the Practices in American Juvenile Courts," Institute For Policy Analysis, Eugene, Oregon, June, 1977, unpublished.

8. Joe Hudson, Steven Chesney, John McLagen, "Restitution as Perceived by State Legislators and Correctional Administrators," Minnesota Department of Corrections, St. Paul, September, 1977, unpublished.

148

9. Joe Hudson, Steven Chesney, John McLagen, "Parole and Probation Staff Perceptions of Restitution," Minnesota Department of Corrections, St. Paul, September, 1977, unpublished.

10. Joe Hudson, Steven Chesney, John McLagen, "Survey of Operational Restitution Programs," Minnesota Department of Corrections, St. Paul, September, 1977, unpublished.

11. Minnesota Department of Corrections, unpublished research, St. Paul, Minnesota, October, 1977.

12. Roger O. Steggerda and Susan P. Dolphin, "Victim Restitution: An Assessment of the Restitution In Probation Experiment Operated by the Fifth Judicial District Department of Court Services," Polk County Department of Program Evaluation, December, 1975, unpublished.

13. David A. Lowenberg, "Pima County Attorney's Adult Diversion Project's Second Annual Report (October 1973-September 1975)," Tucson, Arizona, October 29, 1975, unpublished.

14. Gerald T. Flowers, "The Georgia Restitution Shelter Program," Program Evaluation Section, Georgia Department of Offender Rehabilitation, September 30, 1977, unpublished.

Part V: Service Restitution

12 The Win-onus Restitution Program
Dennis A. Challeen and
James H. Heinlen

Win: to fight, endure, struggle, to desire to gain victory
Onus: responsibility for a wrong
Restitution: giving back to the rightful owner something that has been lost or taken away

Inititation of Program

In the fall of 1972, the Winona County Court started an experiment with alternatives to the traditional sentences of fines, jail, and probation for adult misdemeanants. The program was aimed at the nonviolent, first-time offender. The basic premise of the program was to impose positive sentences that would repay the victim, the community, and the offender. (The offender was also considered a victim.) The word *positive* is used in this context as meaning sentences productive for society in a personal, responsible way, as opposed to *negative,* implying fines (economic hardship), jail (loss of freedom), or probation (conditions on freedom), all of which are nonproductive for the victim, society, and the offender. A basic principle was evolved: *if you've wronged someone, it is your responsibility to make it right with the person you have wronged or to the community as a whole, and at the same time do constructive things for yourself to improve your self-esteem and social position.* Using this principle, the penalties imposed on offenders by the Winona County Court were repaying the victim (money or services), repaying the community (working for a charitable organization), and doing constructive things for oneself (for example, attending a vocational school class or Alcoholics Anonymous).

The program was developed upon three premises: first, that most offenders are "losers" with low self-esteem and a feeling that they are not part of the mainstream of society and are not respected by others; second, that the traditional court practices of imposing harsh, degrading penalties reinforces the already poor self-esteem of the offender and encourages the offender to respond to the crisis by negative acts or childish attempts at manipulation; and third, that the further offenders involve themselves in the criminal justice system, the more difficult it becomes for them to free themselves of the negative pressures that have caused their problems.

Definition and Rationale for Restitution

Applying the foregoing premises, all sentences are aimed at enhacing the self-esteem of the offender and at the same time making things right with the victim and the community. The first step was to humanize the atmosphere of the court in order to reduce its authoritarian quality. The simple Transactional Analysis principle of treating a person as an adult so the person will respond as an adult (whereas treating a person as a child will encourage the person to respond as a child) was applied. The offenders were then allowed to become involved in their own sentencing, which was accomplished by giving them some options. The sentences were molded to fit the offenders' needs and at the same time allow them to choose the form of restitution. (The offender, with the guidance and support of the court service office, presents the sentence to the judge. The judge then accepts, modifies, or rejects the proposed sentence.) Thus the responsibility for the sentence is placed on the offenders. Once the offenders have committed themselves to the court with "their sentence," the responsibility shifts to them to carry out the sentence and the usual manipulation and excuse finding are eliminated. If offenders fail to carry through "their sentence," the court simply imposes a traditional fine or jail sentence and the alternative restitution is withdrawn. Experience shows this happens in about one out of twenty-five cases.

The Population Served

The program is offered to nonviolent adult misdemeanants—those convicted of, for example, disorderly conduct, theft, simple assault, shoplifting, driving while intoxicated, reckless driving, or vandalism. Welfare recipients or dependent offenders are also admitted to the program by reason that their economic status makes fines and jail inappropriate penalties. It is estimated that less than 10 percent of the total misdemeanor, petty misdemeanor, and traffic arrests in the county are involved in the program or are suitable to the Win-onus Program. Winona County, Minnesota, has a population of forty-seven thousand. Three colleges and a vocational school add an additional eight thousand young people, mostly in the crime-producing age bracket.

The Restitution Process

Step One. The offender enters a plea of guilty or is found guilty after a trial. The judge decides after questioning the offender whether the restitution program is appropriate for the offender. If so, the offender is referred to a court service officer.

Step Two. The offender and the court service officer meet in private to discuss the program. If a victim is involved, restitution to the victim is discussed. If there is no direct victim, restitution to society in general is discussed. The court service officer then enters into the problems and goals of the offender, for example, alcohol treatment, drugs, marital problems, unemployment, and so on. The offender is given a list of possible alternatives, (see appendix 12A) and the offender is given options to select from. Negative or degrading restitution is strongly discouraged. The possibility of failure to perform a sentence is discussed as well as the usual fine or jail sentence if there is failure.

Step Three. A proposed sentence is arrived at either on the first meeting or on a subsequent meeting between the court service officer and the offender.

Step Four. The offender and the court service officer return to court for sentencing at a time set up by the court service officer. The proposed sentence is offered to the judge. The offender is encouraged to speak up and present the sentence for approval.

Step Five. The judge accepts the sentence, modifies it or rejects it. The sentence is almost always accepted by reason that the court service officer discourages any unreasonable sentence before it gets to the court for approval or rejection.

Step Six. The sentence is imposed.

Step Seven. The Court Services Department supervises and sentences. Proof of compliance is required from all parties connected with the sentence. Credit for work service is given at $2.50 per hour. Ten dollars worth (four hours) of work service equals one day in the county jail. Completion of an Alcoholics Anonymous program, vocational school classes or similar courses equals $100 or more. A blood donation equals $15. Upon completion the Court Services Department reports the result to the clerk of court's office and the case is closed. Thereafter, the offender is encouraged to continue self-improvement courses and is invited to come back to court services for counseling on any future problems that may arise. If the offender fails to comply with the alternative sentence, a bench warrant is issued and the defendant reports to court and the usual jail or fine sentence that was stayed is imposed. In this type of sentencing, the court must rely heavily on the Court Services Department.

Instances of offender restitution have involved benefits to the victim, the community, the offender and offender's family, or most often to some combination of these. Some examples: a young offender coached Little League Hockey; another cleaned the total carpeting in a large church; another young man, a math major, spent hours tutoring slow junior high math students; twenty young offenders developed an ecology project and cleaned up twenty-two miles of ditches along a four-lane highway that ran through the county; four youths from college coached a basektball group at the YMCA; others painted park benches for the Park Department and many worked for the Bicentennial Committee. Other offenders worked with youth groups, in homes for the elderly, shoveling sidewalks for shut-ins, picking up litter in parks and streams, doing maintenance work for the Historical Society, working with retarded children, donating blood to the Red Cross, working on church projects, repairing government buildings, working in day care centers, participating in sportsmen's club wild life projects, erasing graffiti from buildings, and so on. In one case, a middle-aged shoplifter agreed to a sentence of volunteering twenty hours to a rest home. She liked it so well, she put in over fifty hours. There was a definite change in her personality: she became less selfish and more outgoing.

Victim Involvement

If there is a victim of the crime, the victim is always contacted about the loss sustained and is repaid if at all possible. The court service officer must be on guard to protect the offender from being victimized (by the victim). Exaggerated losses are referred to conciliation court for litigation, and any repayment of loss revolves around the determination of damages by the conciliation court judge. Victims are repaid in money damages or in like services. Reactions to offender and victim involvement have been most encouraging. The offender gets to meet the victim of the crime on a personal basis. This is something that does not occur when the offender is sent to jail or pays a fine. The offender often learns that the person hurt is a "nice guy" and didn't deserve the problems the crime created. The victim, likewise, learns that most offenders are not the stereotyped "bad guy" they have learned to suspect. In fact, we have had at least five cases in which the victim has hired the offender after this work restitution encounter.

Problems

A restitution program of this type is only as good as the Court Services Department makes it. Community involvement and cooperation is necessary. Judges also must have the courage to try this program: fines and jail sentences are the easiest and safest for judges and clerks to administer. Restitution programs can be embarrassing to a judge if a thief steals while doing restitution. Liability coverage must be obtained. We have had one minor claim in five years. The question of loss of fine revenue must be explained to the legislative body. (We have found our program has had little effect on fine revenue as more than 90 percent of fines paid are for minor traffic violations.) The general public tends to believe that anything less than a stiff fine or jail sentence is leniency. However, repaying the victim has become popular in recent years. We have found that restitution appeals to both conservatives and liberals when completely explained.

Evaluation

The Win-onus Project has been evaluated through cooperation with Winona State University. A study completed last July reveals for the years 1973, 1974, 1975, and 1976, that of 815 offenders who committed various offenses and were involved in restitution sentencing, there were only 22 repeaters for a four-year recidivism rate of 2.7 percent. (See appendix 12B.) A similar study of recidivism for those sent to the Winona County Jail during the same period of time revealed a repeating rate of 27 percent. In addition, thousands of dollars were returned to crime victims, thousands of hours were contributed to charitable organizations, and much time was spent by the offenders in improving their social status.

Conclusions and Recommendations

Those involved with the program feel that three innovative, constructive steps have evolved that make this program work in a modern court system. First, sentences are aimed at improving the offenders' self-image and responsibility toward society, with the recognition that offenders are also in need of restitution to themselves for what they lack socially. Second, restitution is self-imposed with options to the offenders, and their participation in the sentencing process is extremely important. Third, negative or degrading restitution is avoided if at all possible.

Future Aims

"Group sessions for losers" are now being organized whereby offenders will be given options to participate in weekly peer group sessions using Transactional Analysis and Gestalt methods to confront their problems. Also, a program involving the community where offenders can choose to repair acts of vandalism caused by other unapprehended offenders is contemplated along with a "clean up the county" program where eyesores such as abandoned automobiles and litter can be removed to landfills. The Court Services Department is expanding its availability to any people who need help with any problems, regardless of whether they are presently involved with the court system, by acting as a broker to get "losers" into contact with community agencies that can help them with their problems. This is a project of "preventative medicine" aimed at curbing future criminal acts.

Appendix 12A
Sentencing Alternatives

An offender may request to donate his time or his services to any charitable or governmental agency. Many offenders have come up with their own ideas. The following have been accepted.

Alternatives the Help Others

Work at YMCA
Work at YWCA
Work for American Red Cross
Work for Boy Scouts
Work for Girl Scouts
Work for Church organizations
Help a victim of vandalism
Shovel sidewalks or do yard work for invalid persons or senior citizens
Paint and repair government buildings
Clean streets or parks
Work in high schools
Work in colleges
Work in vocational schools
Work in Winona Volunteer Services
Work in St. Anne's Hospice
Work in Sauer Memorial Home
Work in Tri-County Poverty Program
Work in Watkins Memorial Home

Work in group homes
Pick up litter on highways
Clean litter from lakes and streams
Donate blood
Become a volunteer probation officer
Work for historical society
Work in day care centers
Work in Big Brother Program
Work in Mental Health Center
Work in children's homes
Work for Minnesota Society for Crippled Children
Work for Sportsmen's Club projects for wildlife
Work in Winona County Fairgrounds
Erase "graffiti" from public buildings
Work in special projects or organizations
Work for Winona Art Center
Repair vandalism done by others

Alternatives that Help the Offender

Personal counselling
Alcohol education clinic
Driver's improvement clinic
Vocational education classes
High school or college
Family services
Vocational rehabilitation Center
Medical treatment

Legal counselling
Alcoholics Anonymous
Alcohol and drug abuse programs
Mental health center treatment
State hospital treatment
Marriage counselling
Group counselling
Employment counselling

157

Surrender driver's license

Sell or junk automobile

Refrain from owning an automobile for a given time

Stay away from ex-wives, ex-husbands and/or relatives and certain individuals

Stay out of a certain bar (disorderly conduct)

Stay out of a certain store (shoplifting)

Sell, surrender, or destroy weapons

Appendix 12B
Four-year Study (1973, 1974, 1975, and 1976) of Recidivism Rates in Winona County Court for Offenders Involved in Alternative Sentencing

	Total offenses	Repeat offenses	Percent of recidivism
Disorderly Conduct	118	6	5.1
Shoplifting	175	5	2.9
Driving while Intoxicated	294	9	3.1
Assault	63	1	1.6
Theft	113	1	0.9
Criminal Damage to Property	52	0	0
	815	22	2.7

Independent study made in cooperation with Winona State University Political Science Department, David S. Miller, Intern.

13 Community Restitution Comes to Arizona
Robert Keldgord

Initiation of Program

According to an old adage, "Necessity is the mother of invention." It was, in part, because of necessity that a community restitution program was "invented" in Arizona. The specific case was that of a drunken driver who was convicted of vehicular manslaughter. As a result of his previous convictions, the defendant had been sentenced to jail—only to be released upon completion of his term and to return to his pattern of excessive drinking, and driving.

His offense had cost the taxpayers a substantial sum of money, but, although he was employed, the defendant had little money with which to pay a fine (in effect "restitution" to the taxpayers), and, clearly, previous incarceration had made little impact upon him.

At this point the sentencing court decided, upon the recommendation of the probation officer, that the defendant would be required as a condition of probation to donate service to the community in order to "repay" the community for the costs the taxpayers had incurred as a result of the defendant's crime. It was further determined that his community service should be at the County Hospital, where he would work for an alcohol counseling program and where he could observe, firsthand, the misery caused by those who drink and drive.

From this seemingly insignificant start in September, 1975, there has developed a distinct program that is referred to as "CRISP"—Community Restitution in Service Program. The rapid growth of the program has exceeded the original expectations of the courts or the probation officers.

In Arizona, probation is administered at the local, county level, and insofar as can be determined, only one of Arizona's fourteen counties presently utilizes the concept. That jurisdiction is Pima County (Tucson), a jurisdiction with a population of some five hundred thousand persons, and the second most populous county in Arizona.

Definition and Rationale for Restitution

Restituion, as utilized in Pima County's CRISP program, is a service provided by selected probationers to the community, by which the offender has the opportunity to repay the community for costs incurred as a result of the probationer's law violation.

The rationale behind the CRISP program is that probationers who do not have the financial means to pay monetary restitution to the community, either in the form of a fine (which goes to the county's general fund) or in the form of a traditional restitution order, can satisfy their obligation by providing service. In addition, the rationale holds that the CRISP program offers the probationer the opportunity to develop a sense of responsibility, to learn work habits, to improve work habits, and to learn job skills.

Population Served

Between January 1, 1976 and June 30, 1977, 129 probationers, representing some 4 percent of the total probation population, were assigned to the program.

CRISP participants are overwhelmingly male (estimated 90 percent male). In addition, CRISP participants are young. Sixty-two percent are between the ages of eighteen and twenty, and 38 percent are between twenty-one and twenty-five years of age. Eighty-seven percent of the CRISP probationers have never married. Sixty-two percent are Mexican-American, 38 percent are Anglo, and 6 percent are black. Thirty-eight percent of the participants have not completed high school while 24 percent have done post-high school work. (See table 13-1.)

The Restitution Process and Victim Involvement

The issue of possible restitution first arises in the presentence investigation phase. At this point, the investigation probation officer seeks to ascertain the

Table 13-1
Profiles of Crisp Participants, General Pima County Adult Probationers, and General Population of Pima County

	CRISP participants	Adult probationers	Pima County population
18-25 years old	100%	65%	13%
Male	90%	90%	49%
Anglo	38%	67%	70%
Mexican-American	62%	20%	24%
Black	6%	11%	3%

degree of loss incurred by the victim as a result of the crime. This factor is determined either by letters that the investigating probation officer sends to victims, by personal interviews with the victims, or in some cases by both means.

The investigating probation officer also conducts an examination of the defendant's financial status and his ability or inability to pay a fine, pay court costs, or make monetary restitution. The investigating officer also makes a determination as to the defendant's ability to participate in community service.

The information collected by the investigating probation officer is then presented to the sentencing court as part of the presentence report. In this report, the probation officer may recommend to the court that, if the defendant is granted probation, an appropriate condition of probation would require community service.

When the defendant is sentenced, the court imposes conditions of probation in those cases where probation is granted. Immediately after the court hearing, the probationer reviews the conditions of probation with the field probation officer (the officer who will supervise the defendant's probation). Both the officer and the probationer sign the conditions of probation, and a copy is furnished to the probationer. The CRISP assignment may be directed by the court, as is the case in 75 percent of the instances, or by the probation officer, as is the case in 25 percent of the instances.

Sometimes an effort is made to assign the probationer to a CRISP activity that has relation to the crime. For example, a Tucson barber who was convicted of stealing from Salvation Army "drop boxes" was required to donate haircuts at the local Salvation Army Men's Social Service Center every Tuesday night. Some young men who were convicted of arson were required to donate service to the Tucson Fire Department. Sometimes, a probationer goes "above and beyond" the requirements of his probation. In addition, sometimes, unexpected benefits accrue to the probationer: approximately 3 percent of the probationers involved in CRISP have obtained permanent employment as a result of their community service.

When it has been determined that the probationer is to provide community service, the matter is referred to the departmental training officer, who coordinates the program. The probationer is then assigned to a specific CRISP activity that is consistent with the probationer's other activities, such as his employment schedule if he is employed, or his class schedule if he is a student.

The CRISP coordinator, assisted by the probation officer-aide, periodically checks with the private, nonprofit agency or the governmental agency to which the probationer has been assigned to determine if, in fact, the probationer has performed the assigned duties. This information is then transmitted to the probationer's field officer.

If a situation develops when the number of assigned CRISP hours are too great to be completed by the probationer, due, perhaps, to a change in his employment, the probation officer will either modify the number of hours assigned or will petition the court to modify the number of hours assigned.

Problems

The CRISP program suffers from one major problem. That problem is the lack of adequate financial support, which, in turn, has precluded the hiring of adequate staff, the maintenance of adequate records, and the purchasing of sufficient equipment to be used by CRISP participants. Pima County's CRISP program can best be described as a bootstrap operation. It exists without benefit of any special federal grant, and with only minimal financial support from the county. The program is coordinated by the department's training officer, while the day-to-day operation of the program is achieved by a probation officer-aide, who is assisted by two CETA-funded social service aides. Moreover, it must be conceded that Pima County's Probation Department is not likely to receive adequate sums of monies with which to operate or expand the CRISP program.

Evaluation

In the spring of 1977, the Probation Department, utilizing the services of a graduate intern from the University of Arizona and another graduate student from the same University, sought to evaluate the CRISP program.

Through a process that involved questionnaires, personal interviews, and telephone interviews, efforts were made to ascertain if those agencies to which CRISP participants were assigned had experienced satisfactory communication with the Probation Department, if the agency's needs had been met and if skills had been taught to probationers.

Simultaneously, efforts were made to determine if those community residents who had received CRISP services on a referral from an agency had experienced satisfactory results from the program. Further, effort was made to determine how much prior knowledge the recipient-residents had of the CRISP program.

Finally, inquiry was made of probationers who had participated in the CRISP program to determine if they had learned work skills, if existing work skills were utilized, and if proper tools and supervision were provided. Results of the survey revealed the following:

Seventy-two percent of the agencies reported that their needs had been satisfied.

Twenty-six percent of the agencies reported that they had taught some skills to probationers, primarily in the areas of warehousing, landscaping, maintenance, plumbing, cooking, and child care.

Ninety percent of the agencies reported that they had experienced adequate communication with the Probation Department.

One hundred percent of the community residents reported that their needs had been met. The residents reported that, in 83 percent of the cases, the services provided by CRISP probationers had been "excellent," while 17 percent reported that the services had been "good."

Seventy-five percent of the community residents reported that they had no prior acquaintance with the CRISP program, and 100 percent reported that they would be inclined to utilize CRISP services again.

None of the probationers felt that they had learned work skills while on the CRISP assignment, although 3 percent apparently learned sufficient skills to secure permanent employment with the host agency.

Sixty-five percent of the probationers reported that some use had been made of existing skills, while 20 percent felt that they possessed no skills which could be utilized.

In 20 percent of the cases, the probationer's participation in CRISP was supervised by the Probation Department. In 80 percent of the cases, supervision was provided by the requesting social agency or governmental agency.

A number of probationers complained that they lacked adequate tools with which to work. This problem was alleviated, in part, when the Catalina Council of the Telephone Pioneers of America, a service organization comprised of AT&T employees, donated over three hundred dollars in equipment for the program.

In addition to this evaluation of the CRISP program conducted for the Probation Department by two graduate students in the spring of 1977, the Department has maintained statistics on the program. A review of the department's statistics, based on the period January 1, 1976, to June 30, 1977, reveals the following:

Three participants, or 2.3 percent of the total group, failed to comply with the condition of probation that required CRISP activity. The probation of these three persons was revoked.

The total number of CRISP hours assigned to probationers was 15,136. The number of hours assigned per probationer ranged from a high of 1,040 to a low of 10, with a mean average of 121.5.

When the total number of CRISP-assigned hours (15,136) was computed at the prevailing minimum wage, the dollar value to the community of CRISP-rendered services was $34,812.80.

CRISP referrals were made to forty-two agencies, ten of which are local governmental agencies, such as the County Hospital, County Juvenile Court Center, County Health Department, County Parks and Recreation Department, County Nursing Home, County Animal Control Center, and the Tucson Fire Department.

Included among the thirty-two private, nonprofit charitable organizations to which CRISP referrals were made are the Salvation Army, St. Vincent de Paul Society, Tucson Metropolitan Ministry, Community Food Bank, Family Service Agency, Multiple Sclerosis Foundation, Jewish Family Service, and Tucson-East Mental Health Center.

The Probation Department has also sought to determine the strengths and problems of the program, and has been able to identify the following strengths:

exceptional support from both the superior courts and the lower courts;

the fact that the program can provide rapid delivery of service, with a minimum of "red tape";

exceptional support by community social service agencies and by local governmental agencies;

general community acceptance.

The community restitution program as operated by the Pima County Adult Probation Department is a sentencing alternative available to the courts, and is a viable alternative to incarceration, the imposition of a fine, or the imposition of monetary restitution.

14 Off Days Sentencing Program
Anthony Macri

The Off Days Sentencing Program was started to provide a needed service for the community, to preclude excessive association of less serious offenders with offenders who have committed more serious crimes, to save the taxpayers money, to give the judges an alternative to jail sentencing, and to avoid embarrassment for defendant and family associated with the defendant's remaining in jail.

The Setting

The setting for this restitution program is Metropolitan Dade County, Florida, a sprawling metropolis comprising twenty-seven municipalities and a population of over a million and a half people. The program operates from the Dade County Training and Treatment Center, an annex to the County Jail. It is a maximum-medium penal institution averaging 625 inmates which operates as a rehabilitation center with vocational and academic programs. The center confines a conglomerate of young and old, alcoholics and drug addicts, traffic offenders and armed robbers, contempt of court cases, plus 150 unsentenced defendants who are awaiting trial and are at this institution because of crowded conditions at the main jail. The maximum sentence is one year; the minimum five days. Of the 625 inmates, 450 are incarcerated because of criminal charges and the remaining because of traffic violations, misdemeanors, and involuntary committments due to excessive drinking. The judges in this jurisdiction had previously established the practice of weekend sentencing for minor adult offenders. This program builds on this practice and substitutes weekend community service work for weekend incarceration.

The first step in establishing the program was to find a substitute victim who needed and wanted the program. A meeting was arranged with the head of Dade County General Services who subsequently called a meeting of department heads. Three of six department heads were interested and planning was underway to develop public work sites through County General Services. Next, judges were contacted to explain a new element in the already existing weekend program—the use of weekenders for work projects with the incentive of letting the offender return home at night. The judges accepted the program and agreed to blanket permission for all who volunteered to enroll in the experiment unless specifically stated to the contrary in the court commitment.

167

Definition and Rationale for Restitution

In this program restitution is provided by making payment in service to a substitute victim—a community organization or a governmental agency. Projects to improve the environment of the community, such as cleaning debris from the rivers, canals, waterways, public parks, and road sides, are of high priority. The rationale for restitution resides in the concept of justice as heeding the rights of all. Restitution is both practical, and just in the present sense. In the old system of sentencing offenders to serve weekends, nothing constructive was accomplished and in reality the community was burdened with costly expenditures. By enrolling the offender in a community work program the sentence became constructive and economical. In addition, the offender who has violated the rights of others, even in minor ways, is making restitution. This type of sentence compensates the community through good works and should help the offender to realize responsibility to self and others. Thus the rights of offenders and those suffering are both respected.

The Population Served

The population served in this program are mainly blue collar males from the lower middle class. They range in age from nineteen years to sixty with a mean of thirty years. The majority were convicted of traffic violations or misdemeanors. A few criminal offenders are involved in the program at the special request of a judge. The average income is about one hundred and fifty dollars per week. The men are usually married and have dependents. Most have some alcoholic or drug use tendencies. A few professional people and a few women have been involved in the program. To date we have had 286 people involved in the program.

The Restitution Process

At the time of sentencing the defendant receives a specific number of weekends to be served at the Dade County Training and Treatment Center. All offenders are required to report on Friday evening for the first weekend at the center. This overnight experience gives them a small understanding of confinement. On Saturday mornings at 6:00 A.M. the project director and the two work foremen visit the cells and briefly explain the program to all who are eligible. Volunteers are removed from the cell and taken to the office where they are enrolled in the program, given a work assignment, briefed on the rules and regulations, and given a short history of the experiment. Transportation is supplied to and from the job sites but the offender may also use his own vehicle. (More than half the participants have suspended driver's licenses and depend on transportation made available by the program.) Efforts are made to assign people to work sites in their neighborhood and consistent with any special skills they possess. Originally all work sites were provided by the Department of General Services, but as the program developed more challenging types of work were needed. Jobs such as counseling at the state youth hall, working at a girls' delinquent center, and assisting cottage supervisors at a retardation institute have been developed. The project director and two foremen determine work assignments and removal from the program, resolve transportation problems, approve change of assignments, review work sheets, and so on.

Offender reaction to the program has been positive. Ninety-five percent of eligible persons are volunteers and many of the participants have said they were grateful for not having to spend another night in jail. Others like the idea of not being separated from their family. The majority feel it is better than just sitting around in a cell.

Persons in the community who have heard about the program consider it an excellent idea. The initial contact of offenders with the supervisors and workers is frequently one of suspicion but positive accomplishments and association usually break down these prejudices.

Problems

One of the first problems encountered was acceptance of the offenders by county work foremen. Many of these men have had previous experience with inmates and have developed a general distrust of prisoners. In most instances the problem solved itself through the good works the men accomplished. In some cases, however, a workable relationship was not established and the site was closed. Corrections work foremen do not stay on the job site but try to visit each place twice a day checking on attendance and problems that may arise. If the county supervisor does not take an interest and oversee the men, the project fails. In some situations offenders had to be hand picked for a sense of responsibility and maturity.

Initially the program experienced a high number of "no shows," when a man would come one week and miss the following or come on Saturday and miss Sunday. This was solved by insisting that anyone who did not show and failed to notify project staff must return to the center for the following weekend. This action has reduced but not eliminated the problem of "no shows." Accident was a main concern of many people who inquired about the program. In the first year the program had three semiserious accidents.

Irresponsibility on the part of some participants in the form of leaving early, coming late, drinking, and so on, presented a problem. Initially program staff were tolerant of everyone because of strong desires for the program to succeed. Subsequently staff have learned to be strict and have decided that it does not pay to risk the success of the program because of the irresponsibility of a few. The present approach is to insist on responsible behavior from the participants or to remove them from the program.

Evaluation

Since August, 1977, an evaluation sheet has been filled out by each man completing the program. Thirty-seven participants have completed the questionnaire. The majority of the men were in the program because of traffic offenses and were sentenced to an average of five weekends in custody; this was the first custodial sentence for all respondents. Twenty-two of them reported that they would have lost jobs had they been required to serve straight terms and that their family would have required welfare or other assistance. All respondents agreed that under the circumstances the program was of help to them and that they preferred the program to being incarcerated. Thirty-six thought that the work they performed was worthwhile. Between January and September, 1977, 286 men entered the program and 259 have successfully completed it. A cost analysis suggests that the program results in considerable savings to the community.

Personnel contact with the offenders (supervisors and men working with the participants) has generally been positive. Some of the offenders involved in the program have continued to donate their time as counselors and others have made material donations to some of the institutions. This is a positive step in assisting offenders to become aware of community problems. The program provides an alternative to jail sentences for minor adult offenders and does so in a manner that contributes to the good of both the community and the offenders involved.

Part VI: Monetary Restitution

15

Victims' Assistance Program
Camden H. Raue

Initiation of the Program

Early in the 1970s, Judge Marshall Young, District County Judge for the County of Pennington, the Pennington County Board of Commissioners, and other Rapid City area residents thought there was a definite need for a program that would benefit victims of crime and delinquency.

Information in regard to such programs was sought and obtained and a request for federal funding for a pilot Victims' Assistance Program was prepared. The application for funding was submitted to the South Dakota State Crime Commission requesting LEAA funds. In 1973 this application was funded by the South Dakota State Crime Commission and in October of 1973 the Pennington County Victims' Assistance Program was initiated at the juvenile court level in the county of Pennington.

During the first year of operation the program received national attention in that it was designated as a "Promising Project" under LEAA guidelines. Due to this fact and its overall acceptance within the Rapid City-Pennington County area, funding for a second year of operation was requested from the South Dakota Crime Commission. Second-year funding was granted and the program again operated at the district county court juvenile level.

In July of 1975 the program went under the direction of the South Dakota Unified Court System with partial funding from the Pennington County Board of Commissioners. In November of 1975, the program operation was extended to include victims of offenses that had been committed by adults at both the misdemeanant and felony level. The program is presently operating under the direction of the Seventh Circuit Court, a division of the Unified Court System of the state of South Dakota.

Definition and Rationale for Restitution

Restitution refers to money paid or services performed by an offender who has admitted guilt or who has been found guilty of an offense that caused loss to a victim. The rationale for restitution is that when possible an offender should be held responsible for losses caused by an illegal act and ordered to make good that loss.

If an adult offender pleads guilty or is found guilty of an offense where it appears that a victim suffered financial loss, that offender may be required by the court to pay restitution to cover the loss incurred by the victim. Such restitution payments may be required at both the misdemeanant and felony court levels. The restitution may be ordered as a condition of probation at either the misdemeanant or felony level or it may be ordered at a misdemeanor court level as a condition of suspended sentence.

The amount of restitution to be paid is the result of an investigation by a court services officer connected with the Victims' Assistance Program. This investigation includes contacts with investigating law enforcement agencies and with the victim of the offense. A victim case file is prepared and an amount of restitution to be paid is determined from the information obtained. The restitution itself is in many cases paid directly to the Victims' Assistance Program by the offender and when paid in full, or when the restitution that can be obtained has been obtained, the restitution is forwarded to the victim.

Such a program at the court level of the criminal justice system accomplishes several objectives: it makes the offender responsible for loss that was caused by his offense; it gives the offender an opportunity to make good or repay before other court sanctions are imposed; it helps the victim recover losses and in so doing improves the victim's attitude toward the criminal justice system; it gives the sentencing judge an alternative other than fines or incarceration; it creates a situation in which the victim has some say or input in sentencing.

The Population Served

The population that is served consists of persons who live within the four counties (Pennington, Custer, Fall River, and Shannon) of jurisdiction of the Seventh South Dakota Circuit Court. In 1975 total population of the circuit was approximately 93,500 of which about 60,000 lived in or near Rapid City.

Victims' assistance or restitution efforts at the adult offender level began in November of 1975. Since that time 320 victim cases have been investigated involving 270 adult offenders. Of those 270, 236 were male, and 34 were female. Through September of 1977, $23,979.48 in restitution has been collected.

The Restitution Process

The process begins when there has been a plea of guilty or a finding of guilt in a case where there is an indication of victim loss. This holds true for both felony and misdemeanor offenders. There are exceptions to the above. One is if the prosecutor or the defense requests victim loss information to be used prior to a finding or a guilty plea entered. As both prosecution and the defense are aware, there exists the possibility of restitution being a part of the judge's sentence. Or the judge may want restitution or loss information before sentencing when it is a part of the case in question.

In those cases where there is an indication of victim loss, the court services-victims' assistance investigator obtains victim loss information from law enforcement reports, copies of prosecutor's complaints, law enforcement interviews, and so on. This information is used to make a victim case file. If loss is not apparent in the information obtained, the victim is contacted and additional information in regard to loss is requested. The victim is also advised as to where the case is within the system and further made aware of the possibility of restitution being ordered.

The victim is also made aware that the Victims' Assistance Office can and will provide assistance in the areas of collection of ordered restitution, return of property being held by law enforcement agencies, and in providing additional information in regard to where the case is within the system. In addition to this, the victim is made aware that other types of questions can and will be answered, for example: what are the chances of full recovery? should an insurance claim be filed? can the victim sue in civil court? how long does the offender have to pay before further action could or would be taken by the court? what sort of person is the offender?

When an adult is ordered and/or agrees to pay restitution, and it has been ordered or agreed that the restitution be paid to the Court Services Department, the offender is contacted either in person or by a letter from the Victims' Assistance Office and advised as to how much restitution is to be paid, where that restitution is to be paid, how it is to be paid, how the restitution figure was arrived at, and how long the offender has to pay the money in full. In some cases a set schedule is laid out by the sentencing judge. In other cases the offender has a set period of time, six months, nine months, and so on, for the full amount to be paid. In still other cases the offender would have the length of a set probation period in which to make restitution payments in full.

When payments are made, they are deposited in a Seventh Circuit Court adult restitution account, which is a no-cost, non-interest bearing checking account with a local bank in the Rapid City area. When the offender has paid restitution in full or when as much restitution as can be obtained has been obtained, the restitution is forwarded to the victim by the Victims' Assistance Office. The money is accompanied by a letter explaining the facts surrounding the collection and payment.

In cases in which payment has been ordered or agreed upon and is not being received, the Victims' Assistance Office will send letters to the offenders, at the request of the supervising court services officer, reminding them of the amount owed and also the time still remaining to pay before further action would and could be taken. When and if the time for complete payment has passed without full payment, the victim-offender case information along with the documented efforts of the supervising court services officer and the Victims' Assistance Office files are forwarded to the sentencing judge for his consideration in regard to further action.

That action might take the form of a warrant for failure to comply, probation violation action, an extension of time allotted to pay in full or no action at all. In the event that the sentencing judge chooses not to pursue the case, it is closed and the victim is advised that there will be no possibility of restitution recovery through the court.

Victim Involvement

The victim involvement in the adult restitution process varies according to the type of offense that has been committed. In the case of questionable or unknown amounts of loss or injury at the time of the offense, the victim is contacted to determine if, in fact, he did suffer a loss as the result of the offense. Some victims even though suffering dollar loss do not wish to request restitution. Other victims may and do inflate their loss or place unreasonable value on property lost or stolen. In those cases an effort is made to resolve the difference and to arrive at a figure that appears to be fair and just. If no agreement can be reached or agreed upon by the offender, the victim, and the victims' assistance investigator-court services officer, the victim is advised that an effort will be made to collect a lesser figure or that he can pursue relief and satisfaction through civil process.

In some cases the victim has received payment for losses due to insurance coverage. In these cases, the full amount of loss is ordered or requested and the insurance company is paid when restitution is received. If there was a deductible clause, the victim receives that amount and the insurance company the balance.

Major Problems Encountered

The Pennington County Adult Victims' Assistance Program was an addition to an existing victims' assistance program that had been in operation at the juvenile level for two years. Therefore, many of the day-to-day operational problems in such a program had surfaced and been dealt already.

One problem that continues to exist is the amount of time available between finding and/or guilty plea entrance sentence being imposed. In many cases it is difficult or impossible to obtain adequate victim loss information prior to sentencing. In these cases the sentencing judge may order the amount of loss to be determined by the Victims' Assistance Program and restitution to be paid. If the figure that is obtained appears to be unreasonable or is not a figure that the offender's counsel can or will agree to, the facts may be taken before the sentencing judge in an effort to resolve the issue.

Another problem has been with the ability of the victim to understand the intent and purpose of such a program. Some victims feel that it is the *responsibility* of the sentencing court to collect the payment. Some victims also do not understand the fact that restitution cannot be extracted from an offender and the only alternative that the court has is to impose additional sanction.

Also, problems exist at the adult restitution or Victims' Assistance Program level regarding the inability of the sentenced offender to make restitution payments. As might be expected, many of the offenders are not in a good position to obtain well-paying jobs, and/or many of the offenders have additional problems such as lack of education or alcoholism. In some cases it becomes necessary for the sentencing judge to impose a suspended sentence or to violate the individual's probation due to his failure to pay restitution.

Evaluation

The Pennington County-Seventh Circuit Court Adult Victims' Assistance Program at present does not possess any type of structured evaluation procedure. Quarterly program reports are prepared which contain statistical information in regard to numbers of cases, numbers of offenders, amounts of dollars collected, amounts of dollars ordered, and so on. This information is submitted to the immediate program supervisor, that being the chief court services officer in the Seventh Circuit. Copies are also forwarded to the Seventh Circuit Court Administrator's Office, and to the office of the presiding judge of the Seventh Circuit Court for evaluation. These reports are also available to the Unified Court System, Director of Court Services in Pierre, South Dakota, and to the office of the Chief Justice of the South Dakota Supreme Court, Pierre, South Dakota.

16 The Oklahoma Department of Corrections Restitution Program
Mike Patterson

Initiation of the Program

During the 1976 legislative session, Senate Bill 571 was passed and signed into law, establishing a formal, statewide restitution program, to be administered by the Oklahoma Department of Corrections beginning October 1, 1976. The law revises probationary sentencing and establishes the restitution program. In regard to restitution, the statute states:

in addition, order Restitution to the victim according to a schedule of payments established by the sentencing Court if the defendant agrees to pay such Restitution, in the opinion of the Court, if he is able to pay such Restitution without imposing manifest hardship on the defendant or his immediate family and if the extent of the damage to the victim is determinable with reasonable certainty. Provided, however, that such order for Restitution shall be made in conjunction with Probation and will be made a condition of the suspended sentence.[1]

Definition and Rationale For Restitution

The concept of the restitution program in Oklahoma is to reimburse financially the victims of crimes, by direct repayment through the department of corrections. Presently, loss crimes make up the majority of the cases in this program, with bogus checks and forgery heading the list. The nonresidential, financial-type restitution program that is presently operating in Oklahoma was selected over the other types of programs because of its relatively low operating cost. The necessity of an increased staff in both a service program and a residential program increased the cost to a level that the Oklahoma Legislature was not prepared to expend for the implementation of a restitution program.

The main goals of restitution under the Oklahoma program are to aid the offender, the victim, and the state. An offender placed on probation under this program benefits from the unique opportunity to get a "second chance" (although a defendant cannot be placed in this program if the conviction is a third felony charge). Both offenders and the state would benefit from the expected reduction in Oklahoma's prison population. Many times in the past, judges were forced to sentence an offender to a term in prison merely to insure that an adequate punishment was imposed for the crime committed.

179

Restitution has definitely become a viable alternative to incarceration: the courts may now select the most appropriate punishment for each offender.

The Population Served

The characteristics of the offenders who are involved in the Oklahoma Restitution Program are very similar to those of the offenders in other programs. The majority of the offenders in the Oklahoma program are white males with a median age of twenty-five. Very few of the offenders have completed any additional education after receiving a high school diploma. In the sample of offenders that was selected for this study, it was found that 53 percent are married while 47 percent are single. In a similar study that was conducted in January, 1977 it was discovered that the majority of offenders involved in the program earn from four to eight thousand dollars per year.

The type of crime involved has a definite influence on whether restitution is ordered in a given case. Oklahoma's program consists mainly of property loss crimes. An explanation given by several prosecutors in Oklahoma for the small number of minority participants is that members of minority groups do not commit crimes in which restitution could be a factor.

During the initial year of operation, 1,214 offenders took part in the program. Of this total, 294 offenders successfully completed their court-ordered obligations to 457 victims. The victims were made up of individuals and businesses. The present case load is comprised of the remaining 920 offenders.

The Restitution Process

The restitution process in this program was especially designed to enable the "restitution unit" to make quick and accurate disbursements to the victims. The entire process involves not only the department of corrections, but local governments as well.

When probation is ordered by the court, the prosecuting attorney may file a restitution schedule with the court clerk. If the court approves of the restitution schedule, it becomes a part of the judgment and sentence, which is forwarded to the restitution unit by the court clerks.

When the judgment and sentence is received by the restitution unit, an account is established for the offender utilizing the information that is contained in the restitution schedule. All money received from the offender is posted to the account that has been established and disbursements are made to the victims on a pro rata basis. The use of the pro rata system is normal procedure unless otherwise designated by the sentencing court. At the present time, the average span between the receipt of the money from the offender and the disbursement to the victim is three days.

The restitution unit is involved in only one major decision in the entire process: this concerns delinquency of the court-ordered payments. Under the procedures that the restitution unit follows, each defendant is allowed a thirty-day grace period within which to be delinquent in payments. When the grace period has expired, a "failure to pay" notice is forwarded to the district attorney's office. A carbon copy of this notice is also forwarded to the offender's probation officer informing him of the situation, so that he will be aware of the most recent developments concerning his client. This also provides the probation officer with the opportunity to discuss the situation with the offender and try to determine the reason for his delinquency.

The district attorney's office is involved in two decisions within the restitution process. The first decision is activated by the receipt of the "failure to pay" notice, and involves whether or not a "violation report" on the offender is necessary. If so, this request will be made to the restitution unit. In turn, the restitution unit will forward the request to the probation officer, who will submit a "violation report" to the district attorney.

The facts presented by the probation officer are taken into account when the district attorney's office makes the decision whether to apply for a revocation of sentence. The decision must be made at this point whether the offender is simply refusing to conform to the court order. Generally, if the offender is unable to meet the obligation, the district attorney's office will work with him to have the court order altered to something more realistic.

During the revocation hearing, the judge must decide whether the offender should be incarcerated for his failure to pay or if an extension should be granted. Generally, only one extension will be granted by the court. If the offender is again brought before the court, incarceration will most likely result.

If the court-ordered restitution has created a hardship for the offender or his family, they may petition the court for a change in the terms of the order. This privilege is granted to the offender in the same law that created the program.

Victim Involvement

Victim involvement in the Oklahoma program is strictly on a voluntary basis. Unlike the program in Minnesota, where the offender and victim enter into a contractual agreement, a victim in this program is not required to be involved in the restitution process at any time. No personal contact is required between the offender and victim after the case has been adjudicated. At no time is victim involvement encouraged.

Problems

Necessary information not being forwarded to the restitution unit by the courts has been the only major problem in the program. Lack of information can be attributed to two situations that have existed in the program since its inception. First, there was a communications breakdown regarding the type of information that was required by the restitution unit. There have been great efforts made recently to educate the court clerks through the restitution unit and the Administrator of the Courts. However, the problem still exists to a certain extent in the smaller rural counties of the state. Secondly, some court clerks were reluctant to conform to the new program's system. Once again, through persuasion by the Administrator of the Courts' office, most of these court clerks have been convinced that the new procedures should be followed.

More often than not, the case in which the confusion exists are ones that were in process during the transition between local and state control. Because of the informality involved in the restitution cases that were locally controlled, accurate documentation was not always kept. Therefore, when it came time to forward the needed information to the restitution unit, it was not in written form.

Before any disbursements can be made on a particular case, written documentation must be on file with the Department of Corrections. This is the major reason for the twenty-three thousand dollar balance in restitution receipts. Fortunately, the problem is disappearing, and most of the new cases that are being received by the restitution unit contain all of the needed information.

Conclusions and Recommendations

The restitution program in Oklahoma is one that had an excellent base at the local level. Even though some problem was experienced during the transition period, the program can be used as a model for other programs. Now that a solid base of operation has been established on the state level, some expansion should be considered for the program. Two possibilities are the following:

1. Restitution could be used as a condition of an offender's parole. The courts could sentence an offender to prison and still have the option of ordering restitution. Then if the offender is granted an early release, restitution would become a condition of the parole order.

A provision for this type of expansion was signed into law during the 1977 legislative session. However, no concentrated effort has been made at this time, by either the courts or the Parole Board, to implement this phase of the program.

2. The establishment of a victim compensation program, which would be administered jointly by the restitution unit and the Division of Community Services, both of which are within the Department of Corrections. Each prisoner being retained in a community treatment center on work release would be required to pay no more than 5 percent of his salary to be applied to the compensation of all victims of crime.

In conclusion, the program in Oklahoma has been built on a solid base and is now operating at a high rate of efficiency. At the present, the yearly salaries for the restitution unit's personnel supporting the restitution program is $19,100.00. This definitely is a small investment for the return of over $175,000.00 to the victims of crimes in Oklahoma.

Note

1. Oklahoma Statutes 23 Section 991 (a) (b) (c) (d).

17 Postincarceration Restitution
Ted Nelson

Initiation of the Program

In 1976 the Corrections Division of the Oregon Department of Human Resources received a two-year grant from the Law Enforcement Assistance Admin--
istration to establish and maintain a twenty-man work release center with the
emphasis on developing a restitution program for convicted incarcerated adult
felons in the state's penal institutions.

Definition and Rationale for Restitution

Everyone agrees that restitution is a good idea, but a clear definition of restitution is needed to help in the formulation of program guidelines, selection criteria, and goals. The corrections division was faced with an array of questions.
One was: should the program include exclusively monetary restitution or should
restitution in service or kind be used? Once the program grant was approved
and staff were hired, different types of restitution were explored. Advice was
solicited from the State of Oregon Attorney General's Office and after nearly
a year of research, the selection criteria for the restitution program were final-
ized. A decision was reached to focus attention on monetary restitution only
during the formative stages of the program. Service restitution was put on the
back burner because of some legal questions arising out of possible injury to the
clients while fulfilling their obligation.

    With the decision to focus on monetary restitution, the staff found two
specific areas that needed clarification from the state's attorney general. Who
would determine the amount of restitution to be paid and to whom would the
payments be made—to the victim or some intermediate agency? The decision
was made to implement three primary categories for monetary restitution:
concurrent probation restitution obligation; court-ordered restitution obligation; and voluntary financial restitution.

    Individuals who are incarcerated in a state penal institution often have a
concurrent probation obligation for another crime that may carry a restitution
obligation. Individuals who fall into this category are tracked through the system and when they become eligible for the work release program, arrangements
are made with the sentencing court to begin restitution payments. Some judges
in Oregon order restitution in addition to a sentence of time in one of the

state's penal institutions. Once the individuals become eligible for the work release program, arrangements will be made for these *court-ordered restitution* cases to begin making restitution payments. Some convicted felons in penal institutions wish to make *voluntary restitution* to the victim(s) of their crime. When this occurs, contact with the sentencing court is made to determine if an amount for restitution had been ordered. Staff strive to set the amounts from court orders, even in the case of voluntary restitution. If no court order exists, then staff search out other means to determine the amount that is fair and equitable to both the client and the victim. Presentence orders may be used as a resource, and if no monetary value is documented, clients are interviewed as to what they feel are the amounts owed. Contact then is made with victims requesting what they think are the amounts owed. When the two figures are compatible with one another, the voluntary restitution agreement is completed. When the two amounts are not compatible, both the victim and the client are informed of the two figures. If the disparity cannot be settled, both parties are informed of this and the matter is dropped. Both parties are informed that the victim has the right to take the matter to civil court upon release of the client from official detention.

The Restitution Process

Any convicted felons incarcerated in one of the three state penal institutions is eligible to participate in the Oregon Restitution Program if they qualify and are approved to take part in the state's work release program. Once a client is approved to take part in the work release program and transfers to one of the nine community corrections centers in the state, center staff complete a file search and interview the client to ascertain if a possible restitution obligation exists. If an obligation exists, the center staff contact the sentencing court to request an updated report on the obligations and documentation as to any payments made. When this is received, another interview with the client is held outlining the status of his responsibilities in regard to the obligation. The client is advised of the possible consequences that could result if the obligation is not addressed. The financial situation of the client is then discussed and a financial statement worksheet is completed to show the client what his current financial situation is and the projection for the future. With completion of the sheet, the client and counselor gain a better picture of the amount of money the client can afford to pay towards the restitution obligation.

Once the financial statement worksheet is completed, the counselor and client will complete a restitution contract and forward a copy to the sentencing court outlining the payment schedule and date the first payment will commence. Copies are also made available to the client. Payment is made through the client's work release trust account which has already been established upon enrollment in the work release program. All monies received by the client while on the work release program are deposited into this account.

If for any reason the client can not fulfill the obligations of the restitution contract, the counselor will notify the court of the circumstances and whether the payments will be resumed.

All money transactions fall under the guidelines of the work release program. The client receives receipts for all deposits and withdrawals from the work release trust account. All withdrawal requests must be approved by the client's counselor. All restitution checks are sent to the county clerk's office of the sentencing court for court-ordered restitution and concurrent probation obligation categories. Checks are mailed directly to the victim in the cases of voluntary restitution. Personal contact between the client and victim is allowed only if both parties request it. In all cases, the recipients of the restitution checks are notified that the conditions of the restitution contract are valid only while the client is enrolled in the restitution program.

Problems

Many problems have become evident after nearly one year of operation. The grant proposal outlined the establishment of a work release center in the Salem, Oregon area with an emphasis on establishing a restitution program. The first problem encountered was gaining governmental and citizen approval of the site for the center. The project suffered a six-month delay while concerned agencies and citizens were allowed thoroughly to study the proposal.

Problems with grant income also had to be worked out. As in the other eight community corrections centers throughout the state, enrollees of the Salem center were expected to pay maintenance and transportation charges. However, the Salem center was federally funded and money collected for client maintenance and transportation had to be deposited into the center's account. During this period of time, a multitude of minor problems had to be solved in regard to the daily operation of a full time community corrections center.

The State of Oregon Attorney General's Office was contacted and an official opinion was requested on the legalities involved in collecting and disbursing money from client accounts under the heading of restitution. Questions that needed answers were: who sets the amount of restitution that is to be collected? how will the money be disbursed and who should receive it? should restitution be paid to insurance companies who have covered the victims losses? is there any liability of the Corrections Division if a full remittance to the victim is not accomplished? do the current *Oregon Revised Statutes* covering disbursements from client accounts allow for the payment of restitution on a voluntary basis? These and many more questions had to be researched and studied to determine if the program would succeed. The attorney general's office found that only the judge could set the amount of restitution owed, and only in the cases of voluntary restitution could the client and victim settle on the amount of restitution that should be paid. The attorney general's office decided that restitution should not be paid to insurance companies that covered the victim's losses during the commission of a crime. It was felt that the money should be paid to the victim via the court in court-ordered cases and that the victim had the responsibility to contact their insurance company to make a settlement. The current *Oregon Revised Statutes* did cover the question of restitution in the disbursing of client funds from the work release trust account.

Once the legal questions were settled, work began on developing a policy and procedure for line staff to follow when the question of restitution arises. While work on a policy and procedure manual was in progress, staff realized a problem that would be encountered by the clientele. There was only one place in the state where someone with a restitution obligation could go while on the work release program—the Salem Community Corrections Center. If an individual planned to reside in an area other than Salem, a conflict would develop as to where placement should be. Staff were also concerned with being able to reach women clients. There is only one women's community corrections center in the state, which is located in the Portland area. To resolve this potential problem, staff requested a word change in the original grant to include the eight other community corrections centers for program participation.

Probably the most important problem experienced was education of the state's circuit and district court judges. For many years the judges had used restitution as a condition of probation. Many judges were reluctant to impose restitution along with incarceration primarily because they felt there was not an avenue available to them by which to collect the amounts owed. To combat the problem, staff have educated our field staff so they may inform judges of the program during their routine visits. Newspaper and television publicity has been used throughout the state to familiarize both the public and local officials with the new program. An interview conducted by the Oregon Judicial College with the project manager was published and sent to each circuit court judge indicating to the judges that a system now is in effect to carry out their restitution orders for incarcerated individuals.

Evaluation

The Corrections Division evaluates the project in three primary ways. First, the project manager is responsible to appear before the Corrections Division Policy Committee in person once each quarter to report on progress made and problems experienced. At the close of each quarter, the project is also evaluated by an independent consultant to the administrator of the division. This consultant visits the center several times each quarter and reviews center records and interviews with staff. The goals and objectives of the project are addressed and a statistical and narrative report is submitted to the Law Enforcement Assistance Administration for their review. Once the project is completed, the independent consultant will complete a final evaluation of the project in terms of the money spent and the goals reached.

By November, 1977 a limited number of participants were in the program. Eight work release enrollees have participated in the restitution program. Six of the eight have successfully completed payments on court-ordered and probation obligation restitution orders for a total of $1,633.19 collected and disbursed to the sentencing courts.

In the 1977 Oregon legislative session, approval was granted to continue the restitution and work release center when federal funds cease. On January 1, 1978 the restitution and work release center became partially funded by the state and on June 1, 1978 the center will be funded entirely by state funds. We plan to continue the program of postincarceration restitution, and as the program continues we may be able to expand our restitution program into other areas.

The 1977 legislative session also passed a House Bill 2012 that provides for the collection of restitution obligations from individuals paroled from any state penal institution. The bill states that the Oregon Parole Board will establish a schedule of payments to be made by the client and this payment schedule will be forwarded to the original sentencing court. The client's parole officer will monitor the payments made and report to the parole board the progress that has taken place. The intent of the legislation was to provide continuity throughout the corrections process for the collection and disbursement of monetary restitution obligations. This act is seen as a significant step in making the restitution program in Oregon a workable and practical tool for all concerned.

Part VII: Summary and Future Directions

18

Theoretical and Programmatic Concerns in Restitution: An Integration
Alan T. Harland

An integration of the theory of restitution and the programmatic concerns that it raises would not be well-balanced without drawing attention to four highly related features of the concept that were emphasized by the Second Symposium on Restitution. The first of these is the wide variety of theoretical perspectives from which restitution can be considered. Second and third, respectively, are the diversity of criminal justice stages at which restitution is used, and the crucially different ways it is approached in each of these settings. Fourth is the widespread academic, legislative, and agency interest that restitution has generated since the first symposium, two years ago.

At this second symposium, participants from almost every state in the country, as well as from several Canadian provinces, heard presentations and raised questions about restitution: as a victim compensation measure, and as an offender treatment modality; as a way of restoring equity after a criminal victimization, and as a retributive and deterrent sanction; as a way of diverting offenders from more intrusive contacts with the criminal justice system, and as a way of increasing existing penalties; in the context of pretrial diversion, plea bargaining, sentencing, probation, parole, and in a number of different incarcerative situations.

Restitution Defined

Although it is possible to say with some certainty what restitution *is*, it is less straightforward to determine what it *is not*. Similar concepts, to be distinguished and considered for their independent usefulness, include composition, reparation, restoration; indemnification; compensation; and community service.

In its broadest sense restitution has been used to describe all of the above and more. Speakers at the symposium equated fines with "restitution to the state," and one participant even spoke of an offender "making restitution to himself by making himself whole again." In its narrowest interpretation restitution has been said to refer only to the process by which stolen goods or proceeds are returned to a victim upon conviction of the offender.

Composition is an ancient term given to a sum of money paid by an

193

offender as satisfaction for a wrong or personal injury, to the person harmed, or to the family if the victim died. Originally made by mutual agreement of the parties, it later came to be established by law as an alternative to private vendetta. Restitution is used in this sense under modern law in connection with pretrial diversion programs and some misdemeanor statutes allowing victim-offender compromise under court supervision. However, in its more familiar sense, restitution differs from composition insofar as restitution rarely is viewed as *total* satisfaction by criminal justice decision-makers. Instead, it is used most prominently in conjunction with other criminal sanctions such as probation or parole.

Reparation is a term perhaps most commonly seen in connection with war reparations. It signifies a "making of amends" for a wrong or an injury. It is often used synonymously with restitution although it lacks the strict sense of *returning* something taken from its rightful owner, or the equivalent. Recently, however, restitution has taken on the more generic meaning of simply making up for loss of injury caused by a crime.

Restoration, on the other hand, has the more literal sense of putting back into a former state. As such, it can be taken as merely one form of restitution, as indeed it is under the civil law order of *restitutio in integrum.* Examples of restitution under this meaning might include the direct return of stolen goods or the repair of damage caused.

Indemnification is a term frequently encountered where the government gives indemnity (or compensation) for private property taken for public use. The intent, to paraphrase Mr. Justice Goldberg's familiar expression, is to make the person whole in relation to a loss already sustained. Indemnification also has strong insurance connotations of security against future loss. In both cases an offender could be said to indemnify the victim if restitution were to become a routine component of criminal dispositions. This seems to be the logic behind some "deterrent" claims for restitution, based on the idea that an offender is on notice that he must indemnify the victim for loss or injury due to the crime.

With the exception of linguistic purity, there seems to be little loss in viewing restitution as a combination of composition, reparation, restoration, and indemnification. It would include then, the notions of rendering satisfaction (if only partial), returning what was taken, and/or making amends generally. It is with the remaining concepts of compensation and community service that there is truly a need for definitional clarity and distinction. Confusion of terminology here has led to widely differing assumptions about the nature and purposes of restitution.

Compensation, or more precisely, victim compensation, is a term most frequently used to denote *state-funded* or *public* compensation to crime victims. Employed by approximately one-half of the states in the U.S. (Harland, 1978), compensation schemes make awards to victims of violent crimes, primarily to cover medical and related expenses.

Important distinctions must be considered between compensation schemes and restitution programs. First, compensation schemes have been restricted almost entirely to the victims of violent crimes. Property offenses typically are excluded from consideration. Conversely, as will be discussed below, restitution programs usually have been limited to minor, nonviolent offenders. Second, and most important, compensation schemes provide relief to victims whether or not an offender is apprehended or convicted. In restitution programs, the victim receives only what the offender(s) can be made to provide. It is the introduction of an *offender* into the picture that makes restitution the more confusing and complex issue to be faced (Advisory Council, 1970).

Community service and service restitution perhaps are the two concepts that are the most difficult to distinguish. The two terms are often used interchangeably as they were throughout the symposium, and confusion stems from the many different meanings ascribed to service restitution.

The term *service restitution* has been used to embrace a variety of activities along a continuum reflecting the degree to which the service is or is not related to the offense. At one end of the continuum is service to the victim by the offender(s). The relationship of the service to the offense in this case might be *direct* or restorative, as in the case of vandals repairing the damage they have caused. Alternatively, the relationship might be *symbolic*, as in the case of a joyrider cleaning or servicing the victim's automobile.

Next along the continuum is service related to the offense or the injury caused but performed for a third party, not for the actual victim. This type of service might be work in the burn unit of a public hospital by an offender who has attempted arson. In such a case there may be no victim who has suffered loss, but the penalty can be construed as restitutive insofar as it reflects payment for the potential consequences of the crime.

Finally, in its broadest sense, service restitution has been used to include *any* form of service, whether or not it is related to the harm caused by the offense. Thus, an offender in a victimless crime, or an offender whose victim does not want restitution, might be required to perform service for a charity or for a public works project. This last type of "restitution" more commonly has been called, simply, community service, and programs under this heading are widespread in the United Kingdom (Pease et al., 1975).

The question must be raised, therefore, whether community service and service restitution are one and the same. If they are not, a further question is: where along the continuum does service cease to be restitution and become instead simply community service? If the theoretical assumptions about each are identical, the problem becomes one of semantics. If they are not, there seems to be obvious merit in separating them, especially for purposes of evaluating whether either form of service is bearing out its theoretical rationale.

Practical Implications of Restitutive Theory

Psychological Theory

To emphasize the importance of definitional clarity when putting theoretical constructs into operation, one need only consider the practical implications of one of the major themes of the symposium; that is, the significance of the evident rationality of the restitutive sanction. Keve argued, for example, that if restitution is to be a useful therapeutic technique it must possess the rehabilitative quality of being a *meaningful* sanction. From a psychological perspective Mowrer cited the work of Rudolph Dreikurs in suggesting that for restitution to be optimally effective it should be related to the *natural and logical consequences* of the offense. And, for similar reasons, Utne and Walster contended that *direct restitution to the victim* is likely to produce the best results under equity theory.

The importance of these propositions for program administrators should be obvious when it is realized that the emphasis of the presentations made by practitioners at the symposium fell upon community service rather than direct service to the victim. The fact is that direct service restitution to the actual crime victim occurs rarely in programs operating in the United States. Limited experience in programs that have experimented with direct service reveals that victims are generally unwilling to enter into any direct service relationship with their offenders. In cases where the victim may be willing, program staff tend to be justifiably concerned about the offender's being returned to a potentially explosive situation in which the service recipient may be victimized a second time. Concern for the victim in this situation is reinforced by fears of civil liability on the part of program personnel should anything happen to the victim as result of an unsuccessful offender placement.

Even in cases where the restitution is strictly financial, there may be strong questions as to its meaning for the offender. If restitution is only one part of a package of payments that includes court costs, fines, and attorney fees, the offender may not even distinguish among his payments. Where financial restitution is ordered to a large corporate victim, or to an interested third party such as an insurance company, the meaning imparted to the offender may be clear, but adverse; it might be interpreted by the offender as yet further evidence of societal inequity, where the rich get richer and the poor just pay.

The hardest question to be faced in this context concerns the widespread use of community service by restitution programs. The issue here, as Warren pointed out, is that of how to make the service seem rational to the offender. Picking up litter for the park service, for example, may not always seem related to the natural and logical consequences of a drug offense or an attempted burglary for which no financial restitution is assessed. As many of the practitioners have said, however, service resources are not always broad enough to permit a rational relationship to be established between the service and each offender's crime.

Several suggestions were made by symposium speakers to overcome this problem. Macri, for example, recommended that all offenders be given some type of formal seminar or orientation to explore the question of what they can do in a practical way to compensate for their violation. Judge Challeen would go one step further and allow the *offender* to worry about the rationality of the sanction, by establishing a self-sentencing procedure.

Restitution and Punishment

The central importance of claims for the manifest rationality of restitutive dispositions is reinforced when restitution is considered in the context of traditional theories of punishment. From the deterrent standpoint, dealt with by Tittle, the use of financial restitution allows the offender to compute in advance at least part of the cost of being apprehended. The rational relationship of restitutive payments to the offense in this case lends itself well to the kind of cost/benefit calculus posited by deterrence theorists. Similarly, as McAnany noted, the harm-punishment relationship established by restitutive sanctions seems to approximate quite closely the theory of retribution or just deserts.

Nevertheless, the practical implications of relating restitution to the harm caused by an offender are at least as extensive in a jurisprudential sense as they have been shown to be from a psychological point of view. A hypothetical example will illustrate some of the problems. Two offenders, A and B, break into identical homes on a housing estate. Both steal identical television sets. When leaving the house, both are equally clumsy and break identical-looking vases on a hallway dresser. Both are prosecuted for first degree burglary and given probation for three years.

To this point the principles of justice seem to have been satisfied, insofar as similar offenses have received similar penalties. Suppose, however, that the vase in offender A's case was a rare piece of china worth ten thousand dollars, while B's vase was a good imitation but worth only fifty dollars. A and B are each ordered to pay restitution to the full value of the vases. Suppose further that A is an unemployed father of four, while B is a bachelor whose previously undetected life of crime has made him very wealthy. Are the sentences fair? Does the fact that the physical actions and the intent of both offenders were so similar imply that they should receive similar dispositions? What about A's victim? Should he be considered as contributorily negligent for leaving such a valuable vase in a place where it might easily be knocked over? And, finally, is it relevant that *any* financial payments would represent a much greater hardship for A than for B? The issue of the relative roles of harm and intent in establishing criminal sanctions has been discussed extensively by legal scholars (Austin, 1911). It is an issue of considerably more than theoretical significance for decision-makers in a restitutive system of justice.

One theory of punishment not dealt with explicitly at the symposium is incapacitation, which undoubtedly has had the greatest impact of all upon the nature of restitutive programming. Generally speaking, the research described by Warren, and by Hudson and Chesney illustrates that where restitutive and incapacitative needs collide, restitution will rarely be used. Similarly, the program experiences described by practitioners at the symposium show that restitution is used almost exclusively for nonviolent, low-risk offenders whose offenses are often quite trivial. Several implications follow for program administrators from this restitution/incapacitation conflict.

First, it seems inevitable that if restitution programs are to deal with more serious offenders, provision must be made for more realistic earning possibilities within an incarcerative setting. Second, and more important, restitution programs must be monitored very closely to determine exactly *how* restitution is being used. Especially when it is used mainly for minor offenders, for example, who would not normally receive a severe sanction, restitution may *increase* the level of intrusion by the state, as opposed to reducing it through acting as a means of mitigation of other sanctions.

The practice of adding restitution to existing sanctions is familiar in currently operating programs and can be seen as an example of "widening the net" of criminal jurisdiction under the guise of benefitting offenders. To do so would be contrary to the admonition given to participants by Commissioner Schoen at the outset of the symposium and will obviously have serious cost implications for restitution programs.

Restitution and Crime Victims

The fact that a juxtaposition of the two terms *restitution* and *victim* has become so common today is an interesting commentary upon the almost faddish acceptance of innovations in the field of criminal justice. Only a few years ago, if the term *restitution* was heard at all, the context might more typically have been one of quasi-contracts, or remedies in a tortious or other civil law setting. See, for example, Carlston (1954).

The feverish growth in popularity of restitution as an offender treatment or punitive sanction is undoubtedly related to current disenchantment with more traditional alternatives: see, for example, Lipton, Martinson, and Wilks (1975) and von Hirsch (1976). Reasons for the increasing attention to restitution as a victim compensation tool are illustrated in the presentations of several of the symposium speakers.

Viano, for example, stressed the need to consider restitution in the wider context of victimology, and more general services to crime victims such as those provided by public compensation and victim assistance programs. Underlying this emphasis upon both compensation and victim aid programs seems to be a general feeling that victims have long been neglected, and simply deserve to be helped by, and in, the criminal process. In terms of equity theory, one might say that the victim's need for procedural and substantive equity should now receive the kind of attention reserved in the past for offenders.

McDonald extended this idea, suggesting a more active role for the victim in the criminal process as a whole. And, a utilitarian rationale for this approach has been suggested by Galaway:

Increased victim involvement will likely create more support for the criminal justice system and there is little ground for believing that the victim's input might create injustices in regard to the offender (1977:17).

Contrasting justice for the victim with justice for the offender has been an approach taken frequently by advocates of restitution as a victim compensation mechanism. Although, as McDonald pointed out, it is not intrinsically necessary to argue the merits of victim programs at the expense of offenders' needs, there is no denying the political expediency of capitalizing on the sympathetic public response invoked by the plight of crime victims, especially when it is contrasted with the very unsympathetic public image of most criminal offenders. In addition, there will undoubtedly be instances when conflict does arise among the treatment needs of the offender, the sanctioning power of society, and compensation of the victim. In such circumstances, restitution program staff are faced with the sensitive task of arranging hierarchically the goals of their work.

All of this raises a particularly cogent question for research into restitution. Criminal justice agents and restitution staff are repeatedly placed in a position of observing inequity, becoming distressed by it, and intervening to correct the situation. A significant research need is to identify the *different styles of intervention* and their impact within programs and, more importantly, across different agencies. The equity theorists, for example, ask whether program staff in an offender-oriented setting (for example, probation) empathize more with an offender and share some of his rationalizations about his behavior than do victim-oriented actors (for example, district attorneys) who might share the anger and indignation of the victim. If this is shown to be the case, what effect does it have on program procedures and the types and amounts of restitution ordered? Does the style of intervention lead to different program "models," perhaps on a continuum from a "victim compensation model"—with high emphasis on generous loss estimates and broad offender liability assumptions—to a "treatment model"—with low concern for actual losses and higher concern for offender perceptions and benefits?

Further questions surrounding the introduction of a more prominent role for victims in the criminal justice process include that of the influence it may have on decisions beyond restitution: what might be the indirect effects of restitution program activities upon key decision-makers in the system? Information uncovered for restitution purposes brings victim and incident characteristics more readily to the attention of district attorneys, judges, and parole boards. Do overall penalties, including restitution types/amounts, vary according to such characteristics? Are representatives of organizational victims considered less "deserving" than individual victims? Does the restitutive information assume an independent value to the decision-maker in, for example, assessing the gravity of the offense and hence the penalty required?

Clearly, the need to monitor the effects of restitution programming goes well beyond the question of whether it is used as an alternative or addition to traditional sanctions. It still seems appropriate, therefore, to restate a note of reservation from the first symposium, held two years ago:

Restitution may, indeed, be a magnificent step forward in correctional arrangements, but it appears desirable to take that step, if it is to be taken at all, with a certain self-aware tentativeness (Geis, 1975:249).

Future Directions

From the interest generated by the restitution symposium and the availability of large-scale federal funds for program development, it seems inevitable that restitution will continue to grow in importance in criminal justice. Important factors in the nature of such growth include the actions of legislatures and courts, and the results of major research efforts currently underway.

Legal Developments

The increasing programmatic activity in restitution will inevitably lead to a parallel rise in legislative and judicial consideration of the issues it raises. Indications from existing programs show that resolution of these issues has extensive implications for the criminal justice process.

In Oregon, for example, judicial limitations upon the way in which restitution can be used (see, for example, State v. Stalheim, 275 Or 683, 522 P. 2d 829

[1976] [direct victim only]; *State* v. *Getsinger,* 27 Or App 339 [1976] [no restitution to insurer of crime victim]) have led to legislation that defines broadly the types of activities for which restitution may be imposed, and which expands the definition of who may be a victim or "aggrieved party" for purposes of restitution (H.B. 2012, 1977).

Interestingly, in *Getsinger* the court noted explicitly that the restitution statute is "a rehabilitative tool of the criminal law." However, in the federal courts, dispute over the purposes of restitution (punitive—*United States* v. *Bowens,* 514 F.2d 440 [9th Cir. 1975]; or rehabilitative—*United States* v. *Hix,* 545 F.2d 1247 [No. 76-1222] [9th Cir. Nov. 26, 1976]), has reached the Supreme Court for resolution (*United States* v. *Durst,* et al., 20 CrL. 4203, [1977]). Once again, the impact of such rulings is more than theoretical since, in this case, a decision that restitution is "punitive" might make it an impermissible sanction under the Federal Youth Corrections Act, which the district court in *Bowens* held to be "an avowedly non-punitive, rehabilitative statute."

Further issues that would appear likely for attention include questions of the relative culpability of victims or implicated third parties, and the effect of restitution on the plea bargaining process. The question here, of course, is whether restitution may be ordered for offenses that are dropped as a result of a plea bargain or whether it may only be ordered for offenses upon conviction. To choose the former has implications for the presumption of innocence, while to adopt the latter position could alter the nature of plea bargaining in the United States.

Because restitution has received so little explosure in the past, it is likely that program administrators and legislators will now be faced with decisions for which there is little or no judicial precedent. The interest in expanding the use of restitution seems so strong at the moment, that such precedent should not be long in coming.

Restitution Research

In addition to the results of local evaluations of restitution programs, reported by Hudson and Chesney, two research projects are underway on a national level. In the adult system, as Warren explained, the Criminal Justice Research Center in Albany, New York is evaluating restitution programs in seven states across the country (Harland and Warren, 1978). A similar effort is being undertaken in the juvenile justice system (Schneider and Schneider, 1977).

Both these major research projects are studying restitution not only in traditional terms of program effectiveness and efficiency, but also from a variety of theoretical perspectives. By approaching evaluation on a differential level, asking for what offenders, with what victims, in what kinds of programs, restitution does and does not seem to achieve the goals set for it, these research projects should provide a wealth of invaluable information for program planners and administrators.

In the meantime, it seems inevitable that the number and variety of programs will continue to grow rapidly. Indications from the symposium are that much of this growth will be in the area of community service, rather than the more recognizable forms of restitution. If this is so, then much can be learned from the experiences with this sanction in the United Kingdom (Pease et al., 1975).

Whatever direction restitution does in fact take, there can be little doubt that its new-found impetus will take it into every part of the criminal justice system. Very few innovations have been accepted so widely in the past by the different actors in a system across which there is so little agreement about goals and objectives. The difference with restitution seems, so far, to be that there need not be agreement as to its purpose before it can be supported.

References

Advisory Council on the Penal System (1970). *Reparation by the Offender.* London: H.M.S.O.

Austin, J. (1911). *Lectures on Jurisprudence.* 5th ed., R. Cambell (ed.). London: J. Murray.

Carlston, K.S. (1954). "Restitution—The Search for a Philosophy," *Journal of Legal Education* 6:330-339.

Galaway, B. (1977). "The Uses of Restitution," *Crime and Delinquency* 23(1): 57-67.

Geis, G. (1975). "Restitution by Criminal Offenders: A Summary and Overview," in J. Hudson (ed.) *Restitution in Criminal Justice* Lexington, Massachusetts: D.C. Heath, 1976. pp. 246-263.

Harland, A.T. "Victim Compensation: Programs and Issues," in B. Galaway and J. Hudson (eds.) *Perspectives on Crime Victims.* St. Louis: C. V. Mosby Company (in press).

Harland, A.T. and M.Q. Warren. *National Evaluation of Adult Restitution Programs: A Description of the Project,* Research Report #1. LEAA. NILECJ. Washington, D.C.: U.S. Government Printing Office, 1977.

Lipton, D.; R. Martinson; and J. Wilks (1975). *The Effectiveness of Correctional Treatment.* New York: Praeger.

Pease, K.; P. Durkin; I. Earnshaw; D. Payne; and J. Thorpe (1975). *Community Service Orders.* London: H.M.S.O.

von Hirsch, A. (1976). *Doing Justice.* New York: Hill and Wang.

Selected Bibliography

Azrin, Nathan H., and M.D. Wesolowski. "Theft Reversal: An Overcorrection Procedure for Eliminating Stealing by Retarded Persons." *Journal of Applied Behavior Analysis* 7 (1974): 577-581.

Barnett, Randy E. "Restitution: A New Paradigm of Criminal Justice." *Ethics* 89 (1977): 279-301.

Bernstein, Jesse. "A Study of the Evolution of the Concept of Restitution and Recently Enacted Victim Compensation Laws in New York and Other Jurisdictions," Ph.D. dissertation, New York University, 1972.

Berscheid, Ellen, and Elaine C. Walster. "The Effect of Time on Tendency to Compensate a Victim." *Psychological Reports* 25 (1969): 431-436.

_____ . "When Does a Harm-Doer Compensate a Victim?" *Journal of Personality and Social Psychology* 6 (1967): 435-441.

Brickman, Philip. "Crime and Punishment in Sports and Society." *Journal of Social Issues* 33 (1977): 140-164.

Cameron, Bruce J. "Compensation for Victims of Crime: The New Zealand Experiment. *Journal of Public Law* 12 (1963): 367-375.

Canadian Corrections Association. "Compensation to Victims of Crime and Restitution by Offenders." *Canadian Journal of Corrections* 10 (1968): 591-599.

Carrington, Frank. "Victim's Rights Litigation: A Wave of the Future?" *University of Richmond Law Review* 11 (1977): 447-469.

Chappell, Duncan, and L. Paul Sutton. "Evaluating the Effectiveness of Programs to Compensate the Victims of Crime." In *Victimology: A New Focus*, edited by Israel Drapkin and Emilio Viano, v. 2, pp. 207-220. Lexington, Massachusetts: Lexington Books, 1974.

Cohen, Irving E. "The Integration of Restitution in the Probation Services." *Journal of Criminal Law, Criminology and Police Science* 34 (1944): 315-321.

"Compensating Victims of Crime: Individual Responsibility and Governmental Compensation Plans." *Maine Law Review* 26 (1974): 125-148.

"Compensation of the Criminally Injured Revisited: An Emphasis on the Victim?" *Notre Dame Lawyer* 47 (1971): 88-119.

Deming, Romine R. "Correctional Restitution: A Strategy for Correction Conflict Management" *Federal Probation* 40 (1976): 27-32.

_____ . *Divergent Corrections.* San Francisco: R & E Research Associates, 1977.

Dockar-Drysdale, Barbara. "Some Aspects of Damage and Restitution." *British Journal of Delinquency* 4 (1953): 4-13.

Prepared by Cynthia May, Criminal Justice Reference and Information Center, Law Library, University of Wisconsin, Madison.

Drapkin, Israel, and Emilio Viano, eds. *Victimology: A New Focus.* Lexington, Massachusetts: Lexington Books, D.C. Heath, 1974.

Edelhertz, Herbert. *Public Compensation to Victims of Crime.* New York: Praeger, 1974.

———. *Restitutive Justice: A General Survey and Analysis.* Seattle: Battelle Human Affairs Research Centers, 1975.

Eglash, Albert. "Creative Restitution, A Broader Meaning for an Old Term." *Journal of Criminal Law, Criminology and Police Science* 48 (1958): 619-622.

———. "Creative Restitution: Some Suggestions for Prison Rehabilitation Programs." *American Journal of Correction* 20 (1958): 20.

Fogel, David, Burt Gallaway, and Joe Hudson. "Restitution in Criminal Justice: A Minnesota Experiment." *Criminal Law Bulletin* 8 (1972): 681-691.

Fogelman, Sylvia. "Compensation to Victims of Crimes of Violence—The Forgotten Program," Unpublished M.S.W. thesis, University of Southern California, 1971.

Fry, Margery. "Justice for Victims." *Journal of Public Law* 8 (1959): 191-194.

Galaway, Burt, Joe Hudson, and C. David Hollister, eds. *Community Corrections: A Reader.* Springfield, Illinois: Charles C. Thomas, 1976.

Galaway, Burt. "Issues in the Correctional Implementation of Restitution to Victims of Crime." In *Considering the Victim,* edited by Joe Hudson and Burt Galaway, pp. 351-360. Springfield, Illinois: Charles C. Thomas, 1975.

Galaway, Burt, and Joe Hudson. "Restitution and Rehabilitation; Some Central Issues." *Crime and Delinquency* 18 (1972): 403-410.

Galaway, Burt. "The Use of Restitution." *Crime and Delinquency* 23 (1977): 57-67.

Georgia, Department of Corrections and Offender Rehabilitation. *The Restitution Shelter Program in Georgia.* Atlanta, n.d.

Gold, Alan D. and Judge P.J.T. O'Hearn. "Restitution and Compensation and Fines." *Ottawa Law Review* 7 (1975): 301-329. Working Papers 5 and 6 of the Law Reform Commission of Canada.

Goldstein, Naomi. "Reparation by the Offender to the Victim as a Method of Rehabilitation for Both." In *Victimology: A New Focus,* edited by Israel Drapkin and Emilio Viano, v.2, pp. 193-205. Lexington, Massachusetts: Lexington Books, D.C. Heath, 1974.

"Governmental Compensation for Victims of Violence." *Southern California Law Review* 43 (1970) no. 1, entire issue. Symposium.

Havers, M. *Reparation by the Offender.* London: Society of Conservative Lawyers, 1971.

Heinz, Joe, Burt Galaway and Joe Hudson. "Restitution or Parole: A Follow-up Study of Adult Offenders." *Social Service Review* 50 (1976): 148-156.

Hudson, Joe, and Burt Galaway, eds. *Considering the Victim: Readings in Restitution and Victim Compensation.* Springfield, Illinois: Charles C. Thomas, 1975.

Hudson, Joe et al. "Diversion Programming in Criminal Justice: The Case of Minnesota." *Federal Probation* 39 (1975): 11-19.

Hudson, Joe, ed. *Restitution in Criminal Justice.* Lexington, Massachusetts: Lexington Books, D.C. Heath, 1977. Based on papers presented at the First International Symposium on Restitution.

_____. "Undoing the Wrong." *Social Work* 19 (1974): 313-318.

Hudson, Joe, Burt Galaway, and Steven Chesney. "When Criminals Repay Their Victims: A Survey of Restitution Programs." *Judicature* 60 (1977): 312-321.

Jacob, Bruce R. "Reparation or Restitution by the Criminal Offender to his Victim: Applicability of an Ancient Concept in the Modern Correctional Process." *Journal of Criminal Law, Criminology and Police Science* 61 (1970): 152-167.

Jacobson, William T. "Use of Restitution in the Criminal Process: People versus Miller." *UCLA Law Review* 16 (1969): 456-475.

Klauzer, Randall W. and Paul G. Quinn. "Victim Restitution: New Colorado Legislation." In *Proceedings of the 106th Annual Congress of Correction of the American Correctional Association, Denver, Colorado, August 22-26, 1976*, pp. 239-242. College Park, Maryland: American Correctional Association, 1976.

Laster, Richard E. "Criminal Restitution: A Survey of its Past History and an Analysis of its Present Usefulness." *University of Richmond Law Review* 5 (1970): 71-98.

McAdam, Michael R. "Emerging Issue: An Analysis of Victim Compensation in America." *Urban Lawyer* 8 (1976): 346-366.

McDonald, William F., ed. *Criminal Justice and the Victim.* Beverly Hills: Sage, 1976.

MacNamara, Donald E.J., and John J. Sullivan. "Making the Victim Whole." *Urban Review.* 6 (1973): 21-25.

Marvus, Marvin. *Victim Compensation and Offender Restitution: A Selected Bibliography.* Washington, D.C.: National Criminal Justice Reference Service, 1975.

Minnesota Restitution Center. *A Viable Correctional Alternative for Dealing With Property Offenders in the Community.* St. Paul, 1975.

Moran, Richard and Stephen Ziedman. "Victims Without Crimes: Compensation to the Not Guilty." In *Victimology: A New Focus*, edited by Israel Drapkin and Emilio Viano, v.2, pp. 221-225. Lexington, Massachusetts: Lexington Books, D.C. Heath, 1974.

Mueller, Gerhard O.W. "Compensation for Victims of Crime: Thought Before Action." *Minnesota Law Review* 50 (1965): 213-221.

_____. "Society and the Victim: Alternative Responses." In *Victimology: A New Focus*, edited by Israel Drapkin and Emilio Viano, v.2, pp. 85-101. Lexington, Massachusetts: Lexington Books, D.C. Heath, 1974.

Multnomah County District Attorney. *Victims... Who Cares?* Portland, Oregon, 1976.

National Center for State Courts. *Recommendations for Improving the Use of Restitution as a Dispositional Alternative as Administered by the Connecticut Adult Probation Division.* Washington, D.C.: American University School of Law, 1975.

"New York Crime Victims Compensation Board Act: Four Years Later." *Columbia Journal of Law and Social Problems* 7 (1971): 47-48.

Newton, Anne. "Aid to the Victim, Part 1: Compensation and Restitution." *Crime and Delinquency Literature* 8 (1976): 368-390.

———. "Alternatives to Imprisonment; Day Fines, Community Service Orders, and Restitution." *Crime and Delinquency Literature* 8 (1976): 109-125.

Prime, Terrence. "Reparation from the Offender, I." *Soliciter's Journal* 115 (1971): 859-861.

———. "Reparation from the Offender, II." *Soliciter's Journal* 115 (1971): 880-882.

Purchase, G.E. "Reparation by the Offender." *Justice of the Peace* 140 (1976): 329-330.

Read, Bill. "How Restitution Works in Georgia." *Judicature* 10 (1977): 322-331.

"Restitution and Compensation: Fines." *Canadian Journal of Criminology and Correction* 17 (1975): 1-23, 29-42.

"Restitution and Criminal Law." *Columbia Law Review* 39 (1939): 1185-1207.

"Restitution for Consumer Fraud Under Section 5 of the Federal Trade Commission Act." *Valparaiso University Law Review* 10 (1975): 69-125.

Rothstein, Paul F. "How the Uniform Crime Victims Reparations Act Works." *American Bar Foundation Journal* 60 (1974): 1531-1535.

Rubin, Sol. "Fine and Restitution." In *Law of Criminal Correction,* by Sol Rubin, pp. 253-302. St. Paul: West Publishing Company, 1973.

Samuels, Alex. "Compensation and Restitution." *New Law Journal* 120 (1970): 475-476.

Schafer, Stephen. *Compensation and Restitution to Victims of Crime.* Montclair, New Jersey: Patterson-Smith, 1970.

———. "Compensation of Victims of Criminal Offenses." *Criminal Law Bulletin* 10 (1974): 605-636.

———. "The Correctional Rejuvenation of Restitution to the Victim of Crime." In *Interdisciplinary Problems in Criminology,* edited by Walter C. Reckless and Charles L. Newman, pp. 159-168. Columbus, Ohio: Ohio State University, 1965.

———. "Corrective Compensation." *Trial* 8 (1972): 25-27.

———. "Restitution to Victims of Crime—An Old Correctional Aim Modernized." In *Criminological Controversies,* edited by Richard D. Knudten, pp. 310-320. New York: Appleton-Century-Crofts, 1968.

_____ . *The Victim and His Criminal, A Study in Functional Responsibility.*
New York: Random House, 1968.
_____ . "Victim Compensation and Responsibility." *Southern California Law Review* 43 (1970): 55-67. Symposium.
Schultz, Leroy G. "The Violated: A Proposal to Compensate Victims of Violent Crime." *Saint Louis University Law Journal* 10 (1965): 238-250.
Serrill, Michael. "The Minnesota Restitution Center." *Corrections Magazine* 1 (1975): 13-20.
Sethna, Minocher J. "Compensation of Victims of Offenses." In *Victimology: A New Focus,* edited by Israel Drapkin and Emilio Viano, v. 2, pp. 167-174. Lexington, Massachusetts: Lexington Books, D.C. Heath, 1974.
Skogan, Wesley G. "Victimization Surveys and Criminal Justice Planning." *University of Cincinnati Law Review* 45 (1976): 167-206.
Steggerda, Roger O. *Victim Restitution: An Assessment of the Restitution in Probation Experiment Operated by the Fifth Judicial District Department of Court Services, Polk County, Iowa.* Des Moines: Polk County Department of Program Evaluation, 1975.
Stewart, J. E. and S. Rosen. "Adequacy of Compensation Worthiness of Recipient and Their Effects on Transgression Compliance to Render Aid." *Journal of Social Psychology* 97 (1975): 77-82.
United States Congress, House Subcommittee on Criminal Justice, *Crime Victim Compensation*: Hearings on Victims of Crime Compensation Legislation, 94th Cong., 1st and 2d sess., Nov. 4, 18; Dec. 9, 15, 1975; Feb. 7, 13, and 27, 1976.
United States Congress, Senate Committee on the District of Columbia, *Compensation of Victims of Crime*: Hearings on S.2936, 91st Cong., 1st sess., 1970.
Waller, Louis. "Compensating the Victims of Crime in Australia and New Zealand." In *Victimology: A New Focus,* edited by Israel Drapkin and Emilio Viano, v. 2, pp. 175-192. Lexington Massachusetts: Lexington Books, D.C. Heath, 1974.
Walster, Elaine, G. William Walster and Ellen Berscheid. *Equity: Theory and Research.* Boston: Allyn and Bacon, 1978.
Washington County, Department of Public Safety. *Washington County Restitution Center.* Washington, D.C.: Law Enforcement Assistance Administration, 1975.
White, Anthony G. *Restitution as a Criminal Sentence: A Selected Bibliography.* Monticello, Illinois: Council of Planning Librarians, 1977.
Williams, Vergil L. and Mary Fish. "A Proposed Model for Individualized Offender Restitution Through State Victim Compensation." In *Victimology: A New Focus,* edited by Israel Drapkin and Emilio Viano, v. 2, pp. 155-165. Lexington, Massachusetts: Lexington Books, D.C. Heath, 1974.

Index

About the Contributors

Dennis A. Challeen is a county court judge in Winona, Minnesota.

Steven Chesney is a research analyst at the Minnesota Department of Corrections, St. Paul, Minnesota.

John T. Gandy is an associate professor at the College of Social Work of the University of South Carolina, Columbia, South Carolina.

Alan T. Harland is the project coordinator for the National Evaluation of Adult Restitution Programs at the Criminal Justice Research Center in Albany, New York.

Elaine Hatfield is a professor in the Department of Psychology and Sociology, University of Wisconsin, Madison, Wisconsin.

James H. Heinlen is a court service officer for Winona County in Winona, Minnesota.

Robert E. Keldgord is chief of the Pima County Adult Probation Department in Tucson, Arizona.

Paul W. Keve is a professor at Virginia Commonwealth University, Richmond, Virginia.

Anthony Macri is project director for the Days Off Sentencing Program of Dade County in Miami, Florida.

Patrick D. McAnany is an associate professor in the Department of Criminal Justice, University of Illinois at Chicago Circle, Chicago, Illinois.

William F. McDonald is associate professor of sociology and research director of the Institute of Criminal Law and Procedure, Georgetown University, Washington, D.C.

O. Hobart Mowrer is a research professor emeritus in the Department of Psychology, University of Illinois, Champaign, Illinois.

Ted Nelson is program manager for the Salem Community Corrections Center in Salem, Oregon.

Mike Patterson is a restitution accountant for the Oklahoma Department of Corrections, Oklahoma City, Oklahoma.

Camden H. Raue is director of the Victims' Assistance Program of the Seventh Circuit Court, Rapid City, South Dakota.

Charles R. Tittle is a professor in the Department of Sociology, Florida Atlantic University, Boca Raton, Florida.

Mary K. Utne is a research associate of the Police Foundation, Washington, D.C.

Emilio C. Viano is an associate professor in the Center for the Administration of Justice, the American University, Washington, D.C.

Marguerite Q. Warren is a professor at the School of Criminal Justice of the State University of New York, Albany, New York.

About the Editors

Burt Galaway received the M.S. (social work) from Columbia University and is a candidate for the Ph.D. (social work; sociology) from the University of Minnesota. He has had professional experience in child welfare and corrections and has been a past director of the Minnesota Restitution Center. Mr. Galaway is currently a faculty member of the School of Social Development, University of Minnesota, Duluth, and has had previous teaching experience at the School of Social Work, University of Minnesota, Minneapolis, and at Mount Mercy College, Cedar Rapids, Iowa. He is a coauthor of *Social Work Processes* (1975), *Considering the Victim* (1975), *Community Corrections: Selected Readings* (1976), and *Restitution in Criminal Justice* (1977). Mr. Galaway has published numerous articles in the areas of child welfare, restitution, and victim compensation in professional journals.

Joe Hudson received the Ph.D (social work; sociology) from the University of Minnesota. He is presently Director of the Victim Services Division for the Minnesota Department of Corrections. He formerly worked in the Department as Director of Comprehensive Planning, Director Research and Development, and as Director of the Minnesota Restitution Center. Dr. Hudson has had previous professional experience working in adult prisons, a diagnostic center for juvenile offenders, and residential treatment centers for children. He has been a faculty member at the School of Social Development, University of Minnesota, Duluth, and at the School of Social Work, University of Minnesota, Minneapolis. Dr. Hudson is coauthor of *Considering the Victim* (1975), *Community Corrections: Selected Readings* (1976), and *Restitution in Criminal Justice* (1977). He has also published numerous articles in the areas of restitution and evaluation research in scientific and professional journals.